D0271452

DALGLISH
MY AUTOBIOGRAPHY

DALGLISH
MY AUTOBIOGRAPHY

Kenny Dalglish
with
Henry Winter

Hodder & Stoughton

First published in Great Britain in 1996 by
Hodder and Stoughton
a division of Hodder Headline PLC

A CIP catalogue record for this book is
available from the British Library

ISBN 0 340 66011 2

Typeset in 11 on 13pt Palatino by
Hewer Text Composition Services, Edinburgh
Printed and bound in Great Britain by
Mackays of Chatham PLC

Hodder and Stoughton Ltd
A division of Hodder Headline PLC
338 Euston Road
London NW1 3BH

CONTENTS

CONTENTS

This book is for my mum Cathy, my late dad Bill and sister Carol for all the sacrifices they made for me, for their unending support and the discipline they instilled in me; for my wife Marina, her dad Pat, mother Martha and sister Catherine, and my children Kelly, Paul, Lynsey and Lauren and everyone who has helped me throughout my career. I will never forget what they have done for me; and finally for the people of Scotland, who sent me down south on missionary duty. It's been harder than I expected!

This book is also for all the families who lost their loved ones at Hillsborough and Heysel. I never stop thinking of them.

ACKNOWLEDGEMENTS

My thanks to Henry Winter, Football Correspondent of the *Daily Telegraph*, for listening to my story so carefully and recording it so faithfully. I would also like to thank Roddy Bloomfield, my publisher at Hodder & Stoughton, his assistant Laura Brockbank, and copy-editor Marion Paull. Many thanks also to John Keith for his excellent and comprehensive statistics section.

Photographic Acknowledgement

For permission to reproduce copyright photographs, the author and publisher would like to thank the *Daily Mirror*, *Liverpool Daily Post & Echo Plc*, *Manchester Daily Mail*, *Mercury Press Agency Ltd*, *Daily Star*, Harry Ormesher, Tom Fitzpatrick, George Ashton, *Daily Express*, *UPI*, Steve Hale, Allsport Photographic Ltd, Terry Mealey (Photography) Ltd, Popperphoto.

FOREWORD

Alex Ferguson CBE, Manager of Manchester United

I HAVE ARGUED with Bobby Charlton that the best Scottish team would beat the best English team. Bobby would say: 'How can you possibly say that?'

'Well,' I would tell him, 'straight away the strikers have got you knackered: Dalglish and Law.' Bobby just laughed.

I have known Kenny since he was a young kid. I knew his family and his wife's family. When Kenny was a young lad, his family moved to a block of flats overlooking the Rangers training ground and Kenny used to come and watch us train almost every day, whenever he skipped school. He was friendly with some of the young Rangers players, like Alex Miller who became Hibs manager. Alex kept saying to Rangers, 'You should give my pal Kenny a try.' There was a bit of mickey-taking of Alex because of it. People would say, 'Who's your friend?' Then Kenny went and signed for Celtic the next year. Rangers really missed the boat because Kenny was a dyed-in-the-wool Rangers fan. He went on to be a great player with Celtic.

He was a right-half as a young kid at Celtic. I was starting to fade away from the Rangers scene but I played against him in a reserve game. He man-marked me. I said to him, 'You'll need a doctor for this.' He just looked at me! He got stuck in, but I scored.

Kenny had unbelievable vision and strength as a player. He was really aware of people around him. He had great balance and was a good finisher, courageous too. People often forget that the one quality great players need is courage. Kenny is as brave as a lion. He would take a kick from anyone and come back for more. All the great strikers, like Pelé and Law, had wonderful talent, which incorporated things like balance, but they also had the extra part, the courage.

Before Kenny became manager of Liverpool, they won titles with teams that were functional. They ground out results, with simple, effective teams. They had a great side in the 1980–81 era with Graeme Souness, Jimmy Case and Dalglish. But when he became manager, Kenny brought players of flair into the Liverpool set-up. He signed Peter Beardsley and John Barnes and took Liverpool a stage further than they had been before. They had a fantastic season in 1987–88. Liverpool walked away with the League. They beat us by nine points. Their first defeat was in March at Everton. That was an incredible season.

We had two seasons competing with Kenny and Blackburn for the title; one we won, one we lost. After they had beaten us in 1995, I dropped Kenny a line, congratulating him. It was a change from the mind games we used to play.

I think Kenny did use mind games. He would come out and say that he wouldn't change his players for any players in Britain or the world. 'My players have my confidence,' Kenny would say. What he was saying was the old Churchillian thing, that 'we would take them on the beaches, we'll fight them in the air, we have the best of human resources.' That was the message he was trying to get across to his players. I'm sure he did get the message across. The one problem I had with Blackburn was how resilient they were. Newcastle probably mirror Kevin Keegan in that they are a rollercoaster type of team whereas Kenny is stubborn, which comes from his Scottish background. Kenny's team mirrored him as a player and as a person. Blackburn wouldn't give in. They were snatching games that season. They got a win at Everton when they were being slaughtered. They would always come out of games with something because of their grit and resilience. That was my big problem, my big worry. That's why I had to try to talk them out of it.

All the stuff about a feud between us is nonsense. We had one argument, the famous one at Liverpool. Kenny came by with his baby when I was giving a radio interview and told the reporter that he would get more sense out of the baby. But that's the only time we've ever had an argument. I picked him for the Scotland team. I was the manager of his testimonial team.

As a person, Kenny's witty. He can be a bit complex at times. You may ask him a question and he'll say, 'What do you want to know for?' He's got that suspicious Scottish nature about him. It takes time to get his trust. Kenny has associates, colleagues, but only a few true friends. There's nothing wrong with that because, at the end of the day, you only need six people to carry your coffin. We are not close but I am on friendly terms with him. Whenever we meet we always get on well. Cath and Marina have always got on well, too. We are not close simply because we live in different worlds. He was at Liverpool; I was at United. There was never going to be a big mix there. When he was at Blackburn, he was challenging us so there was not going to be close contact. After Hillsborough, I rang him up. I knew what he would be going through and I could detect when I phoned him that he was down. I remember him saying, 'You wonder what it's all about.' I understand what he was saying. Kenny is a man I shall always respect.

Alex Ferguson
July 1996

—1—

GROWING UP AND CELTIC DAYS

M Y ADULT LIFE has simply been a time of trying to fulfil childhood dreams. I spent the early part of my life moving between housing estates in Glasgow, dreaming of growing up to become a professional footballer. Most boys in Glasgow shared the same dream. Few actually made it but that fact never stopped a young boy dreaming of stepping out in an Old Firm derby, or of scoring the winner for Scotland at Wembley. I was just a normal kid, conjuring in my mind visions of footballing glory yet living with the reality of life on housing schemes with no real amenities. I had a beloved ritual on Friday nights when my family lived on an estate at Milton. It was the special moment of the week; the memory refuses to fade. I would wait patiently for the ice-cream van to arrive, eager to spend the thruppence my parents had given me. Then, clutching my ice-cream and flake, I would rush home to watch Harry Lime in 'The Third Man' on television. What a treat, the social highlight of the week!

My two sporting loves – football and golf – were with me from those uncomplicated early days. A group of boys on the estate, including me, played football all the time. If we were lucky, somebody would bring a golf club out and we would take turns with that, too. At the first hint of summer we'd be off to the public park in Milton. There were tennis courts there and during Wimbledon fortnight we would hire rackets and have a go at that, trying to bang the ball over the net, occasionally succeeding.

We would try any sport we could afford. It kept us happy and busy. If athletics were on television and everybody was talking about the Olympics or some big athletics meeting, the Milton boys used to have races around the block. It was a childhood of sport and dreams. I even played cricket, but that was a mere distraction. Football has always been my love, an obsession really. Even now, after all these years, I still relish the prospect of playing, even if it is only a training match or a testimonial.

Growing up in Glasgow, there was always a game of football going on. There were two or three parks near where I lived so I could play with two or three different sets of lads. Goalposts were readily to hand – we just put our jackets down. Eventually, with my main gang of football mates from Milton, we went big-time – we got posts and nets. A friend's dad was a plumber and he constructed these ingenious posts out of little conduit pipes. We could unscrew them and carry them to and from the park. How proud we felt. Soon, we had even formed ourselves into a team called Milton Milan. One Christmas we were all given Milan strips. That was a brilliant moment. We felt a cut above all the other kids with our own kit and goals. It was not a bad team, either; Ian Ross played with us and he went from Milton Milan to Liverpool and Aston Villa!

Every waking thought was consumed by football. My dreams at night were probably filled with match-winning displays against England. All I thought about was football. If there weren't enough players for a game, we would play head football. You could head it or chest it but if you touched it with your hands you couldn't shoot. All the time, without realising it, I was developing skills that would lead to a career in football. In those games or knockabouts, I wasn't deliberately preparing to become a professional footballer. I just played football for the love of it. There was nobody teaching me. I taught myself simply by playing and playing, every hour of the day that I could.

I watched games too. My dad was a real Rangers fan. He used to take me to Ibrox to see the Rangers play. Harry Lime was good but the real highpoint of the week was going to Ibrox to see my first idol, a burly South African centre-forward named Don Kitchenbrand, nicknamed Rhino. I don't know why he became my first hero; maybe because he was a centre-forward and scored goals, the dream of most Scottish boys. Kitchenbrand left Rangers when I was quite young. My father said I cried. I can still recall the thrill of going to see other players, like Dougie Baillie, a centre-back who now works for the *Sunday Post*. Dougie was a big fellow who could head the ball further than most people could kick it. One of my earliest memories is of him taking a penalty for Rangers reserves. The goalkeeper briefly turned his back on Dougie. In that split second Dougie shot. You would have expected him to score, with the keeper facing the other way, but the ball hit the keeper's heel and flew out. A great save!

Jim Baxter was special to me, as he was to millions of Scots. He was a truly great player. I will never forget how he broke his leg in Vienna, limped off and just collapsed on the snow. The memory of that moment will never leave me. It was such a powerful image, spelling out the commitment and acceptance of danger demanded by football. Another skilful player I used to love watching was Ian McMillan, so clever and quick. I remember one goal he scored at Kilmarnock. McMillan must have been 18 yards out. He waited until a defender ran across the goalkeeper, momentarily blocking the keeper's view, knocked it back across the defender and the next thing the keeper knew the ball was lying in the back of the net. A really clever goal. Even without me knowing it, McMillan must have influenced me. If some of my game carried echoes of McMillan, and my father insisted it did, that's a huge compliment to me because Ian McMillan was such a canny player. All the time, I was absorbing knowledge from watching greats like Jim Baxter and Ian McMillan. Their tricks and skills lodged in my mind. I would practise them until they were second nature.

Denis Law became an immediate idol of mine the moment I saw him at Hampden Park. Most Scottish kids idolised Denis. He had played in Italy, played for Manchester United, played for Scotland. I couldn't stop thinking about him. Some people just have a charisma about them and Denis had it in abundance. Denis was a great goalscorer and a scorer of great goals. Maybe even the blond hair attracted people; the way he held the cuffs of his shirt in his hands; the way he saluted when he scored. He just looked a likely lad, but in a nice way, not arrogant. He wasn't too perfect. He had a couple of fights, just skirmishes really, whilst he was playing. Everyone can relate to that. It shows he had a passionate side. That does no harm. Passion like Law's is a vital part of football. If you have passion in your heart you've a chance in football, in life as well. I know there are an awful lot of people who have passion and commitment, but who haven't been sent off like Denis. I'm sure Denis wasn't proud of how he behaved in clashes with the likes of Ian Ure, but such indiscretions made Denis human. There was nothing to admire in those incidents yet they somehow added to his glamour.

One of my proudest possessions is Denis Law's No 8 shirt which I acquired in my early years as a professional at Celtic. In the autumn of 1972, Celtic played Manchester United in a testimonial for Bobby Charlton. After the game, I caught up with Denis in the tunnel and asked whether I could have his shirt.

'No problem, wee man.'

'Thanks a lot,' I replied.

I was completely thrilled. Then Jock Stein, Celtic's manager, came into the dressing-room and said: 'Hand in the shirts, lads, they are all going in for a charity auction.'

'No chance,' I told Big Jock. 'I'm bagging mine. I'll pay for it if I have to.'

It went straight in my bag. No one was going to take it off me, not even Jock Stein, who we all feared and respected.

After watching idols like Denis and Ian McMillan play, whether at Ibrox or Hampden, I would rush home, run into the back-garden if it wasn't raining, and kick a ball about with my dad until our tea was ready. The goal was very simple – a clothes-pole was one post, a metal stick the other. My dad always encouraged my football. He inherited his love of the game from his father, who had been on the committee of a club called Strathclyde Juniors, now disbanded. My father was not a bad player when he was younger. Sadly, any ambitions he might have had ended when a lorry ran over his ankle.

The background that I was born into, on 4 March, 1951, was a Scottish working-class one. We weren't poor, there was none of this running around with no shoes on. I was lucky. My parents, Bill and Cathy, did everything they could for me. Whatever they could afford, my sister Carol and I could have. We were typical

Scottish working-class but my background wasn't Labour orientated or SNP orientated. It was football orientated. The only time I've voted, it was for the SNP. I was only 18. I don't vote now. I can't be bothered. Maybe if political parties got some football personalities standing for election, I would vote for them! I imagined my father was Labour.

We first lived in Dalmarnock, near Parkhead, the home of Celtic Football Club, but we soon moved to Milton. Our house had a loving atmosphere but my parents would clip me round the ear if I misbehaved. That tended to make me shape up pretty quickly. I have always believed in discipline. As a professional footballer, I was dedicated. Discipline is a value that seems to be disappearing from today's society. Many young people misbehave because they have nothing to look forward to when they leave school, but the parents have the biggest responsibility. Discipline must prevail at home if children are to behave outside. My mum and dad brought me up to believe in fundamental principles, like having good manners and knowing right from wrong. I was taught to appreciate other people and what they have done for me. Learning such values gave me a good basis for life.

We were a simple, straightforward family. My dad was a diesel engineer with a motor company. My mother looked after the house. My dad gave his wages to my mum and got his pocket-money in return. It's the same principle as I've got now with my wife, Marina. My upbringing has been described as a Protestant one but we never made a big fuss over religion. It didn't bother us. I wanted to go to the Catholic school at the end of our street simply because they had just laid down a gravel football pitch. My two wee mates went there and I wanted to be with them. It was irrelevant to me that it was a Catholic school and that my friends were Catholic. I never thought about the religious side. Although I would go and watch Rangers, it was because I was interested in football not Protestantism. Many Glaswegians are ingrained with bigotry. I have never been able to accept that. I supported Rangers but I looked upon my Catholic footballing companions as friends not lepers. I have never discriminated against people, unlike all the tens of thousands of religious bigots who chant at Old Firm games. I don't think a lot of them realise what the chants are, all that glorifying of ancient bloodshed. Fortunately, Glasgow's bigotry seems to be lessening. Society in general is changing up there. Glasgow has a bad reputation but, apart from the religious bigotry, it is no worse than other cities.

Religion meant little to me. I only went to Sunday school because my friends did. In the summer, I would tell my mother I didn't want to go to Sunday school and we would have an argument. When I got a bit older, I joined the Boys Brigade, but not the local one. I went to the one at Possil Park because it had a better football team. At school, my main interest was focused on the school football team. Although I was above average academically, later I wished I had studied harder. As someone who is perceived as being uncommunicative, I'm sure a lot of journalists wish I had studied harder too!

I spent some time in my lessons dreaming about playing. During breaks, or at the end of the day, I hurried off to start a game. My footballing career, which took me to three World Cups as a forward or attacking midfielder, had the strangest of beginnings. I started out in goal for my primary school at Milton Bank. I made the mistake of playing well in my first game, keeping a clean sheet in a 2–0 victory over a team called Chirnside. Eventually I began to play out of goal. When I moved on to High Possil, I played for Possil Park YMCA. Possil had a reputation for nurturing players – Eddie Kelly went on to Arsenal, Johnny Hamilton to Hibs and Rangers and Robert Russell to Rangers. Soon I began representing Glasgow Schools. We had a really good team and in 1966 won the Scottish Schools Cup. My father's mother used to come and watch. She once berated a reporter for spelling our surname 'Dalgleish'. She'd looked over his shoulder to see what he was writing. My father tells the story that she was critical of me to him at half-time during one game. Afterwards, I asked my father what my grandmother had said about me.

'Behave yourself,' he said. 'She's forgotten more about football than you'll ever know.'

There was clearly football in the Dalglish family.

That year I gained my first Scotland recognition after suffering rejection at a trial stage. After playing in the first two rounds of trials for the Scottish Under-15 Schools side I wasn't selected for the next round. The manager of the Glasgow Under-15 team I played for felt I should have been included and he was a bit upset that I hadn't been. So when the Scottish Schools team had a game against the Glasgow Under-16 team, he put me in the city team hoping to persuade the national selectors to change their minds. They didn't, at least not immediately. I was left out of the side that played the first game against Wales, which was drawn. But I was selected for the second game against Northern Ireland which we won 4–3. High Possil gave me a smart blazer and trousers. I felt so proud, smartly dressed and representing my country. We won 4–3 at the Oval, Glentoran's ground in Belfast, and then drew 1–1 with England at Ibrox. Dave Thomas, who was at Everton when I was at Liverpool, played. So did Tommy Craig, who went on to Aberdeen and then south of the border. It was a very high standard.

From 15 to 16, I played for Glasgow United. At the time everybody expected Rangers to ask me for a trial – even me. Rangers were certainly aware of me. I was representing Scottish Schoolboys and was known to be a Rangers fan. It would have been an obvious step. Rangers' chief scout, Jimmy Smith, apparently told people watching Scottish Schoolboys matches that he thought I would end up at Ibrox. But no one ever asked me. I never knew why. At the time I was disappointed because the team I followed, and wanted to sign for, didn't seek me out. My bedroom even overlooked Rangers' training ground. Although in hindsight it's worked out for the best, and I haven't done too badly, I still don't know why Rangers never came in for me.

The club on my doorstep were not showing any interest but others from further afield were. I was invited down for trials at Liverpool and West Ham in August 1966. I played for Liverpool B against Southport A. Ian Ross once said that Bill Shankly never knew that I was at Liverpool as a teenager, but he must have done. He and Reuben Bennett gave me a lift back to the YMCA where I was staying during my trial. They dropped me at the lights near the YMCA and watched me walk over. Liverpool wanted me to stay on a couple of days, but I told them that I needed a couple of days at home because I was going to West Ham for a trial at the weekend. The real reason was that Rangers were playing Celtic at Ibrox that night. I caught the train back up from Lime Street and went straight to the match.

I soon saw Shanks again. Liverpool's first team were due to play at West Ham the same weekend as my trial. As I walked through to the players' area at Upton Park, Shanks came along in the other direction. I was overwhelmed with embarrassment. I couldn't speak to him. I just kept my head down and hurried past. I heard his voice shouting 'Kenny, Kenny' but I said to myself 'just keep walking, just keep walking'. I regret not talking to Shanks, but I was only 15 and very shy. If anybody spoke to me I'd blush. West Ham were very good at making me feel at home during my trial. Their manager, Ron Greenwood, was particularly thoughtful and even gave me a pair of boots; but I didn't really want to leave Glasgow, so I returned home and carried on playing for Glasgow United. We had such a good team, with players like Vic Davidson and Freddie Pethard, that Celtic invited us to play against their provisional signings under the lights at Barrowfield, their training ground. Jock Stein and his assistant, Sean Fallon, watched us win 3–2 with me scoring. Afterwards, Big Jock said he 'liked the No 4' but that he'd heard I was going to Ibrox. Fortunately Celtic still came in for me which was just as well given Ibrox's apathy. I certainly wasn't going to ignore Celtic's interest simply because I supported their biggest rivals. My dream was to become a professional footballer. The location was just a detail. A couple of days after the Barrowfield win, our manager was asked to go up to see Mr Stein at Celtic Park. He talked with my dad and Bob Keir said I couldn't get any better than Celtic.

My father understood the sort of footballing education I would receive under Jock Stein at Celtic. So when Sean Fallon came to our flat, in May 1967, he did not need long to convince my family to let me sign. Sean and his wife had been on their way to a seaside hotel to celebrate their wedding anniversary. Sean was keen to talk to my parents and decided to stop by on the way. His wife waited outside. She told Sean later that she hoped I was worth ruining their anniversary for. They were too late for the hotel and had to turn back. I don't think Sean was too disappointed at what his visit led to. A myth has developed that I wasn't in the living room when Sean and my father spoke. I was; it was my future they were discussing after all. I sat in the corner listening. Their conversation was fairly straightforward, just talking about football generally. Sean wasn't trying to persuade my family that Celtic was the right place for me to go. My parents knew that anyway. After an hour it was agreed I would go training with Celtic. My mum then decided to show Sean around the flat. I panicked. My bedroom wall was covered with pictures of Rangers players and Celtic's assistant manager was about to see my room. I managed to get most of them down before Sean saw them. It didn't bother him.

There was no finance involved in my signing for Celtic, as there can be nowadays. Even then, parents could make a few quid. When I was 15, somebody came up to the school and said: 'I represent a big club. I want to speak to your dad. Where does he work?' I told him and off he went. He explained to my dad who he was and which club he represented. He then said: 'But we are not getting involved in any auction.' 'Get away,' my father said. He was angry that financial considerations should be deemed more important than the quality of environment I would be committing myself to. Money wasn't important. I was never offered anything – I must have been a bad player!

A couple of days after Sean's visit a slip of paper came through the door. It was from the Scottish Football Association confirming that I had signed provisional forms for Celtic. A Rangers fan was off to Parkhead! I was not the only one. Danny McGrain joined at the same time and we used to catch the No 64 bus from Argyle Street in the centre of Glasgow to Celtic Park. I had got to know Danny when I was playing for Glasgow Under-15s and he was in the year above. We once played each other and became very good friends. I've been through a lot with Danny. I was best man at his wedding. I can remember the two of us sitting at an Old Firm game in 1967 after we had signed provisional forms. Rangers were leading 1–0 and got a penalty. Kai Johansen, a Danish full-back, took the penalty which hit the bar. The ball came out and he hit it again with the goalkeeper nowhere. This was obviously a free-kick to Celtic because the rule was that someone other than the penalty-taker had to touch the ball next. It was so frustrating because there was another Rangers player standing next to Johansen who could have tapped it in. Of course, Celtic went up the park and equalised. Danny jumped up cheering. 'What are you doing?' I said. 'Do you want Celtic to win?' That was typical of me. That's how involved I was with Rangers. Even though I was training at Celtic, I would go on the Rangers supporters' bus to Ibrox to watch my heroes in blue. Celtic never knew, but even if they had done I think they would have accepted it. It would have been different if I had been missing training to go to the games. I can remember coming from training at Celtic Park to go and watch Rangers and Leeds on the big screen at Ibrox when Johnny Giles scored a penalty in a 2–0 victory for Leeds.

I continued living near Ibrox. Jim Craig, one of the Lisbon Lions, stayed close by and often gave me lifts to Celtic Park. All Celtic's players were really helpful. Later when I moved to another part of the south side of the city, Bertie Auld or Billy McNeill would pick me up. In training, they were always willing to help. Big Jock encouraged them to look after the younger players. I don't know what the Lisbon Lions thought of me as a player, I just know that they conducted themselves quite humbly. It was very similar when I moved to Liverpool in 1977. They were great players, and they knew they were great players, but they were good people as well, not arrogant or blasé. Big Jock wouldn't have let them play or behave any other way. Even with such a welcoming atmosphere, I was nervous. Turning up for training was like playing a Cup final every day. I would sit on the bus, stomach churning. I was so nervous that the first thing I had to do on reaching Celtic Park was go to the toilet.

Celtic was a marvellous place to be. Everyone was so committed to the success of the club. No team can be successful without everyone pulling in the one direction; not just the team on the pitch, but everyone off the pitch as well, from turnstile-operator to director. Celtic's first team were so successful that Big Jock and Sean Fallon could spend time working with the kids, which really helped my development. Most of the training was taken by Willie Fernie, who had been a great inside-forward for Celtic. Willie loved the ball's company as a player. He never changed as a coach. Every Friday he used to come running out for training with the ball, shouting, 'Let's go, lads.' The warm-up was trying to catch him up. In training, Willie would award us extra points for playing 1–2s. Much of our training was two-touch. We were so lucky – all the people who coached us, Big Jock, Willie and Sean, had also played for Celtic. They were steeped in the club's tradition, steeped in the principle that football was a passing game.

To give me some tougher, competitive experience, Celtic farmed me out to Cumbernauld United during my first season at Parkhead. I settled quickly, scoring four goals on my debut and 37 in all. They looked after me really well and it wasn't difficult to fit in. Jim Donald, a mate of mine from Possil YM, was there. Later he was best man at my wedding. It was Cumbernauld's first year in existence. I was there because Johnny Hamilton had left to go to Hibs – he played for Possil YM too – and I took his place. Cumbernauld's ground was fairly basic. It didn't have a stand, just a rail around it. At the end of the season, Celtic brought the Lisbon Lions along to open the new stadium officially. Playing for Cumbernauld was like playing for a GM Vauxhall Conference club. Cumbernauld were a team for guys who were just not good enough to make the professional level, or older players finishing their careers in lower league football. There were not many teenagers like myself because it was so hard. I was playing against grown men every week. There were one or two who wouldn't think twice about kicking me. They never even apologised afterwards. It wasn't because I was young or with Celtic. These old boys kicked everybody. They never isolated people, or thought about making an exception because someone was signed up with one of the big clubs. They were very even-handed! It was a real baptism of fire. They were more wholehearted than vicious, but if an opponent had a kick at me, one of my team-mates would go looking for him.

During the week, I continued my job as an apprentice joiner because my father said it was important to learn a trade. In the workshop, I'd be shovelling shavings, putting a little bit of edging on doors, anything that was needed. Sometimes I went on site and would take messages or run errands. They were always sending the new boys out for things from the ironmongers. We would be given a list of items like nuts and screws and nails. They would often put a sneaky one on the bottom of the list, like 'bubble for the spirit level' or 'left-handed screwdriver'. When I once asked for a 'sky-hook', the ironmonger said: 'First year, son? Just started?' 'Aye,' I replied. 'How did you know?'

The ironmonger said: 'OK, son, I'll go and get you a sky-hook.' Then he hit me with: 'What length?'

That was my initiation. It was all done in good spirit. They treated me well in the workshop. I never had to work Saturdays, which meant I could get to football in good time. Every Tuesday and Thursday I would leave between 4.30 and 5.15 and catch two buses to Celtic Park with my working gear on: jeans, scarf, donkey jacket, hair full of shavings. All the other guys came in from different jobs around Glasgow. Graeme Souness came through from Edinburgh after school.

I could have given up my trade earlier. When I signed for Celtic, Jock Stein asked me if I wanted to go on the ground-staff, but I said no. I preferred to continue working as a joiner until Celtic felt I could go full-time. Towards the end of my first season, I felt I had proven my ability at Cumbernauld, so I went to see Big Jock in his office at Parkhead. Celtic's manager, who was feared by everyone, was surprised to see me, even more so when I asked him: 'Can I go full-time?' Big Jock refused but I was adamant. A couple of days later Big Jock spoke to my dad and warned him: 'Kenny might not get many games in the reserves. He might be better off staying with Cumbernauld for another year.' My dad replied: 'I accept what you are saying, Mr Stein, but if Kenny is going to have a go he's going to have a go now.' Big Jock hadn't expected such determination from me or my father. Eventually he agreed and I signed professional forms.

The reserve side I joined came to be known as the Quality Street Gang, after the chocolates. Somebody used the phrase in a headline and it stuck. It was a smashing side, brimming with good young players, like Danny McGrain, Vic Davidson, David Hay, Lou Macari, George Connelly and Paul Wilson. We never thought of ourselves as the Quality Street Gang. We were just kids eager to do well, to take a chance in life. Along with the quality of coaching, part of the reason for the reserves' success was that all the lads were good friends. We were an interesting bunch. Vic never got the success he deserved. He was a good goalscorer but plagued by injuries and a bit of bad luck. Vic was due to go to Motherwell to talk to them about a transfer, but he couldn't find the place. So he phoned me up.

'Kenny, where's Motherwell?'

'About 20 miles down the road.'

'Will you come and pick me up?' he replied.

So I had to go and pick Vic up, drive him down to Motherwell, and wait around the corner until he came out after talking to them. We have kept in touch since those days.

Danny McGrain was my great friend at Celtic. We were farmed out to different clubs, me to Cumbernauld, him to Maryhill. We used to go back to Celtic Park in the afternoon, knock a ball about, do some work, try to improve ourselves. I roomed with Danny. He was a great player, as good a right-back as Britain has ever seen. Danny had everything. He could tackle, pass, get forward. He was also a regular goalscorer – one a year! We used to tease him that he didn't know how to celebrate because he couldn't remember from the previous year. I have so much admiration for Danny. He has been through everything. He fractured his skull at Falkirk. He had a problem with diabetes after the 1974 World Cup. Three years later, just after I left Celtic, Danny picked up a nasty ankle injury, which he never seemed to shake off. Danny was a great servant to Celtic. He was never envious of anyone moving south, he never felt any animosity towards me, Lou or David Hay, when we got our moves to Liverpool, Manchester United and Chelsea. Danny's philosophy was that we had grown up together and he was pleased to see us getting on well.

Lou was a great goalscorer. He scored a lot of goals for Celtic and then came down south and scored loads more for Manchester United. He, David Hay and George Connelly were the first of the Quality Street Gang to move up into the first team. Danny, Vic and I followed. Lou was an instinctive finisher; he had an uncanny ability to be in the right position at the right time in front of goal.

It was a pity what happened to George Connelly. He had so much skill. George could keep the ball up for hours. He was so good at joining the attack. In the end George just decided he had had enough of football. On one Scotland trip, he just disappeared. It was quite funny actually. We flew from Glasgow to London for a connecting flight to Europe. At London airport, while we were looking for our onward flight, someone noticed that George was missing.

They were great times. I would hang about with Danny, until

we all got girlfriends and went our own ways. In pre-season, we used to train morning and afternoon. At lunch, we would go over to a place near Hampden. It was run by the man who would become my father-in-law. Marina used to work in there. After the game on a Saturday, the reserves would go in there for a meal. I used to go over with Vic because we lived that side of town. I eventually asked Marina for a date. We started going out with each other and it kicked on from there. Nothing romantic!

Danny and I were just normal people. We used to hang out quite a bit with some players from other clubs. We'd go into the city centre after training for something to eat at the George Young coffee bar. There was a big crowd from Partick Thistle, some of the young Rangers lads, one of the boys used to come through from Hearts. It used to be a good crack. My meal was always macaroni cheese with double chips and a Coke. If we didn't head into town, Danny and I would often go off and play golf. When Vic came, he used to strap his fingers up, but he always came off with bleeding hands. We still don't know how he did it. We used to have some good laughs. There was a table-tennis table at Celtic Park; even the first team would join in with us. There was a real feeling of togetherness – that showed on the park.

We used to have a carry-on with some of the ground-staff who were a bit younger and naive. One of them once had a rash on his face so we told him: 'Put Algipan on it. That will clear it up.' The next day he looked like Roger Radish. Another day the same member of the ground-staff wanted a haircut. One of the reserves said he was training to be a barber and gave him the most terrible haircut I have ever seen. It was a real mess with chunks missing. We offered to put some boot polish on his head so people couldn't see the gaps. We loved being at Celtic Park but we never had the run of the place. There were no liberties taken. Big Jock allowed us to have a laugh but never to excess. We were never destructive, there was never anything broken. Every player was expected to treat the people who worked at Celtic Park with respect. One of the cleaners from my early days is still there. So is the groundsman, who has been telling my son stories about me, now that Paul's a player at Celtic. I told Paul not to listen, they weren't true.

There was pressure on us. Everybody has pressure on them. It just depends how much pressure you can take. Everyone has a breaking point. I was under pressure to get in the reserves, to establish myself there, then to get into a position where I would be offered a new contract. Then there was pressure to progress into the first team, to establish myself there, to be successful; then international responsibilities. It's a relentless, pressurised cycle. Every time I climbed a rung up the ladder, or tried to realise a target, it brought different stresses. Always, in the back of my mind, there was a feeling that there might be a disappointment coming my way, somewhere, sometime.

It didn't help that I was so shy off the pitch. If someone spoke to me I would blush, go completely red. There was no real embarrassment on the football side. I just went out and played. I probably thought more about football when I was not playing. If I'm watching somebody play I'll be thinking 'if they get a cross in now, the other team are really in trouble'. Or if I see a tackle, I'll wince. But when I was playing, I would be involved in incidents like that four or five times in a game, without thinking about them, without flinching. My mind was focused solely on the game. I would expect things to happen and I was ready for most of them.

The reserve games were fairly physical. It was good because we were a young group, and playing against older players. I remember playing against Jim Baxter in a 1–1 draw at Ibrox. Rangers had a strong team out that day. I played well in the first half, but in the second half, Baxter walked me all over the place. After the game, my dad took me to one side and said: 'Why did you follow Baxter?'

'I never did,' I answered.

'Well,' my dad said, 'wherever he went, you were never far away from him. He just walked you out of the game.'

Baxter didn't make me follow him, I just did it. I learnt an important lesson that day – that I should play so as to make him come looking for me. Playing against such experienced professionals as Baxter was part of my education.

It was always my dream to play at Ibrox. It is an amazing stadium, although I had a problem when I first played there, for Scotland Schoolboys. I had trouble hanging my clothes up because the pegs were so high. The Rangers players were all big lads. I had to stand on the bench to hang my jacket up. Maybe that's why they never came for me – I was never big enough! My overriding memory of Ibrox from those days is the sheer size of the goalposts. They were different from most other places: big square ones, four inches thick. The Ibrox crowd were unbelievable. A few years later, I remember going on the team bus from Celtic Park to Ibrox for an Old Firm game. The Rangers supporters were all coming out of pubs along Paisley Road West, shouting at us. I saw two guys who lived in the same block of flats as me screaming abuse at the bus. When they saw me looking out of the bus window, their jaws dropped. They waved at me, then carried on giving us stick! On the pitch I was never singled out by the Rangers fans. Maybe that was because nothing rhymes with Dalglish, although listening to many football chants it's obvious that rhyming is not that important.

Playing at Ibrox was part of my dream but also part of my education. Big Jock was determined to give us experience, even if only of being part of a squad. When we were still new to the reserves, Big Jock took us with the first team on European trips. Vic Davidson and I went to Basle. We trained with the team but didn't strip for the match. We sat in the stand. It was great experience which took some of the tension away when we really did play at such places. For a European tie with Waterford some of us kids were even on the bench. It may not sound too glamorous but it was a European tie. When we were 18 we went on tour to America, Canada and Bermuda. Some of the Lisbon Lions were injured, so Vic Davidson and I were drafted in. Vic and I were totally naive. We woke up in the four-star hotel without a watch between us. We didn't think to phone reception to ask the time. Hotels were new to us. It was light outside, so, although it seemed pretty quiet, we thought we had better get up. We went outside and soon saw a clock – 7.30 in the morning.

'Well,' I said to Vic, 'what are we going to do with all this time?'

'Let's go for a haircut,' he suggested. 'That will fill in some time.'

We found a place that was open and the barber said: 'What would you like?'

'Just a wee bit off, please,' we replied. The whole lot came off! We'd been scalped. It must have been a reservation!

It was an unbelievable trip. We played Manchester United in Toronto. I was on for a half against George Best and Paddy Crerand. Brilliant! We went to New York and Boston to play American teams. At the start of the second half in Boston, they kicked off and two extra players ran on, one from each side, so they had 13 on the pitch. They ran up the park and scored. We pointed out this fairly blatant infringement to the referee. He let the goal stand but ordered the two extra guys to leave. Crazy but funny. We also played some games in Bermuda on a beautiful pitch like a bowling green. Every day brought a new experience which helped shape me into a professional footballer. Every day working under Big Jock was the best education a young footballer could have.

—2—

LIFE IN PARADISE

I STILL SENSE Jock Stein's presence. Rarely a day goes by without the Big Man featuring in my thoughts. It's hard to believe he is not here anymore. Big Jock was the most important figure in my football education. He was a visionary. He had the idea of putting No 9 on my back and then withdrawing me into the middle of the pitch. My role was to take the ball from the back four and link with the front two.

'This is a position I think you will be able to play,' Stein told me. 'I don't know if anyone is playing this at the moment, but we'll try it and you'll make it work.'

Big Jock outlined the role and then sent me out to put it into action. We tried it in a Celtic reserve game and it worked. He made me the type of player I became. Much of my success is down to him.

Jock had great presence. A tremendous aura surrounded him. If he walked into a packed room and you had your back to the door, you would know Jock was there. The people who were his friends in the managerial game, men like Bill Shankly, Don Revie and Sir Matt Busby, reflect the respect he was held in. It was unusual for somebody up in Scotland to be considered in the same league as those three, who had all done so well in England, but Jock was. He really studied the game. He thought deeply about tactics and gave inspired team-talks, especially before Old Firm matches. He would often give team-talks to the reserves. I certainly remember the team-talks Big Jock gave when things were going badly. The heat of his anger could rip the paint from the dressing-room wall. Big Jock would accept it if players performed badly but had given their all; he left people in no doubt about how he felt about lack of effort. I didn't know whether he did this for effect but certainly when any first-teamer played for the reserves, and didn't give everything, he would get a right blast from Big Jock. Not many people won arguments with him, and if you did win the argument you weren't there for too long afterwards.

Stein wouldn't suffer fools gladly. If we misbehaved we were punished. He tried to instil a code of discipline among the young lads. Our hair wasn't supposed to be too long, we had to be on time. Big Jock was a hands-on manager. He took charge of my first professional game, getting together a reserve team of new professionals who had just returned from being farmed out. I came back from Cumbernauld, Danny McGrain and Paul Wilson from Maryhill, Vic Davidson from Ashfield. The game was against Greenock Morton and Big Jock thought we'd get battered. We lost only 5–4. It was meant to be a test of mettle, and a learning experience, for us. We probably learned as much about Big Jock as he did about us. At half-time, Big Jock came into the dressing-room at Cappielow and told our goalkeeper that he should have come for one of the crosses. The goalkeeper had the nerve to answer back: 'It's not my fault, it's their fault.' Big Jock responded by walking over and shutting each of the small windows so that nobody outside could hear. Then he went off his trolley, pouring verbal abuse on the keeper and us. Everyone knew there and then exactly where they stood. Answer back at your peril.

You had to be strong to stand up for yourself against Big Jock, but he was constructive. We knew everything he said and did was for our benefit. He used to come out and help at some of the matches. He always had time for us kids. He was always very good to me. Early on in my time at Celtic, I was in the squad for an Old Firm reserve game which used to coincide with the big game. Living near Ibrox, I just walked across the road, waited for the Celtic bus to come and then walked in with the reserves. They told me that Big Jock had been looking for me at Celtic Park. He must have wanted to say a few words because he knew how much playing at Ibrox meant to me. That shows how great a manager Big Jock was. Sean read out the team and, to my surprise, I was playing. I thought I was too inexperienced. It was a very generous thought and one that made me even more determined to play well for Jock Stein. We won that day, Joe McBride scoring the only goal.

At that time I played midfield for Celtic and centre-back for Scotland's Under-18s. Big Jock knew I preferred midfield but put me at centre-back for Celtic as part of my footballing education. If a couple of my passes were intercepted and put us in trouble, Jock would immediately punish me. 'I'll put you at the back to make you learn a lesson,' he would say. So he put me at centre-back after I had been guilty of some errant passing. He felt that from centre-back I could see the problem bad passes created. After three or four games he switched me back to midfield during a reserve game we were winning against Dundee United at Tannadice. I was only there about two minutes when another of my passes was intercepted, put us in trouble and Big Jock put me straight back into defence! When I came off, I received the usual abuse from Big Jock. Although his comments were constructive, they were expressed in a very vociferous manner; but I had to learn. I soon settled down in the middle of the park, from where I would try to influence attacks. Big Jock once said very generously that 'with a player like Kenny, you don't talk about positions. You just give him a jersey.' We did talk about positions. What Jock meant was that because I so loved playing, he knew that although I might not do everything right I would always try my best.

The Lisbon Lions were still winning. Big Jock recognised that players of the Lisbon Lions' quality could carry one kid so I eventually got the shout. Giving me my debut did not rank as one of the greatest gambles of Jock Stein's managerial career. It was on 25 September, 1968, the second leg of a League Cup quarter-final against Hamilton Academical, and Celtic led 10–0 from the first leg. There was not much chance of an upset. I came on in the second half in a 4–2 victory. At least I got a mention in the *Celtic View*, the club's paper, which said I was 'highly promising'.

My League debut didn't arrive until 4 October, 1969. When it did come, it was completely unexpected. The day before the first team faced Raith Rovers, Big Jock came into the boot room after training. I was in there putting my boots away.

'You're not playing for the reserves tomorrow,' he said.

'Oh, all right,' I replied, trying to hide my disappointment.

'Kenny, you are coming with us.'

'Eh?'

'You are playing for the first team.'

All I could say was: 'Oh, that is all right.' I was beside myself with pleasure and pride but trying to be mature and relaxed about getting my first start.

'Don't tell anyone,' Jock warned me.

'Oh no. I'll not tell a soul.'

'Well,' Jock Stein said as he was going out of the door. 'Go and get some rest.'

When my dad came in from work, I told him. He was delighted.

As kick-off approached, I sat in the dressing-room, a complete bag of nerves, trying to get ready. Then in walked Bobby Murdoch, one of Celtic's greatest ever players. Bobby was recovering from shoulder surgery and had just returned from a health farm where he'd been to get his weight down. I looked at Bobby standing there and thought: 'He looks in really good shape.' He actually weighed less than when he won the European Cup. Bobby sat down next to me while I was getting ready. He asked me whether I was nervous.

'No,' I said, 'I'm all right, Bobby. Thanks.'

'Well,' he replied, 'you are putting your boots on the wrong feet.'

I looked down and it was true. Maybe it was having Bobby nearby, or simply the prospect of making my debut, but I had been tugging my right boot onto my left foot. I sorted myself out and we won 7–1. What made it even more special for me was that some of the Raith Rovers team were ex-Rangers, heroes of mine, like Ralfie Brand and Jimmy Millar, players I grew up watching. That game is still fresh in my mind. At one point, the ball went out for a throw-in. One of the lads I used to play football with near Ibrox threw the ball back to me. I remember hitting a volley, from right to left, to John Hughes for one of the goals. It was a brilliant occasion. I played in some big games, a couple of semi-finals in fact and even a European Cup game in 1970. Celtic led KPV Kokkolan 9–0 from the home leg, so it was not too much of a risk bringing me on in the second half of a 5–0 win!

I was getting nearer a regular first-team place. The breakthrough came following a run of goals which read like a golf card: 4, 3, 1, 6, 4, 4, 3. The first eight arrived in a 10-day period at the end of the 1970–71 season, playing in three games against Rangers reserves. We won 7–1, 6–1 and 4–1. That was the culmination of an amazing season, with Vic Davidson, Lou Macari and me scoring more than 80 goals. Then came Frank Beattie's testimonial at Kilmarnock when I scored six out of our seven. A few months after that game, Joe McBride, who had been one of Celtic's most natural goalscorers, said to me: 'You would have got more if you hadn't been embarrassed. Never be embarrassed about scoring.' It was true. I was only a wee boy and I was playing against a guy whose testimonial it was. I felt like I was humiliating Frank Beattie when I should be honouring him. But I had to score, although during the game, as the goals went in, I became more embarrassed with each one.

Celtic went on a pre-season tour of Ireland, where I scored four in a 6–1 win at Limerick. It could have been more – I hit the post twice as well. It was a great trip. Celtic Football Club going to Southern Ireland were always going to get a good reception. It was like Rangers going to Northern Ireland. In Cork, Vic and I decided to get a round of golf in. There was this wee boy caddying for us. At one point he said: 'It's going to rain.' The weather was fine, not a cloud in the sky, so I said: 'Don't be so stupid.' When we reached the furthest point of the course, it lashed down, absolutely bucketed with rain. We got soaked through. After we'd dried out in the hotel, we settled down for our meal. The food wasn't that good, so somebody was sent out to buy fish and chips for the whole Celtic party. It was that kind of trip.

I still didn't know what to expect when we returned to Glasgow. I felt I was playing well and I was certainly scoring, but there was such competition for places up front. Lou, Bobby, Tommy Gemmell, Harry Hood, Tommy Callaghan and I were vying for a couple of positions. I knew how hard it would be to establish myself ahead of players of their calibre, but I was determined. The pre-season warm-up tournament called the Drybrough Cup was coming up. Big Jock picked me for the first game, Dumbarton at home, and I knew this was the opportunity to force my way in. We won 5–2, with four goals from me. Big Jock left me in and I scored a hat-trick in the 4–2 victory over St Johnstone. This made it difficult for Big Jock to leave me out. Although we lost the Drybrough final, 2–1 to Aberdeen, I had come of age. My development, physically and mentally, was improving and that resulted in better performances. It certainly helped that I was playing with some very good players.

One of the greatest was Jimmy Johnstone. He got himself in trouble off the pitch but everyone enjoyed Jimmy's company. He was a great wee fellow, full of eccentricities. Jimmy hated flying which made European trips awkward. Now Big Jock was a bit of a psychologist, so before one tie he told Jimmy that if we beat Red Star Belgrade by two clear goals at home he wouldn't have to fly to the second leg. Jimmy tore them to shreds. At the final whistle, as Celtic celebrated a 5–1 victory, Jimmy danced in delight, doing a delirious jig.

'All the best with the second leg, lads,' he kept shouting at the players, 'I'm not having to fly.'

Big Jock came in just before the second leg and said: 'Jimmy, the Yugoslavian press want to give you an award. If you don't play, there's going to be a riot. You've got to go. You can't let the public down.' Jimmy was not pleased, but he had to go.

I remember Jimmy's testimonial, which he shared with Bobby Lennox. He shared everything with Bobby. Jimmy and Bobby were one of the few Siamese twins to have been separated successfully! They were unbelievable friends. Wee Jimmy was panicking that nobody was going to turn up for the game. Of course, there were 40,000 there. Honest to God, they would have stood on broken bottles to watch Wee Jimmy. For me, it was a privilege to be on the same pitch as him.

I had waited so long to be part of the first team. Now, at the start of the 1971–72 season, we had three games in just under a month at Ibrox, because Celtic Park was being redeveloped. We didn't seem to miss the comforts of home. We won 2–0, 3–0 and 3–2. The one I remember best was the first one, our League Cup meeting on 14 August in front of 72,500. We were winning 1–0 when John Hughes went clean through and was pulled down. I was delighted but I didn't want to celebrate too much in case somebody missed the penalty. Celtic's captain, Billy McNeill, came running up to me.

'Go on, you take it,' he said.

'Get lost.'

'Go on,' he insisted, 'take it.'

'Billy, do me a favour,' I pleaded.

'Take it,' he replied. 'You took them for the reserves.'

'Aye, but not before a full house at Ibrox.'

'If you could take them then,' Billy insisted, 'you can take them now.'

He handed me the ball. I will never forget the ensuing sequence of events. All the Celtic fans were cheering. The photographers ran behind the goal. I placed the ball on the spot, looked around at all the thousands of people focusing on me. 'Jesus,' I thought as I took a couple of steps back. I turned to face the goal; behind it was a green-and-white sea of Celtic fans. I looked down at the ball and saw my bootlace was undone. I stooped down to tie it up. I don't know how long that took, maybe 10 seconds, maybe less. People afterwards made a fuss about it, saying I was being cool or trying to unsettle Peter McCloy, Rangers' goalkeeper. I wasn't. My bootlace just needed tying. I stepped back, looked up and everyone fell still: the cameramen, the fans, big Peter McCloy. I knew he went the same way for every right-footed penalty-taker. He always went down on his left knee to go to his right. That suited me because I wanted to put it to his left. I ran up and put it where I wanted and just hoped that he would do what he normally did. He did. Then the whole place was in uproar. One of the Celtic players threw me up in the air. What a moment! My first senior goal had come against the team I grew up worshipping. At Ibrox too. My dad was delighted. It was irrelevant that he had been a staunch Rangers fan. All that mattered to him was how I fared.

We won 2–0 but, while the Celtic half of Glasgow was celebrating, I sat at home. I never went out that night. Those who play for Celtic and Rangers are always taking a bit of a chance going out after an Old Firm game. If there is a result either way some punter is bound to be upset and give you some stick. After one of the next games against Rangers, both of which Celtic won, with me scoring, I decided to go out. I had arranged to meet Marina in town. I got a lift off one of the lads and stood waiting for her at a bus-stop. I was reading the evening sportspaper, minding my own business. Out of the corner of my eye I could see two Rangers supporters, talking to each other and looking at me.

'Hurry up, Marina,' I was saying to myself, 'just come and pick me up.'

These guys started walking towards me and one of them said: 'Excuse me. I've got a bet on with my mate.'

'What's it got to do with me?' I replied, trying to hide my nerves.

'My mate says you play for Celtic and that your name is Dalglish.'

'Me?'

'Aye.'

'Not me,' I lied.

'I knew that,' the Rangers fan said. 'My friend's an idiot. I've just won a couple of pints off him.'

'Aye, very good,' I said, relieved as they walked away, still arguing. Then Marina's dad drove up with Marina in the back.

'Are you daft?' he said. 'Why are you hanging around here? Where are you going?'

'Just up the road to a disco.'

He turned to Marina and said: 'Get him in the car and the two of you get out of town. Take him out to the airport hotel restaurant for something to eat. You won't be bothered there.'

A funny incident happened one Saturday night. We went to a club and the doorman wouldn't let us in, saying: 'Thirteen . . . you're too young.'

Marina kept arguing that she was 18, but I said: 'Just leave it, Marina. We're not getting in here. Let's go some place else.'

Perhaps the doorman had the last laugh . . . he might have been the Rangers supporter who lost the bet at the bus-stop! So, instead of going to the nightclub, we went for a Chinese meal. Age is no barrier to getting a table in a Chinese restaurant.

The rivalry between Celtic and Rangers was intense but the

two sets of players got on well. I had quite a friendship with Sandy Jardine. I even made a record with him, which unfortunately my kids still have a copy of. Sandy and I called ourselves the 'New Firm'. Soon after the record came out, he man-marked me in an Old Firm match. That was no problem. There was a competitive rivalry between the players but there weren't the religious undertones that scar some of the fans' relationship. On Scotland trips the two sides were very friendly. Ronnie McKinnon, Willie Henderson and Jimmy Johnstone were all close. Jim Baxter was great mates with Paddy Crerand and Billy McNeill. My generation was close too. Derek Johnstone who played for Rangers was smashing company. There were many Old Firm players in the Scotland squad. Big Tam Forsyth used to kick me in Old Firm games, yet he was a friend. 'Scrambled Egg', as we called Rangers' John Greig, was a smashing bloke, but put a blue shirt on him and show him a green-and-white one and he was a different person, totally committed, which is what you would expect. Old Firm games are like weddings – if people did not have them on video they would struggle to recall much about what happened. They were so intense, so competitive and flew by in a flash. Rangers always seemed to be physically stronger than us, especially during Jock Wallace's time. He used to be a hard taskmaster with the fitness. Rangers used to train at Gullane, running up and down the sand-dunes to strengthen their leg muscles. It is still the case that Rangers players seem to be stronger. This contrasted with Celtic, traditionally full of small guys, keen to dribble. The Old Firm styles were a bit like Scotland–England. English teams always seemed to be bigger and stronger – although not necessarily better – than Scottish teams. Although Rangers did have variety, with ball-players like Henderson, they always seemed so much bigger. I might be alone in thinking that. Maybe it was the memory of trying to reach their coat-pegs that convinced me of their extra physical stature. But if we got our game going better than Rangers did, they couldn't get near us, however much bigger they were.

I never received any verbal abuse from Rangers players. There was none of this 'if you go past me again, son, I'll break your leg' which happens elsewhere. There was never any prior warning. I don't think John Greig ever said to Wee Jimmy: 'You do that again and I'll put you on the track.' There was no courtesy call first. It wasn't nice but it was accepted. It also worked the other way. Celtic were hardly angels. Davie Provan's leg was broken in an Old Firm game. Each side was as bad as the other. Each team had people who could look after themselves and their team-mates. But away from the games, the players of Celtic and Rangers always got on very well.

If you have a competitive nature, you have a chance in football, but it is important to ensure your actions do not inflame the crowd. I was present at the Ibrox disaster of 1971 and, although the deaths had nothing to do with anything controversial on the pitch, it made me realise how important it was to behave properly in case it spilled over. I wasn't playing that day but Celtic had given me a ticket for the away end. I couldn't see what happened, we were too far away. Coming out after the game there was little evidence that a major disaster had occurred. Segregation was very strict so when I emerged from Ibrox we were channelled one way, nowhere near the Rangers end. Apparently the fans who had left early and were making their way down the stairs heard cheers for a Colin Stein equaliser in the last minute of the game. They rushed back up the stairs, colliding with others coming out. It crossed my mind that if I had never gone to Celtic, I could have been standing there as a Rangers fan. But then I wouldn't have left early; I never did. I really felt for the people who lost relatives and friends. Supporters tend to be carried away by the occasion of an Old Firm game, not by events on the pitch. Looking back on my 10 years at Celtic, I can't remember an incident in an Old Firm game which I thought would incite trouble on the terraces. I got kicked to bits by Rangers players but I accepted it. The referee's decision was more likely to incite trouble than a player's action. Although crowd trouble plagued football in '73 and '74, most of it was outside grounds. It has been curtailed an awful lot; everybody was united in their efforts to try to improve the punters' behaviour.

In my first season, I scored 17 goals as Celtic took the championship for the seventh time in a row. We also won the Scottish Cup. Celtic could have had a clean sweep but lost the

League Cup final 4–1 to Partick Thistle. It was an unbelievable result. Partick were 4–0 up but in the second half we could have scored as many as them. Unfortunately, Alan Rough was brilliant in goal. I tapped one in but it was meaningless. We missed out on the treble and I missed out on another prize. There was speculation that I was going to get the Scottish Football Writers' Footballer of the Year award. Apparently I was in the running but because I didn't play well from April onwards I never got it. I couldn't understand the logic. I had played so well from August to April; I don't know what happened to those seven months!

My Celtic career was a special time filled with success. Four championships, four Scottish Cups, one League Cup, 328 competitive appearances and 177 goals. I missed only nine league games while at Celtic. Some joker in the dressing-room said I went missing in a lot of games but I never missed many. I was out for two or three games in my first season. This old guy playing for St Johnstone did me in the first minute. It was our throw-in so I stood ready to receive it. As the ball bounced up, the defender's knee went right into my buttocks. I screamed loudly. I have never felt pain like it. What a strange injury that was – a knee in the fatty part of the backside and I missed 10 days.

The most significant disappointment in my Celtic career was that we didn't set a record of 10 consecutive championships. At the start of the 1974–75 season I was very aware of how desperate the club were to make it 10 in a row. Nine was a magnificent achievement but 10 was something special, a figure that would be remembered for all time. It was almost all we could think about. In December the prospects were very hopeful. I scored a hat-trick in a 6–0 victory over Dundee so we could begin the New Year in good heart. Then came a game I will never forget, however hard I try. The memory of it keeps re-appearing like a bad dream. On 4 January we crossed the city to Ibrox. Rangers were rampant, defeating us 3–0 and knocking our confidence so badly that we only won four of our final 15 League games. The dream was over. The sense of shock was awful. The championship was an annual obsession at Parkhead. I can remember one year when we had the title sewn up before the final game of the season. On that last day, all of us players ran out with the same number on our shorts, the figure representing the number of successive titles. It meant so much to us. I felt that I had let down Celtic, and all the hundreds of thousands who love the club.

Championships meant entry to the most prestigious club competition in the world: the European Cup. We never fared too well in Europe while I was at Celtic Park. The great Lisbon Lions were fading from the scene, one by one. We were never good enough to compete with the very top teams in Europe. Of the many ties, the one that stands out most is a brutal semi-final played in 1974 against Atletico Madrid. Atletico had an Argentinian coach who used two teams – a defensive and completely uncompromising one for away games and an attacking team for home games. The Spaniards had three sent off at Celtic Park. They were kicking us, trying to stop us anyhow. I got kicked but was treated lightly compared to Jimmy Johnstone. Obviously, they considered Jimmy to be the most dangerous opponent. It was a horrible occasion; there was even a fracas off the pitch as well. When we went over to Spain amid heavy security there wasn't a problem, apart from the problem their players presented. Atletico played well. They should have gone on to win the final against Bayern Munich but lost the replay.

European success proved elusive. There was no problem domestically, except in the League Cup where we kept failing in the final. By the 1974–75 season Celtic had lost four League Cup finals in a row. Everyone who wore the green and white of Celtic was determined that this year, in the final against Hibs, we would end such an embarrassing run. We beat them 6–3, Dixie Deans scoring a hat-trick for us while Joe Harper hit three for Hibs. Sometime afterwards, I bumped into Dixie and Joe Harper at a dinner. Joe started talking about that League Cup final.

'It's unbelievable bad luck to score three in a Cup final and still lose,' Joe said.

'Aye, that's terrible,' Wee Dixie said, 'but you never really scored three. One was an own goal.'

'No, no,' Joe insisted, 'I scored three. I've got my runners-up medal. I went home and thought I've scored three goals and all I've got to show for it is a runners-up medal.'

Dixie loosened the buttons on his shirt and said: 'Is that the Cup final you are talking about, Joe?' Dixie had the winner's medal around his neck!

It was ironic that Celtic finally won the League Cup the season we lost the League. Fate clearly decreed we had to sacrifice the championship to win the League Cup. I didn't approve of fate's decision. I would rather have had another loser's medal in the League Cup. After that rare triumph, Celtic carried on losing the League Cup. In my last season, we lost 2–1 to Aberdeen in extra time although we murdered them; and we won the double. Maybe we really were jinxed in the League Cup.

Still, at least I had a full set of domestic medals. In 1975 we did the double of both cups, winning the Scottish Cup by beating Airdrie 3–1 in Billy McNeill's last game. Billy gave me a lift to Celtic Park, where we were meeting the rest of the players.

On the way, Billy said to me: 'This is going to be my last game. I'm going to retire after the Cup final.'

'Thank Christ for that!' I said. We just laughed.

But it was his last game. For somebody who had done so much for Celtic it was brilliant that Billy should go out in such a successful manner, holding up another trophy. He was involved in his first season with a headed goal against Dunfermline when Big Jock came in and won the Cup. So it was a fitting farewell that Billy should be chaired off the field by the players, his hands cradling another trophy. Speculation abounded as to who would replace Billy. I never thought it would be me. I certainly wasn't the obvious candidate; Danny was. I was only a veteran of three seasons. There were older players than me at Celtic. But a couple of days later Big Jock called me in and said he wanted me to take over as club captain. It was not the most auspicious of starts: a 2–1 defeat by Rangers, although at least I scored. It was deflected but I still claimed it. I always claimed them. I even tried to claim the Rangers two.

I have never been a confident person. Becoming captain of the most successful team in Scotland didn't make me more confident. Being captain was a great honour but there was not much to be done away from the pitch. Big Jock would organise everything for the players. Occasionally he would discuss things with me, like commercial matters that affected the players. We would never mention tactics. That was solely Jock's territory. Jock allowed me to have an opinion, as long as I never voiced it to him or anyone else! My thoughts mattered to Jock, but his opinions were set in stone. You couldn't influence Jock. What I tried to do as captain of Celtic was lead by example. I hoped people would take inspiration from my dedication to training and my attitude and commitment on the pitch. My first season as captain was none too successful: only a League Cup loser's medal (another one to add to the collection). Celtic had failed to win a trophy for the first time in 12 years.

It was not a happy time at Celtic Park. Big Jock had been badly injured in a car crash before the start of the season. He was driving back from holiday and was involved in a head-on collision on the A74. He was lucky to survive. Celtic missed his leadership. If a guy of Big Jock's ability is not on your side, it's going to make it much more difficult to be successful. Sean Fallon was thrust into temporary charge but Big Jock was an impossible man to replace, for however short a time. You can't fill a legend's shoes. It was certainly not Sean's fault that we didn't win anything that year. Players have got to take responsibility themselves when they don't win anything. A manager guides players, and points them in the right direction, and then it was up to us. Sean certainly tried to do that. Comparisons between him and Big Jock are unfair. The most important thing about that season was that Big Jock recovered.

Fortunes in football can change like the wind. After a poor season, by Celtic's standards, the next season we did the double, helped by some new players, reinforcements in the shape of Pat Stanton, Joe Craig and Alfie Conn. On 16 April at Hibs, Joe scored the goal that gave us the championship, a tenth in 12 years. Three weeks later we beat Rangers in the Cup final. We were awarded a penalty and Andy Lynch said to me: 'I'll take it.'

'Are you sure?' I replied. I would normally have taken it but he was determined. It was a tense moment when Andy stepped up. A few players couldn't watch but Lynch didn't miss, giving us a 1–0 victory. At the final whistle, we went on half a lap of honour. At Old Firm games it was impossible to go on a full lap of honour. I was running round with Peter Latchford, waving to our fans, when we saw some kids in wheelchairs. We ran over, as excited as they were. We were jumping up and down for joy, sharing our happiness with them. 'Do you want to see my medal?' I asked one wee boy. Of course he did. It was special for me to show it to him because I had promised to give it to my own young son. Paul was only three months old.

I unclipped the box and held it up for him to see. Somebody hit my arm and the medal fell from my hand. We searched everywhere, kicking and pulling at the wooden skirting around the outer edge of the pitch, desperately trying to find the medal. The police came over.

'Get inside,' they told us because all the Rangers fans were still down the other end. The police were worried that they might be antagonised by the sight of Celtic players still on the pitch.

'I'm not going until I've found my medal,' I told the police. I was convinced it was down there. We were on our hands and knees looking for it.

Neilly Mochan came out and said: 'You've got to come in. The police are going off their heads.'

But I was adamant. 'I'm not going in until I find my medal.'

Finally, a policeman came up and said: 'Kenny, we'll find your medal. Please go in before there's any hassle.'

Even though I was desperately upset, I could understand their desire to clear the ground.

So I trudged off into the dressing-room feeling completely disconsolate. Although Celtic had just won the Cup, I was really down. I sat there, thinking I had lost my medal which I wanted so much to give to Paul. Two minutes later the door opened and a policeman came in. He walked up to me, leant over and said: 'There you are, Kenny,' as he handed me my medal. I was almost speechless with happiness. It had fallen inside the umbrella of one of the kids. I was so emotional afterwards that I got on the Rangers coach by mistake. It was the first one to pull up. I climbed aboard, looked around, and said: 'Oh, sorry.' I wasn't trying to be clever. There was a wee bit of irony in that. I had arrived at Celtic as a Rangers fan. Here I was almost leaving with Rangers after what proved to be my last important game for Celtic.

For some time, I had been thinking hard about moving on. I needed a new football challenge. I was settled in my domestic life. Marina and I got engaged in the spring of 1974. At the time, we went to the well-known jewellery area of Glasgow called the Argyle Arcade. If couples are spotted in there they get loads of stick at work, so we sneaked in, trying to stay incognito so word wouldn't get out. Picking the right ring took a bit of time. We found one. Bought it. Took it home. Didn't like it. Came back. Changed it. Saw another one. Bought it. Took it home. Didn't like it. Came back. Changed it again. Thankfully it was third time lucky.

Some people live together before getting married but that was not the right way for us. We were married in November 1974. It didn't change me in any way, shape or form. I was always pretty settled. I was happy to stay at home, resting up between matches. I had been going out with Marina since I got in the first team so there was not much to change in my life. Our wedding day was Marina's birthday as well, which was quite convenient. Jim Donald, my old friend from Possil YMCA and Cumbernauld, was the best man. Billy McNeill came back from Buckingham Palace, where the Queen had honoured him for his services to football. Billy and his wife Liz made it in time for the reception, which we appreciated. It was a great night. All the Celtic lads were there, a few of the Scotland lads, too. As we were about to leave on honeymoon, Big Jock said to me: 'We'll see you for training in two days.' And he meant it. I certainly wasn't going to risk Big Jock's wrath. I was back on time. I think Marina understood. That's the price you have to pay if you want to get married during the season. So we had our proper honeymoon in the summer when Marina was already pregnant with Kelly. It was a wee bit embarrassing, saying we were on honeymoon with the baby due in three months. We moved into our new house after the short honeymoon. It was in Newton Mearns, a suburb of Glasgow. No visitor would know that I had once been an apprentice joiner. I never did any work on it. It was a nice house, a good start for us. Newton Mearns was a friendly area. A good friend of mine lived around the corner and we still saw a lot of our families.

My life has been focused solely on football and family. The family ethos is very important to me, whether it's the family at home or the family atmosphere at work. A family atmosphere pervaded Celtic. From the outside, Rangers were by far the more glamorous club, but Celtic by that time were obviously the more successful. A big part of that success was the atmosphere inside the club. The people were so friendly. It is vitally important to me to feel comfortable where I work. That was one of the attractions of Liverpool, the next and most important phase of my life.

=3=

HEADING SOUTH

W HENEVER anyone asked my dad when I was going to go to England, he would answer: 'In May – when he plays at Wembley!' But by 1977 I had outgrown Celtic. The Lisbon Lions were a distant memory. I had captained Celtic, won every trophy in Scotland, but nothing in Europe. It was time to move on to a club capable of giving me the European success I craved. I didn't want to go abroad so Liverpool fitted the bill perfectly. They were the champions of Europe with the family atmosphere I so needed to make me feel comfortable. I wanted to be at a club where we could celebrate trophies with a tour of the city in an open-top bus, looking down to see all the happy faces sharing our success. If Celtic had toured Glasgow's streets holding out a trophy from an open-top bus, there would have been a riot. There had only been tours of the city after Celtic's and Rangers' European successes.

I knew a lot about Anfield, about its history, its success, its friendliness. Having been on a trial there at 15, I already had a bit of an insight. I was only an unknown kid then but Liverpool's first-team players were friendly. They took time out to talk to me, a quiet, embarrassed schoolboy from Scotland. Players like Ian St John, Ron Yeats and Billy Stevenson, who I used to watch at Ibrox, were open and welcoming. It meant so much to me that Billy Stevenson, one of my idols, would talk to me. And Ian Ross, one of my old mates from Milton, was there. During my trial I wanted to get some autographs. With the other triallists, I went to the first-team dressing-room door, but I couldn't bring myself to go inside. I was too shy. The other boys were saying: 'Go in, Kenny, go in.' I froze. I couldn't take that step into a room full of footballers I admired, men who I could hear bantering with each other. Eventually I plucked up courage and went in. I went up to Billy Stevenson and said: 'Would you please sign this, Billy?' He said: 'No.' As I walked away all the players burst out laughing. Billy was only kidding. He quickly called me back and signed it. It was nice that they could have a joke with me. They treated me as an individual, made a joke of the situation, rather than doing it in an off-hand manner. I couldn't stand players not looking up when they signed autographs, not even registering that I was there. Liverpool were different. I re-played that incident over in my mind many times as I pondered which club I should leave Celtic for.

I thought about Bill Shankly too, a manager who had turned Liverpool into such a footballing institution. Everyone who went to Liverpool could relate to Shanks. He had everybody pulling in the same direction, on and off the pitch. People quickly felt a real affinity for Liverpool because Shanks was totally enthusiastic. He set up a great tradition of making people understand the principles that Liverpool Football Club stood for, almost moulding them to the Liverpool way. This approach was inherited by Bob Paisley, because Bob was part and parcel of the way Shanks worked. The tradition was passed on to Reuben Bennett, Ronnie Moran, Roy Evans and Joe Fagan. It was enshrined in the Boot Room, where the coaching staff met to discuss anything that would make Liverpool more successful. I came to learn more about the Liverpool way while I was still at Celtic. Early in that summer of 1977, a time of many disagreements between Celtic and myself, I was relaxing in the Scotland hotel in Chester before a Home Championship international with Wales. A documentary about Liverpool was on television. They were about to play in the European Cup final. I watched it deliberately. I was looking for the right new employers. I realised what an awful lot of similarities there were between Celtic and Liverpool. What came across in the programme was how closely knit the players were. Liverpool was portrayed as somewhere I could go and feel comfortable. My immediate reaction as the credits rolled was: 'That will do for me.'

The next night we watched Liverpool defeat Borussia Moenchengladbach. It surprised me that a number of the Scotland squad who were playing in England wanted Liverpool to lose. That told me that Liverpool were the team every English club wanted to beat, which aroused even greater respect. Liverpool held many attractions. They had just had a very good season: League champions, European Cup-winners and almost FA Cup-winners. Not bad for starters! The possibility of achieving success in Europe was a significant draw for me. The closest we got at Celtic during my time in the first team were semi-finals, against Inter Milan, and that battle with Atletico Madrid. I was desperate to do well in Europe; the European Cup is the greatest test of a club. A team has to be consistent over two years to become champions of Europe.

Seeing pictures of Liverpool parading the European Cup through their local streets really stirred me up. It upset me that Celtic could never go on a tour of the city; Glasgow was too irrevocably divided. Celtic did it once, from the airport all the way back to Celtic Park when they won the European Cup in 1967. Rangers did it when they won the Cup-Winners' Cup. But those were special occasions, great moments for Scotland, and they hadn't had to beat the other Old Firm team on the way. The desire to tour the city became an obsession with me. I wanted to see the thousands of people turn out to cheer, to see their faces all lit up. I wanted to share the celebration, the excitement, the joy the team could bring to thousands of people. It sounds silly but I just loved that side of success and really looked forward to it. At Liverpool we started to take the kids on the bus as well as the wives. I thought that was great for them. It might not mean much at the time but they would look back and cherish the memory. I said to the players after we had won a trophy: 'Look, anybody can come. If you want to bring your kids on the bus, that's no problem, because my kids are coming on.' Everyone had made a contribution. The bus could take it. If someone had put concrete in the tyres we would still have got round Liverpool. People would have pushed it.

So I knew where I wanted to go. It had to be Liverpool. I was determined to leave Celtic. Often players agitate for moves because they know other clubs are interested. That was not the case with me. In all my time at Celtic I only saw speculation in the papers linking my name with other clubs once, when a newspaper associated my name with Crystal Palace. They had plenty of players from Scotland at the time, people like John McCormick, John Hughes and Willie Wallace. I was still only 19 but I went in to see Big Jock about it.

'Get lost,' he said. 'You've got no chance of going anywhere. You'd better believe it.'

'OK, boss,' I said, and walked out.

I wasn't bothered. I think Spurs might have had a sniff at me but otherwise there was no other interest. Maybe other clubs didn't fancy me or thought I was too rooted at Celtic.

I was ready to uproot myself two years before I eventually did. By 1975 I had achieved every success in Scotland, so I asked for a transfer. I felt awkward doing it. Big Jock was in hospital, recovering from that car crash that almost killed him, and Sean Fallon was temporarily in charge. I knocked at Sean's door, feeling embarrassed but determined to do something about my future.

'Sean,' I said, 'I know you don't need this but I've made my mind up. I really want to go. I'm sorry to give you the hassle at a time like this. You don't deserve it. It might be better for you if you were left out of the equation and for me to talk directly to the chairman. It's certainly not a pleasant thing and I don't want to burden you. But I've got to look after myself.'

Sean agreed that I should see the chairman, Desmond White. After a long discussion with him, I changed my mind. There was also the small consideration that Marina was due with Kelly, so it wasn't the best time to move. There was no financial inducement for me to stay, although I did have the honour of being club captain. In the end, I stayed out of loyalty to Celtic. The club had been good to me. Big Jock and Sean had enabled me to fulfil my dream of becoming a successful professional footballer. I owed them. With Big Jock in hospital I didn't want to leave Celtic or Sean in the lurch. If the circumstances had been different at the club, I would have walked out. In 1975 my loyalty to the club in a troubled situation proved stronger than my desire to leave. That definitely changed over the next 24 months.

I tried again the following summer. Big Jock refused to contemplate it. Negotiations went on, with Celtic trying to convince me to stay and me set on leaving. The whole saga came to a head in the summer of '77. Jock Stein told me before the Scottish Cup final that I had to sign a new contract.

'Why?' I asked.

Jock said that if I didn't sign the club would have to register with the Scottish Football Association that I was being retained but not signed. Such a development would be on the back page of every newspaper. The last thing I wanted was to cause any disruption before the Cup final, particularly as we were chasing the double, so I signed what was, to me, a worthless document. On the Monday after the Cup final, I went up to Celtic Park and told them that I still wanted to go.

'But you signed a contract,' Big Jock said. This really angered me.

'Yeah,' I replied, 'but you know full well why I signed the contract and so do I. Fortunately it's worked out well for everybody. We've won the double. But I signed the contract because I didn't want to disrupt the squad before the Cup final. You know that was the only reason and so do I.'

The board couldn't really argue. It was the truth. In the end they agreed to let me go. Celtic could still have held on to me because of the one-year contract I had signed. But Big Jock would have lost all credibility if Celtic had kept me against my will and it became known, as it surely would have done, that I had signed only for the Cup final, and only on the grounds that I did not want to undermine the team's preparations. Legally, Jock Stein was in the right, but he never really had a leg to stand on. Celtic knew my position. They knew I wanted to leave. I never tried to blame Celtic. I never said it was the club's fault for being unambitious or for not giving me more money. This was a decision for Kenny Dalglish. I had made the decision two years before. I left Celtic as double-winners.

The situation dragged on during that summer. Celtic probably felt that if the uncertainty went on long enough I would have a change of heart. Not a chance. I was adamant about leaving. I went off on tour with Scotland to Argentina where I thought the whole thing over again. Nothing changed my mind. If anything, being surrounded by Scots who had done well in England strengthened my desire to head south. When I rang home Marina told me that there had been speculation in the papers linking me with Liverpool. It certainly could not have come from me. I was thousands of miles away and never mentioned the situation to anyone. When I returned to Scotland, Celtic ordered me to go on tour with them, to Singapore and Australia. It was make-or-break time. I told Big Jock I definitely wasn't going, knowing my absence would cause a real fuss in the press.

'What do you mean you're not going?' Jock said. I stood my ground this time.

'I don't want to go,' I said. 'I've just come back from South America and I don't want to disappear away again.'

Celtic tried to coerce me, claiming the host organisers were keen for me to play but that I didn't have to play in all the tour games.

'I'm not playing any games – because I'm not going,' I told them. They tried to get round me in other ways.

'But Danny's going,' Jock said.

'Well that's up to Danny,' I retorted. 'Danny can go if he wants to go. I've told you I don't want to go. Anyway it's better for you to take players who are going to be here next year.' Big Jock told me to have a think about it.

'Aye, all right,' I said as I left the meeting, knowing full well that my decision was unalterable. I went back up to Celtic Park in the morning and told them again I wasn't going to Australia.

They said: 'If you go to Australia, we will phone up a club we know will be interested in you and you can move when you come back.' This, of course, interested me. After all, my main aim was to leave Celtic Park.

'All right,' I said and went off home.

But when I got home I knew I couldn't go to Australia. I had to leave now. I was determined to force the issue. There had been too many delays. I was worried that Celtic might use the extra time to coerce me more.

I had been told to report to Parkhead that afternoon with my boots. I went back as planned but without my boots. As I arrived, the coach Neilly Mochan asked me: 'Where's your boots?'

'I've got to see the gaffer first,' I said. Big Jock came out. 'What is it?'

'I'm not going,' I told him. 'I'm not entitled to ask you which club you phoned or how you got on but I'm not going.'

Big Jock looked at me and said: 'Your career has just taken a backward step.'

'So be it,' I replied, 'but I'm not going.'

'Sleep on it and phone me in the morning.'

As I was getting up the next day, the phone rang. It was Jock.

'Look, Kenny,' he said, 'just don't bother coming. It's better if we take people who want to play for us.'

'Aye, all right,' I said and put the phone down. My Celtic career was almost over.

The players flew out that day. When the papers realised I wasn't in the party, all hell broke loose. There were reporters camped outside the house but I wasn't there. Ironically, it was an old newspaper man called James Sanderson who got me out of the way. He lived round the corner and phoned earlier to say: 'Come on, I'll take you out of the way.' He took me up to Cathcart Castle for a game of golf.

The newspapers were filled with speculation about when and where I was going. While the first team were away I trained with the reserves. It was pointless staying away from Celtic Park. I wanted to minimise the fuss. When the first team returned from tour, Big Jock asked me if I was still determined to go. Once again I said yes. That Friday, 6 August, the reserves were playing at Stirling Albion. I assumed I would be captain, as I was captain of the whole club, but Big Jock told Brian McLaughlin, the reserves' skipper, to lead the team out. I thought to myself: 'Ooh, oh. There's something happening here. Big Jock must be upset.' Again he tried to talk me into staying.

'No,' I said. 'It's nothing personal, I appreciate everything you've done for me but I've got to go and have a look down south. If I'm not good, I'm not good.'

Four days later, the first team were at Dunfermline. At least I was in the side. We were sitting in the dressing-room before kick-off, waiting for Big Jock to say who was captain. Just when the referee's buzzer went he threw the ball to Danny and said: 'Go on, Danny, take them out.' I was sitting next to Alfie Conn and he said to me: 'Oh well, that must be you off then. I'll be seeing you later.' We went out, played and won. My Celtic career ended at Dunfermline, stripped of the captaincy before a small crowd with even fewer people knowing it was my last game.

After the game, two journalists, Jim Rodger of the *Daily Mirror* and Ken Gallacher of the *Daily Record*, came up and asked what was happening.

'I don't know,' I said. 'Nothing as far as I'm concerned.'

They told me Bob Paisley and Liverpool's chairman, John Smith, had watched the game.

'Honest to God, I don't know anything about it,' I told Jim and Ken. But I soon realised something was afoot. Jock had disappeared in his car. On the bus back, Alfie Conn said: 'You must be off, Liverpool were up here.'

'Well they can't have been impressed,' I replied, 'because I'm going back on the bus with you!'

After we were dropped off at Celtic Park I went over to my father-in-law's pub in Rutherglen with Peter Latchford. I had just settled at the bar when Marina phoned.

'You've got to call the Park right away,' she said. I did immediately. Big Jock came on the phone.

'Do you still want to go?'

'Aye, I've told you I want to go.'

'I cannot change your mind?'

'No.'

'Well, don't tell anybody, just jump in your motor and get straight up to the Park. Would you be interested in going to Liverpool?'

'Aye, I think so.'

'Well get up here, then.' I got going.

'See you later,' I told the people in the pub. 'I'm going up to the ground.'

Big Latch looked at me and said: 'All the best, wee man, all the best.' They sensed what was happening.

I reached the ground at midnight. Big Jock was waiting. He took me up to the boardroom, where Bob Paisley and John Smith were waiting. Big Jock had obviously marked Bob's card about me a long time in advance, saying: 'You've got to take him. He's not available now but I'll tell you when he is.' When it became clear I was determined to leave, Jock kept his word and phoned Bob. 'Kenny's available now,' he said. Bob told John Smith he wanted me. Liverpool had such a simple way of handling transfers. Old Bob would just pick the players he wanted to bring to Anfield and John Smith and Peter Robinson would sort out the deals. They were brilliant at deals. So I walked into the boardroom to meet my next employers. Bob was there as well because new players like to talk to the person who is going to be looking after them. They informed me that the two clubs had agreed a fee. We talked for a couple of minutes. After two years of wanting a move, it was all happening in minutes. I was ecstatic. I returned home about 12.30 and told Marina. She was as excited as me. Although Big Jock had said 'don't say a word to anyone', there was already a photographer outside my house in the middle of the night. It was Eric Craig, from the *Daily Record*, who I knew. 'Oh, all right,' I said to Eric, who took some pictures and left. The newspapers must have been tipped off by someone at Celtic.

I tried to get some sleep. It was difficult because I was so excited. At 8 a.m. I got up and left home. It was all so sudden. It was a bit like going to court and being jailed. You walk down the stairs and that's you away. I went up to Celtic Park for the last time. Jock was there, ready to drive me south to Moffat where Bob and John Smith were staying. I went inside to fetch my boots and bumped into Dave McParland, one of Jock's assistants. I had never been one of Dave's favourites. As I got my boots he said: 'I suppose I've got to wish you all the best.' 'See you later,' I said and got out. That was a wee bit of a sour farewell but saying goodbye to Big Jock in Moffat was very emotional. He shook my hand, said, 'All the best, you little so-and-so,' and hugged me. It was a very moving moment. Big Jock had been the most powerful influence in my career and now, here we were, ending a very successful club relationship. There was no trace of animosity.

In his heart, Big Jock knew that I had to go. He understood my motives. He knew I didn't want to look back in later years and think: 'I wish I had done that.' I needed to prove myself. It was selfish, I know, and Celtic's fans were angry, but footballers only have one playing career and it can end suddenly with a bad tackle. You have to seize every chance. If the decision proved to be wrong, I knew I could come back to another Scottish club. It was always in the back of my mind that some Scottish club would be interested. Big Jock also knew how much I respected him for everything he'd done for me and Celtic. It was time to go. I stood there at the hotel in Moffat and looked at Big Jock. 'I've got to try it,' I said. He understood.

It was a real parting of the ways. Jock drove back north and I headed on south with Bob Paisley and John Smith. We arrived at Anfield where events continued to go quickly. I passed a medical and went to the press conference held to announce my signing. I had arrived. The fee was £440,000, including VAT. Some people said it was a lot of money. It wasn't. Liverpool had sold Kevin Keegan to Hamburg for £500,000. They could claim the VAT back so they got me for £100,000 less than they sold Kevin for. At the time, people might have thought Liverpool had got a bad deal; but, over the years, I was fortunate enough to make a contribution to the club's success, just as Kevin made a tremendous contribution to Liverpool's success in previous years. It was a good deal for everyone. Kevin got what he wanted, which was a challenge abroad. I got what I wanted, a move to England, which was virtually the equivalent of going abroad for me. Liverpool were £100,000 to the good. It was the ideal situation for everybody at the time, but no one was to know how it would turn out. It turned out very successfully for Kevin at Hamburg and it didn't turn out too badly for me. Bob said that even if Kevin hadn't gone he would have signed me. A forward line of Dalglish, Keegan and John Toshack could have been interesting.

Some people alleged I went south simply for the money. That's rubbish. Football has given me everything I own but finance has never been of paramount importance. I never worried about my wages at Celtic. If I thought I was getting decent pay, that suited me fine. If someone else was getting more, good luck to them. Even if I didn't think they were a better footballer than me, they were obviously a better negotiator. I have always done my own contractual negotiations. If I had been going south simply for financial reasons, I would have seen if there was somebody else interested. My prime motivating force was whether I would be happy. If I could see myself being comfortable, the money was not so important. A guarantee of happiness is worth a lot.

I certainly can't complain about the financial side. Liverpool were generous. After I had my medical at Anfield, John Smith called me up to Peter Robinson's room to talk over the details of the personal terms.

'What's the most advantageous way for me to get my money?' I asked.

'Leave it with us,' Peter said. 'We cannot give you your money any more advantageously, but we'll give you a few quid extra.'

'Well,' I said, 'I was happy with what you offered me before, but obviously I'll accept the increase.'

It was all completely above board. I knew I had made the right decision. The way Liverpool treated people was superb. The wages I got were very, very good but were not comparable to the great sums being paid now. That's market forces. Wages have gone through the roof since my day, so maybe I've been unlucky. I missed the gravy train. But as long as the club can survive and the players can live with their consciences, there is no problem. I could live with my conscience with what I was getting paid; Celtic, Liverpool and Blackburn Rovers could certainly survive.

Liverpool really looked after their employees. The board helped me through a very difficult time just after I joined. I had got into financial trouble over a bonded whisky warehouse, which someone had said would be a good investment. It sounded a promising financial proposition at the time, but we ran into problems and lost a lot of money. Fortunately I was young enough to be able to survive it.

I'm convinced my success with Liverpool came about because of the way they treated me. They were down-to-earth, helpful, professional and friendly. On the Wednesday I signed, Ian Callaghan sat with me at lunch. That night, Liverpool's captain, Emlyn Hughes, came over to the hotel to see me. Big Tosh took me up for a cup of tea with Shanks and his wife, Nessie. Shanks said to me: 'Look, son, I've got two pieces of advice for you – don't over-eat in that hotel and don't lose your accent.' I kept to one of them! Shanks was proud to be Scottish.

Ten years on, I was finally a Liverpool player. Things kept happening quickly. The morning after signing I was off training

at Melwood. My new team-mates wound me up, which immediately helped me to feel accepted. During a recent England–
Scotland game, Liverpool's keeper, Ray Clemence, had let a shot
of mine through his legs. So on my first day at Melwood, the other
lads were urging me to give Clem some stick. 'I'll wait a bit,
thanks,' I said. I could hardly go round taking the mickey out of
Englishmen on my first day. I waited until the second day.

We travelled south for the Charity Shield against Manchester
United. At Liverpool, they tend to play down the importance of
the Charity Shield. I know it's not the FA Cup final but that
Charity Shield, my Liverpool debut, was a big, big game for me. It
always is. I can't believe it when people dismiss the Charity
Shield. I even experienced cramp for the first time.

Walking out of the Wembley tunnel, Roy Evans said to me:
'Give them a wave.'

'What do you mean?' I replied.

'They're chanting your name.'

I had not noticed that the Liverpool fans were chanting
'Dalglish'. So I lifted my hand up and quickly put it down
again. I felt self-conscious. We drew; I felt very comfortable
playing with my new team-mates.

There was little time to draw breath. I was soon making my
League debut, away to Middlesbrough. It could not have begun
better, with me scoring after six minutes, following a pass that
had a compliment slip from Terry McDermott. Afterwards, I was
surprised at the positive attitude towards this 1–1 draw. I found it
strange to come to terms with going away from home and being
quite happy with a draw. With respect to other teams, I thought a
team of Liverpool's stature should go anywhere expecting to win.
Drawing at Middlesbrough was considered quite a good result.
At Celtic they would have said that a draw wasn't such a good
result.

My Anfield debut came against Newcastle, who counted
Tommy Craig amongst their number. I had grown up with
Wee Tam, playing Glasgow Schools, Scottish Schools and Scottish Youth with him. Before kick-off, I found Tam looking up at
the sign that declares 'This Is Anfield'.

'How are you, Kenny?' he asked.

'I'm all right, I think,' I told Tam, 'but you see that sign there?

It's supposed to frighten the opposition. I'm terrified by it and it's my home ground.'

Fortunately, the game worked out well. Just after half-time, Ray Kennedy started wandering off down the inside left. I raced towards the box. Ray's pass came in and I clipped the ball past Newcastle's keeper, Steve Hardwick, as he came out. The goal was at the Kop end and I nearly finished up in amongst them. Their appreciation was magnificent. It really touched me. That was the start of the relationship between the Kop and me. It was a special relationship, hard to articulate how strong the bond was. We would share great success in England and Europe.

—4—

LIFE AT LIVERPOOL

WHEN I WALKED into Liverpool's dressing-room for the first time, I received quite a shock. I found myself surrounded by men with hair-driers. 'What is this?' I thought to myself. A lot of Liverpool players had them at training and at matches. This was all very strange to me. I would just wash my hair and then let it dry, but here were all these famous footballers standing in front of the mirror, carefully drying their hair, combing and blowing it into place. After I overcame my concern about the hair-driers, I quickly realised what a remarkable place the Liverpool dressing-room was. There wasn't any practical joking, like the usual Algipan in the shorts or boot polish in the shampoo which happens at every club. The joking was more verbal. At Liverpool, banter was a fine art. There wasn't one player who wouldn't join in. I immediately felt at home; the atmosphere echoed Celtic's dressing-room, where laughter reigned.

Success never created any jealousy between players at Anfield, which is unusual in a football club. Success can generate problems. Suddenly each player wants to be the main man and the so-called stars insist they should be getting any endorsements or sponsorships that are going. That never happened at Liverpool. The team spirit was always strong. Football clubs are like other places of work; people stick with those colleagues whose company they enjoy. But the most important quality is to have a great togetherness on the pitch. There were no cliques at Liverpool. We were all in it together. That was one of the many reasons why Liverpool dominated England and Europe: strength through unity. That can keep you going during periods of adversity. The team had it during tough matches.

Liverpool's special spirit could be seen everywhere. The coach rides from Anfield to training at Melwood or away games were absolutely brilliant. Liverpool used to be a terrible club for pulling people up for mistakes. If a player said something wrong, something simple like 'A Merry New Year' instead of 'A Happy New Year', he would get slaughtered. We used to call them ricks. The banter was unbelievable, particularly when Terry Mac was in full flow. Steve Heighway was bright academically, but that didn't set him apart; he contributed to the banter. Everyone did. They worked to make me feel part of Liverpool. Although most people called me 'Kenny', which was not very original, I soon had other nicknames. Terry Mac used to call me 'Super' because of a headline that went 'Super Kenny'. When Graeme Souness arrived, he called me 'Dog's', a shortening of the Scottish compliment 'Dog's Bollocks'. Sitting on the coach, sharing the banter, I would look around and know I was surrounded by some of the best players in Europe: Graeme, Terry Mac, Ray Kennedy, Ray Clemence, Emlyn Hughes, Joey Jones, Tommy Smith, Phil Neal, Steve Heighway, Ian Callaghan, Phil Thompson, Big Tosh, David Johnson, David Fairclough and Alan Hansen.

What players they were. In goal was Clem. Nobody could choose between him and Peter Shilton as the country's best goalkeeper. Clem had a great defence in front of him. Nealy and Thommo were also England internationals. At left-back, Joey Jones was a Welsh internationalist. Smithy was still playing when I arrived; his goal in the European Cup final had fired him up for another season. There was such competition for places: Smithy, Thommo, Emlyn and Big Al going for the two centre-back positions. Big Al arrived before me, in April, but was not a regular to begin with. Al got in when Emlyn was injured. Emlyn could play left-back as well; he was versatile. You wouldn't say Emlyn was shy, on or off the pitch. Other people didn't like him but he was always all right to me. All that really matters is that Emlyn contributed on the pitch. You can't expect 18 to 20 guys in a dressing-room to all be best friends. No Liverpool player ever carried a grudge on to the pitch. Emlyn must have disliked people within the dressing-room, as well as they him, so it was to his credit that he never let grudges show on the pitch.

Quality ran right through Liverpool. Jimmy Case was a good midfield player, who could move the ball about well and scored a lot of valuable goals. He was unselfish and helped Phil Neal a lot. Nealy could stand on his own two feet but Jimmy was always there, covering and closing down. In the middle, Graeme came in January '78 and replaced Cally. Beside Graeme was Terry Mac, and they complemented each other brilliantly. Terry's strengths were running, passing and finishing. Along with his vision, Terry had another great quality: he was always upbeat. On the left was Ray Kennedy, a clever player, probably the best finisher at Liverpool. He could finish any way he wanted with his left or right foot. Ray was good in the air, he could strike the ball in, he could sidefoot in. Shanks left the day he signed and Bob moved him from attack into midfield. What an inspired move that turned out to be.

Things began to change up front. Kevin's great partner John Toshack was about to go. Liverpool enjoyed fantastic success with Tosh flicking the ball on for Kev, and Kevin flicking it on for Tosh. I don't know if Tosh missed Kevin or whether it was coincidental that when Keegan left, Tosh's time was up anyway. Tosh did have a problem with his thigh. Maybe Liverpool were going through a change of style. Maybe Tosh's departure was my fault. Liverpool obviously didn't think we could form a partnership because they let him go. A partnership between myself and Tosh would not have been the same as between Kevin and Tosh; every partnership has its own identity. It was sad to see him go. He had been a great servant to Liverpool and a great help to me settling in. With Tosh's departure, Liverpool started to play without a big target-man for the first time in quite a few years. The style had to change; I couldn't play the way Tosh played. I would never have reached all those flick-ons. There is a common misconception that Liverpool altered their style radically when I arrived, that they deliberately adopted a more patient passing game. I wasn't the cause. Liverpool had begun passing it across the back about two years before I came. I remember it well – I was there. It was in a testimonial match against Celtic and Shanks had Emlyn and Thommo passing the ball across the back. The principles never changed with me coming in. With different individuals in the team you get slight adjustments in the style of play. It's an obvious asset to play to someone's strengths. If a team has somebody tall up front then they should play high balls, but they must pick and choose when to play such balls. It has to be beneficial and not an obsession. I always felt that a big fellow with a good touch is of more value to a team than a wee fellow with a good touch. It gives the team another option.

It was easy to play for Liverpool because their philosophy was that football is simple. Players had to make themselves available so moves could continue. If I was available, I would receive the ball. If I'd got it, somebody else would make himself available. It was hardly complex. People used to refer to 'the secret of Liverpool Football Club'. You didn't need to be Sherlock Holmes to work it out. The 'secret' of Liverpool's success was that every employee was good at his job. That's no secret, that's common sense. If somebody is good at administration and you employ them, then the administrative side of the club is going to be good. If someone is good at football, then the football side of the club is going to be good. Simple really.

Liverpool enjoyed tremendous respect, inside and outside the game, because of the way we conducted ourselves. We won well, and we could lose with dignity. Supporters of other clubs would want their team to be successful, and they might get a bit fed up with Liverpool's continual success, but they would still appreciate Liverpool's ability and humility. No one begrudged us our success because we avoided excess. Liverpool didn't court publicity. We just got on with our work. There was a tremendous closing of ranks in adversity because we were so close-knit.

That closeness was created by the club's attitude. Liverpool did everything to help me settle in. While Marina and I looked for a house, the club put us up at the Holiday Inn for eight months. The innkeeper was Jack Ferguson, a fellow Scot who knew Marina's father through the licensed trade. He was brilliant. It helped me knowing that Marina was being looked after. She became friendly with the girls at reception and used to go down for tea and toast with them. It's important for the partners to settle in as quickly as the footballer husband; harmony at home is paramount. I was soon settled. I had everything. I enjoyed going to work. Marina was comfortable at the Holiday Inn with the kids. The hotel people were on her side. We'd come down to stay in a strange place and found it wasn't strange because the Holiday Inn went out of their way to help us. If we needed a doctor or a dentist, we'd just phone down to reception and they would organise one. We also felt safe in Liverpool. I remember getting off the train at Lime Street, after a trip back to Glasgow, and walking the 10 minutes to the Holiday Inn. I wouldn't have walked through Glasgow, where the footballing rivalry has a nasty side. On Merseyside, there was a great friendliness to the rivalry between Liverpool and Everton. It was noticeable right away. When I signed for Liverpool, Dave Thomas had just joined Everton. He was staying in the Holiday Inn as well. It turned out that I had played against Dave for Scotland Schoolboys against England Schoolboys at Ibrox. What a nice guy he is. We still keep in touch.

Liverpool was a great place to be, both city and club, even if my first season at Liverpool was a disappointing one domestically, thanks to Brian Clough and Nottingham Forest. They beat us to the League Cup. Forest's keeper, Peter Shilton, was cup-tied so a very young Chris Woods played against us. Woods was magnificent, so we went to a replay at Old Trafford, where we lost to a John Robertson penalty. It should never have been a penalty. Phil Thompson tripped John O'Hare outside the area, which television showed. There was quite a big rumpus about it. But you can't change history. It was the only cup Liverpool had never won, but it would be a kind trophy to us in later years when we won it four times on the spin.

Forest were a hard team to beat, as we discovered in the championship. Cloughie had them well organised. There was Shilts, who was on a par with Clem; they bought Kenny Burns and had Larry Lloyd, John O'Hare, John McGovern, Viv Anderson and David Needham in there. At left-back was Frank Clark, who has gone on to be a successful manager. It was always a tight game against Forest. Liverpool would have an awful lot of possession. We just could not break them down. We never scored the goals our possession deserved, which was partly down to Forest's organisation and their ability on the counterattack, where John Robertson was so good.

Without Forest, Liverpool would have dominated domestically. We were also a team in transition. The arrival of Alan Hansen and Graeme Souness helped. Alan was as good a centre-back as you could find, equally as competitive as Graeme or me. He just showed it in different ways. Graeme was completely nerveless. He was one of the best players in Liverpool's history. He may not have been the quickest but he had everything else. Souey could stop goals, create goals, score goals. He had a mean streak that went along with his creativity. He was strong in the tackle and hurt people, but that's football. People have hurt him, have hurt me. It's a physical game. He never complained. He just got on with it and sorted out his own problems. He has been compared to Norman Hunter. Norman never got the credit he deserved because he was labelled tough and uncompromising. Norman didn't take prisoners but he could play and he could make other people play. Graeme had Norman's steel but he was an even better footballer. It was a sign of Graeme's quality that when he went to Sampdoria they began to win trophies.

With new boys like Big Al, Graeme and me settling in, Liverpool had a strong squad of players. We even had the phenomenon of a 'Super Sub', David Fairclough. Towards the end of my first season, David played six or seven games in a row and had begun to believe he could be a regular. I was looking forward to the next season. I thought David was really going to be an asset. Then he got injured pre-season. Maybe if those six or seven games had been mid-season and David had stretched it to 13 or 14 that might have changed his perception of himself, and his role at Anfield. Certainly when he came on as a substitute, David made a difference. He could pick up the pace of the game the moment he arrived. He was very patient, but I don't think anybody can be totally happy when they are not playing. If the side are playing well, you have just got to grit your teeth and get on with it. When I was sub or not in the side, I would never maliciously wish an injury on somebody but I would be thinking: 'If one player picks up a little injury, if he gets a suspension, or a wee bit of a lapse in form – not enough to affect the team – I'll get a chance to get in the side.' Nearly every player thinks like that.

No one ever grumbled. Liverpool treated their footballers as adults. There was no strict discipline at Anfield; everyone was expected to have self-discipline. The players took pride in themselves. There was always a bit of leeway – everybody can be late once. Those football clubs that try to become monasteries rarely achieve success. Players respond well to being treated like adults. When someone stepped out of line, the best punishment was that he wouldn't get a game. That was a tremendous fear because Liverpool were a difficult side to get back into. If a player had a problem with fitting in at Anfield, he had to change otherwise he was away. Liverpool would never change. A few new signings had trouble fitting in, not because of any animosity from people already within Anfield – that never happened – but because they felt Liverpool was too big for them; players like Frank McGarvey, for example. He came to Liverpool for £250,000 in 1979 and never played in the first team. We all tried to help him. 'Everybody is on your side,' I used to tell Frank. He was surprised how nice everyone was to him. 'Don't be surprised,' I said, 'everybody wants you to be successful.'

Frank was the exception which proved the rule. Anfield was an easy place to fit into. The punters just loved anyone who wore the red shirt and gave 100 per cent. If you gave them that, they would stand by you. This atmosphere was created by Shanks. He set the ground rules. The people who were employed there, from the footballers to the staff upstairs like Peter Robinson, then shaped the club with their own personalities. Every time anybody came there were different shades added but Shanks's guiding principles were always the same. Everybody was equally important. There was no star treatment. Liverpool did things properly but not extravagantly. The people who came to support were basically working-class people. When you get local lads in the side, that's even better, because they feel a real affinity with the club. It sounds a bit corny but Liverpool really is the club of the people. The supporters' warmth was always around us.

Liverpool Football Club was a community within a community. It was such a happy club. We'd enjoy the crack on the bus to training. Back at Anfield the lunches would be bubbling away with more banter and joking. The players would have a laugh with the staff, like May Devine, the cleaner who now does the teas in the press room. She loved the lads and the boys all loved her. For one reason or another, Liverpool stopped doing the lunches a couple of years before I took over. When I became manager, I put them back on. It was good for team spirit. May and Theresa would cook and serve up our lunches in the players' lounge. I loved that. It was great that, after training, the players could come in for a bowl of soup and a bit of stick. To start with, all this was new to me. When we finished training at Celtic that was usually it for the day. Sure, we would go for lunch at a café around the corner, but we had to lay it on for ourselves. At Liverpool, it was laid on for everyone. The banter and those lunches were an important part of the club. Everybody had something to say for themselves. Somebody would come up with a story about somebody else and that would keep the crack going. The camaraderie was brilliant. I've heard it said that it was easy for Liverpool to look after the players because of the success they had, but it was the other way about. Liverpool achieved that success because of the way they looked after people.

Liverpool certainly made me a better player, even a bit more confident. What I don't accept is that my stamina improved as well. I left Celtic in August and by the time I went back for an international match in September, I was supposed to be a yard faster! It was a misconception. There were no reasoned judgements being made either, when I returned to Celtic Park with Liverpool for Jock Stein's testimonial later that season. I came back to show my appreciation for Big Jock. I don't know if the match was anything to do with my transfer. Big Jock was certainly close to Bill Shankly; whether there was agreement from days gone by I don't know. Whoever Big Jock asked would have gone, everyone had so much respect for him. I was glad I went up to play; Jock did so much to help me. I certainly got some stick, going back to the club I'd just left. One section of the crowd slaughtered me while another tried to clap me. But I knew what was in store. The guys in Marina's father's pub warned me.

Maybe they were the instigators! I knew from people who had been at games in the run-up that some fans had been practising chants about me that were none too complimentary. On the way to the game, I told the Liverpool lads what was about to be unleashed. They didn't believe me.

'How can you get stick after the success you had here?' they said to me.

'Just believe me,' I said. 'Don't be surprised if I get slaughtered.'

Just to add to the occasion, my new Liverpool team-mates kindly set me up for even more abuse. Bob had made me captain for the night, which was very nice of him. I knew the lads might try something, an old trick like stopping in the tunnel so I would run out alone. When we came down the tunnel, I kept looking back to check they were still there right behind me. Feeling confident that we would run out together, I came charging out of the tunnel on to the pitch, towards a pipe band, and was immediately engulfed by this nightmare realisation that the boys were still standing back in the tunnel, laughing their heads off. 'Oh, no,' I said to myself as the boos rang in my ears. Then Terry Mac and Thommo ran on to the pitch, chuckling away, and saying: 'Nice to be home, is it? You must have done this club a right turn. You must have been a right good player for this club.' I suppose it was a compliment in a way; they don't boo bad players. But they shouldn't boo anybody unless they leave under bad circumstances, which I hadn't. I was open and fair with Celtic. I had done enough for the club and its supporters. By 1977, before in fact, it had been time to do something for Kenny Dalglish.

I was disappointed by the abuse but that was those people's right. I had been gone for less than a year, but I took great pleasure in scoring two goals against Celtic. That made it for me. If they were going to give me stick, then fair enough. The only way to answer them was on the pitch, and I did that, twice over. After the game Big Jock came up to present us with the cup.

'I don't really want to give you this,' he said.

'I don't really want to take it,' I replied. 'But I'm going to.'

To be fair, a lot of people booed the people who were booing me. The next time I went up there, to play in testimonials for Davie Provan and Stevie Murray, I got a standing ovation. Maybe the stick stemmed from disappointment; they wanted me to stay.

In my second season, Liverpool ran away with the League, finishing eight points ahead of Forest. There were some special games that year. We set the ball rolling with a 7–0 defeat of Tottenham Hotspur – a nice welcome for Ossie Ardiles and Ricky Villa. Bob Paisley said it was the finest performance he had ever seen. Our last goal was superb. The move started with a Tottenham corner which was cleared by Ray Clemence to me. Terry McDermott was on our post defending the corner, but as I knocked the ball to David Johnson, who passed it on to Steve Heighway, Terry was making an upfield run. He was there to meet Steve's cross and head the ball into the Tottenham net. One moment he was in our goalmouth and three passes later he was in theirs to score a brilliant goal, making up unbelievable ground. What a player Terry Mac was! There was another game against Ipswich, which we won 3–0, memorable for Arnold Muhren, making his debut after his move from Holland, trying to pick up Terry Mac. Muhren's tongue must have been dragging on the grass at the end because Terry ran him ragged. It was a fantastic season. We had the finest defensive record in the history of the championship. If you concede only 16 goals you are not going to lose many matches. We lost only four that year. Clem and his defence were outstanding. Thommo was very good at reading the game and completely committed. He was like a stick of rock – if you broke him in two he would have 'Liverpool' written through him. Hansen was brilliant, of course. Nealy was very competitive, on and off the pitch. He took great pride in being captain of Liverpool. He took pride in himself. Alan Kennedy was special – he only scored in finals.

The defence was vital. There are many people within football who say that they don't mind conceding goals as long as they score more. That's all very well but it's difficult to be successful in League championships when you are losing a lot of goals. However, letting in only 16 was probably taking the miserliness a bit too far! Because we conceded so few, every goal we scored became a potential match-winner. I built up a good partnership with David Johnson, the two of us sharing 37 League goals. During a semi-final replay with Arsenal, David collided with David Fairclough, split his cheek open and was concussed. He went off, returned, and played wide right. It was the best he ever played for Liverpool but he can't remember it! David Johnson was known as 'the Doc'. He used to carry one of those old airline bags to training. If somebody had a sore head or a cold, the Doc had a tablet ready. He had a remedy for everything.

It was a great year. I was even voted Footballer of the Year and took great pride in receiving the award from Stanley Matthews. While I felt honoured, such prizes have to be put into perspective. Footballers rarely get personal awards unless the team have been successful. Bob Paisley was Manager of the Year.

Bob trained as a physio after he finished playing, so when someone went down injured, he knew immediately what the problem was. He could tell just by watching a player walking or running whether he had a cartilage problem, a hamstring problem, a bad back or a groin injury. The story goes that Bob didn't want the manager's job, but he thought he would be letting Liverpool down if he didn't take it. Bob was a father figure to everyone at Anfield. Everybody loved old Bob. The general public adored Bob Paisley because he was an ordinary man with no airs or graces, no edge to him. It could have been them doing the job. The cloth cap and slippers wasn't a preconceived image – that was the man. People took to Bob because of it. His manner reflected the club. Although he came over as unassuming, Bob was very decisive. Most of his decisions, over substitutions for instance, turned out to be right. Bob found it difficult to explain why he had done something, but he didn't need to, his actions spoke for themselves. His knack of making the right decisions made Bob a great manager. All the players were grateful just to play under him. He was 'wee uncle Bob' with the cloth cap, always laughing and cheerful; he could nevertheless explode with the best of them. Bob was not a crockery-thrower – I have never ever seen anybody throw crockery nor done it myself – but he let players know they had made a mistake. Of all the people in football who owe a debt to Bob Paisley, mine is one of the greatest. I was deeply saddened when he died.

Bob's success was relentless. Championships arrived in 1980, 1982 and 1983 and continued under Joe Fagan in 1984. New players kept coming in, freshening up the team. Mark Lawrenson was good and probably had a bit more pace than Thommo. Ian Rush, Steve Nicol, Bruce Grobbelaar and Ronnie Whelan also arrived. Buying good players was one of the reasons why

Liverpool maintained their success. It was a replacing process – Whelan came in for Ray Kennedy, David Johnson made way for Rushie, Lawro came in for Thommo.

I will never forget Steve Nicol's arrival in October 1981. Until then, the three Scots already at Anfield – Al, Graeme and me – had been pretty well able to look after ourselves. We had a tradition called 'Jock Picture'. Every time Liverpool won a trophy, the three of us would run around shouting 'Jock Picture. Jock Picture'. A newspaper photographer friend of ours would always be there to snap a picture of us. I've got all these pictures of the three of us jumping up and down with yet another cup at Wembley. Terry Mac tried to sneak in but we wouldn't have it. It was an exclusive club, only for Jocks. The three of us were very patriotic, more so for being amongst the Auld Enemy. On one occasion after training, the three of us headed over to wee Sammy Lee's wine-bar to watch Scotland versus England. We had been excused international duty because Liverpool were about to play in a European Cup final. Al, Souey and I wanted to show our support from afar. We piled into Sammy's. He had the telly all ready and the seats lined up like a cinema. Big Hansen and I walked in with a huge Scottish flag, singing 'Bonnie Scotland'. When Richard Gough scored with a header, there was pandemonium. It was hilarious.

In the dressing-room us three Scots had a wee bit of credibility until Nicol signed. We had built up an understanding that the Scots were the Master Race. We would quote historical facts to the English players to prove it. Some of the most important inventions and discoveries in the world came from Scots, like television, the telephone, penicillin, the steam engine and tarmac. Their names are part of history – John Logie Baird, Alexander Graham Bell, Alexander Fleming, James Watt. Not to mention those other wonders of the world – golf and whisky. Per head of population, the Scots are the most educated race in the world. We did well defending ourselves, and flying the flag of Scottish supremacy, until Nicol came. Everything we had built up, he destroyed in 10 minutes because of the photograph that was taken of him when he signed. There he was with a Tammy on, a silly Liverpool scarf and sillier grin. Unbelievable. Stevie was a lovely guy, a real one-off. He made a great contribution to the success of Liverpool. We nick-named him Chico after one of the Marx brothers.

Big Al used to wind Chico up endlessly. One Friday afternoon we were sitting about at the club, waiting to leave for a game in London. We knew somebody owed Nicol money so I got the girl at reception to write him a message, saying that the guy who owed him had phoned. The message read: 'Meet me at Burtonwood service station on Sunday at 1 o'clock'. Nicol got the message and we heard him say: 'Oh, all right.' Off we went to the match, forgetting all about the wind-up. On the bus to training on Monday morning, Nicol was sitting next to Big Al. It was part of Al's daily ritual to wind him up, as natural as cleaning his teeth. Nicol said to Big Al: 'You must think I'm stupid.'

'What do you mean?' Big Al replied.

'Burtonwood – what a wind-up,' Nicol said. 'I knew it was a wind-up.'

That was it, so we thought. For once Chico hadn't been fooled. But during training, Chico went up to Big Al and said: 'Burtonwood – I only waited an hour!' He'd taken his wife as well. If we didn't call him Chico, we'd call him 'Chips', because he loved chips, or 'Henderson'. When he went on the right wing, he used to think he was Willie Henderson, the old Rangers star.

At the same time as Nicol arrived, Sammy Lee was beginning to settle into the first team. Sammy is a lovely bloke. He would always say 'sorry, sorry, sorry' when he did something wrong. He scored on his debut against Leicester City in 1978. Their goalie went to catch Sammy's shot and it went through his hands and legs in front of the Kop. The wee man was going: 'I've scored! I've scored! I've scored at the Kop!' Ian Rush was starting to settle in too although he wasn't scoring. In the League Cup replay against West Ham he was brilliant. He looked so young and thin when he first came, but he was very quick. Rushie found it difficult at first. Everybody was the butt of somebody's jokes in the dressing-room, but Rushie told me later that this really upset him. That was a pity. It was only meant to make him feel part of it. The only time you should be worried in a dressing-room is when they don't make jokes about you. It means the other players don't care. But Rushie hadn't been used to such banter. He had trouble scoring to start with and was dropped but soon found his feet. It had to happen. Rushie was perceptive and had two good feet. He is one of the most instinctive finishers football has ever seen.

My partnership with Rush proved so good because he could run and I could pass. I would just try to put the ball in front of him. Rushie said that he made runs knowing the ball would come to him. That was true but only because his runs were so clever. If he made a stupid run, I couldn't pass to him. His run was more important than my pass. Rushie was a good passer himself. He could have been a midfielder, could have played a bit deeper, because his range of passing was great. When we played small-sided matches at Melwood, his passing and vision were good; either foot, no problem. We used to call him 'Tosh', an ironic touch, because of his lack of ability in the air. Yet Rushie still bagged a few goals with his head.

Rushie was easily the best partner I've ever had. We could have been made for each other. Every team that's been successful has had a strong tradition of partnerships. You look at Everton, when they had their success, they had Kendall, Ball and Harvey. Arsenal had Radford and Kennedy. Our partnership was natural. By watching each other and talking we soon learned each other's traits. We complemented each other well. We had another role, which people often don't give Liverpool strikers credit for. Bob Paisley told us that we were his first line of defence when any Liverpool attack broke down. Rushie is one of the best strikers at closing defenders down. When the opposition got the ball, Rushie and I worked as hard as we could to keep them pegged back to allow our midfield and defence time to regroup.

Rushie matured, became braver and started to give us stick. He came out of his shell although he remained economical with words. Rushie was friendly, especially with Ronnie Whelan, but after training he would always return home to Flint. The geography of where people live, and whether they are married or single, to an extent dictates who they socialise with. But Rushie was never distant with us. He kept performing on the park, which is really all that matters.

The trophies kept coming in. Finally, after such a long wait, Liverpool won the League Cup in 1981, beating West Ham in the replay with Alan Hansen's header. That summer we lost Ray Clemence to Spurs, which was very disappointing. If Clem felt he had to leave it was best for everybody for him to go. That was his choice. It would have been much better for Liverpool if he had wanted to stay. But off he went and Bruce Grobbelaar stepped up. Bruce turned out to be a great keeper for Liverpool in many ways but it was a rough baptism for him. Clem was a difficult act to follow. Bruce's character helped him through. He was such an extrovert, always bantering. Bruce would stand in the dressing-room and tell stories about fighting in the bush. He was a naturally gifted keeper, with tremendous agility and reflexes. In training he would shout at the players when they were shooting, which was a new experience for me. Keepers are known to be a bit different but he was probably the most individualistic goalkeeper you will ever find.

The League Cup suddenly became a bit like buses. You wait ages for one to arrive and then they come along in a rush. Liverpool reached another final in 1982, against Tottenham. Russ Abbott was at Wembley with his son, Christopher. There was not long to go. So, as Liverpool were losing to Steve Archibald's goal, Russ got up to leave. Somebody shouted at him: 'Russ, you'll need to phone Cooperman to get us a goal.' Cooperman was this mad hero character of Russ's. Russ walked off, got down the stairs, and there was a big roar. He and his son came running back up to find that Ronnie Whelan had equalised. He walked back along the aisle to his seat, sat down, and was tapped on the shoulder by the same fella, who said: 'Where did you find a phone?' Ronnie had taken the game into extra time. People made a big fuss over Paisley insisting we stand during the break, rather than sit on the grass as Spurs were doing. They said it was designed to psych Spurs out, to show we weren't exhausted, but we never sat down during extra time. We weren't really tired. We knew Spurs were in trouble and so it proved. Ronnie and Rushie settled the game.

Around that time, I was well and truly set up for 'This Is Your Life'. Marina was always saying to me: 'You are going to get caught for "This Is Your Life" one day.'

'Don't worry,' I would reply, over-confidently. 'I'll be ready.'

But I wasn't. There was the most elaborate ruse to get me down to London and I never suspected a thing. I was doing some work for KP Crisps, who asked me down to London to help with a presentation for a new product. I thought it was a bit strange but

I agreed. I told them I had to speak to Bob first about getting away early. Liverpool were playing in a fund-raising game at Blackpool for a policeman who was swept out to sea trying to save a dog. After the match I approached Bob who said I could go straight after training the next day. Of course, Bob was in on the whole scheme. The next day, while I was on my way south, Bob and all the players were back at Anfield recording a message for the show. When I arrived at Heathrow, David Ost of KP said the presentation was not until two.

'Let's go to the Post House Hotel and have a sandwich while we are waiting for the car to take us to the KP factory,' he suggested.

'Sure,' I said. I rang home to let Marina know I was catching the 4.45 plane back.

'You make sure you are on that plane,' she said, 'otherwise you won't be getting any dinner.'

So I had a chat with David who was talking a load of nonsense. He was so nervous, I thought he must be having problems at work.

Eventually he said: 'The car hasn't turned up, let's go outside and get a taxi.'

As we walked outside, I thought: 'This is very strange, you never get a taxi rank at an airport hotel. It's normally a courtesy bus.' He shouted for a taxi and one appeared out of nowhere. When it pulled up, Terry Mac got out. I said: 'What are you doing here?' I soon found out. Eamonn Andrews was the taxi driver. He got out and gave me all that 'Kenny Dalglish, family man and footballer, This Is Your Life'. I was completely caught. I never had a clue. As we went to the studios, I was still in shock. It was a lovely appreciation though. Tommy Docherty flew all the way from Australia to be on the show. He had to get permission from the chairman of his club in Sydney. The Doc finished the programme and flew back. 'If they hadn't given me permission, I would have come anyway,' he said.

We were back at Wembley in 1983 to lift a third successive League Cup to go with the championship. Rushie and myself shared 42 goals that season. I won Footballer of the Year, Rushie got the Young Footballer of the Year, which was a nice reflection of the partnership's success. David Hodgson had arrived for

£450,000 from Middlesbrough but that didn't worry the other strikers. I was bought; so was Rushie. Why shouldn't Liverpool buy strikers? Sometimes they had to build up the squad. If I was performing well, I would be the first one to get the nod to play. Hodgy was received with the same welcome as everybody else. He would have been a better player if he had believed in himself a bit more. He was a better player than he thought himself to be. But his signing was typical Liverpool; bringing in new talent kept everyone on their toes.

That 1983 League Cup was special. Not because we beat Manchester United but because it gave us the chance to honour Bob in his final season as manager before retirement. We decided to let him go up and collect the Milk Cup. Managers never went up Wembley's famous stairs, which was a disgrace. It meant so much to Bob because it meant so much to us. We wanted to show our appreciation to someone who did so much not only for our careers but for so many players before us. Bob had been the most successful manager in the history of English football, winning three European Cups and six championships, so he deserved the honour of becoming the first manager to go up the stairs to collect a trophy at Wembley. It was a mark of our respect for the man. He loved it. Back at Anfield, I can remember him walking down the tunnel for the last time, nursing the championship trophy. It was a sad moment, Bob leaving, but he went out holding trophies.

Bob's successor, Joe Fagan, was very humble as well. His neighbours wouldn't have known that he was Liverpool's manager unless they were interested in football. Joe was highly regarded by the players because of his coaching ability. He didn't shout often but when he did everyone jumped and took notice of what he said. Joe was observant, very wise to the world. Like Bob before him, he was also reluctant to take the job but did it because it was Liverpool, the club he loved. What a first year Joe had: championship, European Cup and League Cup. Joe was held in the same respect as Bob Paisley. They were like father figures. Both were good with the players because they could relate to them.

Under Joe, I started dropping more into midfield with Michael Robinson and Rushie up front. In January I broke my cheekbone in a collision with Kevin Moran of Manchester United; he was wearing a support brace on his wrist which caught me. I needed an operation which made my face swollen and discoloured. One day the lads came to see me in hospital, which was kind of them. I had been looking forward to their visit – I missed the chat and banter – but when they walked in the door, all their faces fell. That was worrying because I was feeling good that day. When Mark Lawrenson saw my face he had to be taken to a side-room for a cup of tea. It didn't bother me that my face was a mess. When Joe came in with the papers, he obviously got a fright as well. 'There's the papers,' he said, 'I'll leave them there. I can't stay, thanks, bye.' And he disappeared.

I had a disagreement with Joe the following season, when he dropped me. I had no real problem with him leaving me out. What upset me was that I read about it first in the papers. He called me into his office after training and said that he was dropping me.

'I know,' I said. 'I read it in the papers.'

'What are you going to do about it?' Joe asked.

'There's not much I can do,' I said and left.

I don't know how the journalists knew but they should never have known before me. When I became a manager, I always tried to treat people the way I liked to be handled as a player. If I was going to leave someone out, they might not know until the Saturday when I read out the team, but at least they would be the first to know. That's common sense and vital for team spirit.

It was an odd time, different from other years, and not just because we failed on the pitch. I even began – and ended – an acting career with an appearance in Alan Bleasdale's 'Scully'. The original character was Kevin Keegan which shows how long ago it had been written. I told Alan that I would do it for a bit of a laugh, but not to expect too much. If I had to say or do something on set and got it right first time, which wasn't often, there was real surprise on the faces of all the television people. It was just a bit of fun. I wasn't going for Hollywood. Some people say I've been acting all of my life anyway, so it didn't make any difference.

There was a drama of a different sort in December when our Southport home was burgled. We had gone to see Kelly in her school's Christmas concert and came back to find somebody had paid us a visit, taken medals and everything. The important thing was that there was no damage done to Marina or the kids. The only sentimental thing we never got back was something Paul was given by his grandfather. The rest was insured. I got the medals back. The burglars left them at the Shankly Gates at Anfield. I expected that. Medals are of no value to anybody bar the person who received them. It was silly to take them because they are worthless financially.

It summed up a dreadful season. We definitely missed Graeme, who had gone to Sampdoria in June 1984. There is always a void when someone leaves. It was Liverpool's responsibility to replace players as best they could. Jan Molby came in. Jan could do everything. If he had put his mind to it he could have played anywhere on the pitch. Football wasn't the problem for Jan. The only problems Jan Molby the footballer encountered came from Jan Molby the person. He should have got so much more out of football. Jan has been unlucky with injuries and his weight kept going up and down. It was either a genetic complaint or a problem with his preparation. It was so sad because he was a magnificent player. I remember his first game, on tour in Ireland. Jan scored an amazing goal. Took the ball on his chest, knocked it over an opponent with his knee at the edge of the box, went round someone and then volleyed it into the net. But it was always going to be difficult for him to replace Graeme.

Graeme was a great success abroad. I had been at Liverpool longer than Graeme and it has been suggested that I might have gone overseas. But Graeme was different from me. He had great self-belief. I never fancied going abroad simply because I was afraid. The thing that worried me, and set me against even thinking of playing abroad, was the travelling to and from the games and not being involved in the banter because of the language. I was worried that I might be in the dressing-room and hear team-mates joking and think they were laughing about me, because maybe I had had a bad game. That would have destroyed me. That might surprise people who have a different image of me but that was the thing I really enjoyed: the banter, the chat to and from games, the carry-on, the stories, the reminiscences, the wind-ups. I was never asked to go abroad anyway. Besides, I was perfectly happy where I was. I spent enough time in Europe with Liverpool.

—5—

STRIKING OUT

I WAS SUCH A competitive player that I have punched defenders in my desire to win. It's not something I'm proud to admit, but in the heat of matches it is easy to get carried away. Usually I stayed within the boundaries of good behaviour. I didn't regard myself as a dirty player, simply one prepared to look after himself. Battling against defenders can be a violent business. I have been lucky. Over my career, I never wore shinpads and still never got any bad cuts on the shins. I never broke a leg. My ankle was injured a couple of times when defenders stood on it and once when I went over on it at Anfield. I have been in plaster a couple of times. I was always bruised, but that's inevitable playing in the most dangerous part of the pitch. I would have been disappointed if I hadn't received cuts and bruises.

Intimidation is part and parcel of any defender's game. Their job is to find a striker's Achilles' heel, sometimes literally, to put him off his stride, to get him off the pitch. They are doing their job. Although it's wrong, I just had to accept it. Verbal abuse was common but not something that worried me. If defenders wanted to swear or make derogatory comments, I knew I had nothing to worry about. The opponents to watch out for were the silent operators. They didn't say anything before they kicked you. Norman Hunter used to have a go at me but he was the first one to shake my hand afterwards. Larry Lloyd and Kenny Burns would boot me all over the place, but they knew there was every chance of getting kicked back, which wouldn't have bothered tough defenders like them. Norman, Larry and Kenny respected me because they knew I would stand up for myself. Maybe there is a moral in the fact that the most difficult defender I ever played against was one of the cleanest – Colin Todd. His anticipation was unbelievable. He didn't need to foul because he had already read the situation. Colin didn't need to kick you to get the ball.

The secret is in knowing your trade. If a defender is half-clever, he will go about his work, sustaining the minimum number of injuries. Graeme Souness knew his trade in the middle of the park. He would know when to go for a tackle and when to pull out. He learned through experience. Playing up front like I did was the same. The best approach is that if somebody keeps kicking you, you think: 'I can't have that again. I've got to protect myself.' So I did. Anticipation was my first weapon against defenders who wanted to kick me. My physical and mental strength were important. Sometimes I had to stand up for myself. That was my second weapon, being strong. If opponents sensed fear they would have walked all over me. In professional football it is quite easy for a player to get a reputation for being frightened. If that gets about, then opposing defenders are going to kick you the first chance they have. Fortunately, I never felt fear; I knew I could protect myself. Alert referees would help. Receiving good passes from team-mates would cut out the chances of a defender booting me. A lot of the players marking me wanted to play as well. Banning the tackle from behind curbed some of the worst challenges.

A tough approach mentally and physically was needed for such a hard area of the pitch. I tried to give myself an advantage over the player marking me. I would often nudge defenders to put them off-balance. The only crime was getting caught. It was the same for everyone. Football's a contact sport. For most of my career, I played within the rules. Sure, I used my body illegally to gain benefit sometimes. People did the same to me. That is part and parcel of football. When a ball came in, I would lean into a marker first, to put them off-balance, and then go for it. They would do the same to me, if they could. Defenders would often give me a small push as the ball was played in to me. I would want to go one way but the nudge took me the other, so it would look like a bad pass or a bad run. The ref wouldn't see. It's just good defending. My marker's just eased me out and won that battle; fair enough.

Trying to gain the upper hand is totally legitimate. Some referees would pull me up for backing in, a major part of my game. I still can't see anything in the rules that says it's a free-kick to the opposition if I take a step back when the ball is coming in towards me. I would take the step back to knock my marker off-balance. He would step forward into me to knock me off-balance. That's usual. I would also try to entice someone into a tackle or a push inside the box. That's acceptable. It's unacceptable if you feign it. I would go down if a defender put me down, but if I had a chance to score, or play someone else in, I would keep going. People might argue that I dived but I never did. If I knew a defender was coming in hard, I wouldn't stand there. I didn't want my leg being carried off followed by my body. If defenders were silly enough to come in with a tackle like that, I was not going to be silly enough to stand in their way. Of course I would get out of the way. If that meant diving for cover, then so be it. I once missed a bad tackle coming in and it nearly cost me dear. Bruce Rioch challenged me in the box and nearly broke my leg. He apologised but we got a penalty. He had come in high and late and caught me with a nasty challenge. I learned from that tackle by Bruce.

I would play differently against an opponent who had been booked, knowing he would be in trouble if he stepped out of line again. I would just get the ball passed to my feet more, invite the foul. Bob Paisley taught me that. 'Make sure it's in the box as well,' he added. 'If you are going to get kicked, get kicked in the box, it's worth it in there.' It worked well for me. I had no complaints. We got a lot of penalties at Liverpool, deservedly so.

Foreign defenders were even nastier. The Spaniard Camacho came to Hampden Park with a hard-man's reputation but he got booked early on, after a couple of challenges, and that was him scuppered. He was squealing like a pig because I was going into him, trying to provoke a reaction that might cost him. Camacho was screaming to the referee, complaining about some of my challenges. But Camacho had the problem, he had the yellow card.

I didn't seek any more protection from referees and linesmen than any other player. Most of the bookings I got were for dissent. I never knew how they understood what I was saying! It was dissent born of frustration, with myself or the result or the way the game was going or the referee's inability to do his job properly. I would look to the officials for protection, but if referees didn't protect me I would do it myself. I adopted Danny Blanchflower's attitude: get your retaliation in first or, in his words, 'equalise first'.

My worst piece of retaliation came at Tottenham Hotspur, Danny Blanchflower's old club. My action was disgraceful. I feel embarrassed just recalling the incident. Somebody played the ball over the top and suddenly there was a three-man chase involving me and two Spurs defenders, Don McAllister and Steve Perryman. I was running in the middle of them. I looked to either side and thought one of them was bound to elbow me, so I punched McAllister. My fist was quicker than the linesman's eye. He never saw a thing. The whole thing must have looked like a blur of bodies accidentally colliding, when in fact I had cynically taken one of them out. McAllister was lying on the deck. When he got up, he was raging.

'Look,' I said to him, 'I was bang out of order. Totally. I know there is going to be retaliation and I accept that. But you've only got one chance.' So, sure enough, he booted me at the next opportunity.

'OK,' I said to him, picking myself up off the ground, 'no problem. That's us level.' And on we went with the game.

Our next game against Tottenham was when I went over on my ankle. I was lying in a heap. McAllister came up and said: 'By the way, that wasn't me!' I was out of order at White Hart Lane. I knew I was, and accepted the consequences. But we sorted it out between ourselves. The reason why I did it was taking self-protection to the extreme. It was an unseen, but very real, blemish on my career.

My second worst moment of retaliation came in Europe against the Belgian defender Renquin. He was giving me a right hard time. He booted me from head to toe. The bruises were all down the back of me. There were no bruises on the front because Renquin never faced me. He just fouled from behind. The worst of his fouls came when I was running down the line. I feinted to go to my left but let the ball run. I turned to go for it and he came straight through. I was left bouncing on the track. Renquin was booked. Then he committed more fouls on me that led to another couple of free-kicks, yet he was still on the pitch. I couldn't believe he hadn't been dismissed. So I retaliated. We were defending and the ball broke out. Renquin and I ran back down the other end. He had a tug at me, so I just swung my elbow, caught him right in the mouth. Two teeth came out and landed in the grass. I just kept running. Renquin was lying on the pitch. He got up and wasn't too pleased. There was a gap in his teeth. Elbowing him hurt me as well. My arm swelled up and there were two holes where his teeth had been; the impact had punctured my skin. That was born out of frustration. It wasn't an example to set to anyone. I didn't feel proud or pleased with what I had done but I didn't get enough protection from the referee. I can give a reason for doing it, but not an excuse.

The combination of frustration and a competitive nature is always going to be explosive. My pride and competitive streak ensured that I took defeat badly. I always thought it was my own fault. 'What have I done wrong?' I would ask myself in the dressing-room afterwards. 'Was it my responsibility?' Returning from a defeat, I wouldn't join in with the banter; I was conscious of the fact that we had lost. They would be quiet journeys anyway. I would try my best not to bring the anguish of defeat home with me, but it was difficult. I would have a quiet evening and then have to endure, or avoid, the Sunday papers. I tried to brighten up in time for training on Monday morning. I still hate losing; not because I have grown accustomed to winning, simply because I've let down myself and other people. At Liverpool, I was determined to learn from every game, win or lose. I can remember scoring two or three goals in a match and coming off thinking that I should have done better. Sometimes I would leave the field without scoring and feel: 'Yes, that was all right.' If we had won, but I had played badly, I would still be bubbling in the dressing-room.

The depth of disappointment differs in each person. Some of us were more outwardly competitive. I have been involved in plenty of arguments in the dressing-room, often with

Graeme Souness, one of my closest friends. Commitment is all-important. I always tried to give 100 per cent in every match. I have not come across many footballers who have succeeded with only 95 per cent effort. Those who don't give everything are the ones with the problem. The club can always find another player. When I went into management at Liverpool in 1985, I trusted the guy who gave his all, rather than the one who maybe had more skill but didn't work hard enough to deliver consistently.

Every footballer has an obligation to run until they drop for the team. As a player, I never got carried away with my own importance. I just did what I thought was right and what was best for Celtic and then Liverpool. Bob Paisley called me the conductor of the orchestra. That was embarrassing because there were great players in those Liverpool teams. If you are playing alongside great players it is easy to look good yourself. When players left Liverpool they rarely achieved success elsewhere. Of course, there were exceptions, like Kevin Keegan who became a hero at Hamburg; Ray Clemence at Tottenham; Sammy Lee went to QPR and then abroad; Jimmy Case proved to be a great servant for Brighton and Southampton. But, on the whole, there were not a great many players who enjoyed success after Anfield. The reason for that is simple. At Liverpool, a player would be alongside 10 other good players all on the same wavelength. At their next clubs, they might be playing with only five or six other good players and suffered as a result.

To succeed as a footballer at any club, not just Celtic or Liverpool, involves sacrifices. Preparation and discipline are very important. I spent a lot of time sleeping, or just resting up, conserving my energy. I would spend most of Friday in bed. I sometimes took sleeping tablets the night before games to ensure I was fresh for action. Marina understood. She would rather live with a sleeping husband on Friday than a bear with a sore head on Saturday night if Celtic or Liverpool lost.

I was dedicated because I loved playing and I didn't want to let anyone down. Nowadays some players seek second and third opinions on injuries. In my day we just strapped it up and played on. Once, at Liverpool, there was something wrong with my pelvis. So Joe Fagan's missus got one of my jockstraps and tightened it. She stitched strands of the material together to pull it in a bit. I was OK after that. After warming up by sending some crosses over for Bruce, the pain went away. In today's climate of sensitive footballers, I would probably undergo an operation. I preferred Mrs Fagan's stitching.

The one consistent criticism directed at me throughout my career has been that I lacked a yard of pace. I wasn't the quickest person across the floor. I had run that first yard in my head so I was ahead of the opposition. If the pass is right and the move-ment is right, pace is less important. The opponent wasn't going to get near me. I would only struggle if the ball was hit long over the top. I couldn't play a direct style, with a big striker flicking on for me to run on to. I didn't possess the blinding pace to exploit those balls. Again, that was not a problem because I played with teams who passed the ball to get into positions to score. People tend to remember me as a forward who would receive the ball with his back to goal and then turn. They don't remember the times when I lost possession! Sometimes I knew where my marker was. Other times I took a chance. If a ball was passed to me at Liverpool, I knew there was something on otherwise my team-mate wouldn't have played the pass. The passing was accurate and intelligent and so was the movement off the ball. I could lay it off first time to a supporting player or control it and go myself.

I loved shooting. I am naturally right-footed but I wasn't uncomfortable on the other side. I didn't really work on my left. It just developed through normal training sessions. The more often you try something the more it will improve. I loved scoring goals where the ball swerved in the air. I always knew roughly where the goal was. It was a feeling. Sometimes I had time to look, pick a spot. At other times I just relied on pure instinct.

There is more to scoring than just technique. An awful lot of football is psychological. When I had possession, and intended to shoot, I would first have a look and see where their keeper was. Then the thought wars take over. The keeper might think I was going to put the ball one way, so I would put it the other side. It's a game of bluff and counter-bluff, which has worked for me and against me. It worked one night at Ipswich against Paul Cooper. I had taken the ball and bent it past his left-hand corner a couple of times from 18 yards. Then I got into the box again, looked up and Paul started to step back. He was expecting it to be floated in so I drilled it low. It went in the net as he was going backwards. Then Pat Jennings got the better of me at Highbury. I cut inside David O'Leary and I went to hit it with my left foot towards the right-hand post. Jennings read me like a book.

Of the near-400 competitive goals I scored, it is difficult to select a favourite. Some strikes looked better than others, some carried more significance, in terms of the scoreline or seriousness of the game; but every goal meant something to me. If I had to take one goal with me it would be the one for Scotland against Spain at Hampden on 14 November, 1984. There was a throw-in and I let the ball go past me into the box. With Davie Cooper in support, I went past the first defender, knocked it to the side of the second one and then bent it with my left foot into the top right-hand corner. When I turned to run to the stand, my old man was sitting there in the front row. The look on his face was the same as mine: overjoyed. It was a good goal for Scotland because it helped us beat Spain 3–1, an important step on the way to qualifying for the 1986 World Cup. It equalled Denis Law's record of 30 goals for Scotland and it was my last goal for Scotland.

People who think of me as dour were surprised when my goal celebrations were always so full of smiles. Scoring was just pure pleasure for me. Television cameras would obviously focus on me when I scored and capture my huge smile. That expression of joy wasn't pre-meditated. It wasn't an act. It was simply a spontaneous reaction to scoring. I enjoyed other people scoring goals as well because I enjoyed winning. Nothing compares to scoring but I would be embarrassed talking about goals with the press. Football relies on team-work; also, goalscoring is such an instinctive process that it is difficult to analyse. But the press would insist on asking detailed questions about a goal, like my 300th which I scored in a televised match against Stoke. I checked back and hit it with my left foot to the far post. Peter Fox, Stoke's keeper, couldn't reach it properly and he knocked it in. When I came out after the game, journalists were saying: 'What a great goal, blah, blah, blah, what happened?' 'It was a cross,' I replied and kept on walking. They wrote in the paper that I had joked it was a cross, that I 'modestly described' it as a cross. But I wasn't joking, it was absolutely true. Sometimes it is not genius that sends a ball flying into the top corner – it's luck. If I had tried to claim that the Stoke goal was deliberate, Liverpool's players would have given me fearful stick. It was heading yards wide.

One of my weaknesses as a footballer was a shortage of self-belief. If I had had more self-confidence, I would have been a better player, and maybe a better manager as well. Confidence, or rather the lack of it, was still an issue even when I felt well established at Liverpool. It's the way I am, a chink in my armoury. I wish I had more belief in my own ability. Maybe I have too much respect for other people; although people I respected made me captain of Celtic and Liverpool, and also of Scotland, but I still lacked self-belief. I could have done better for club and country, if I'd had more confidence.

—6—

SCOTLAND

I REPRESENTED Scotland in three World Cup finals and helped them to a fourth. I hold the record number of caps and share with the great Denis Law the record number of goals; but looking back on my long Scotland career, I feel a sense of disappointment, a feeling that I could have achieved so much more, that I could have played so much better for the country I love. The reason why I never did myself justice for Scotland is simple to relate: I suffered from an inferiority complex for a long time. I never felt confident when I was on international duty, surrounded by my idols. I was star-struck, although I had trained and played with Celtic's internationals, and played against a lot of the Scottish lads in the First Division. It wasn't the fault of the other players; they never strutted about or exuded an air of arrogance. The problem lay within my mind. I would look at these well-known talented internationals, then look at myself, and not be able to come to terms with being there. These were footballers I greatly admired, had watched on television, whom I was suddenly playing with. I couldn't cope with that. How I wished I could feel on equal terms with them. I would have loved to have gone on Scotland trips and treated them with respect, not awe.

This feeling of inferiority definitely affected my performance. I always worried what the other Scotland players would think if I made a mistake. I feared they would believe I had let them down, that I should be able to do better, that someone else could do better than me, that I should be dropped. All those questions tugged at my concentration. It was self-destructive on my part. I shouldn't have been like that. There were fellow squad members who I could have talked to about the problem, like George Graham and Bruce Rioch, both people you could have an intelligent conversation with, but I never felt able to broach the subject of my inferiority. I was too embarrassed to discuss it.

I felt that if I could prove myself playing for the best team in Europe, playing in one of the best leagues in the world, I would not feel so inferior when I reported for Scotland duty. It is ironic that people thought I was forsaking my country. It was just the opposite. I fervently hoped quitting Scotland would make me better equipped mentally to represent my country. Success with Liverpool gradually gave me an inner belief, a sense of my own worth. It was while I was at Anfield that I played my best football for Scotland.

It seems strange that it should take so long for me to feel comfortable when I started so young with Scotland. I was still establishing myself in Celtic's first team when the call came. I was sitting by the edge of a hotel pool in Malta, where Celtic were playing Sliema Wanderers in the European Cup. Big Jock Stein strode up.

'You are in the pool,' he said. I looked at him slightly confused.

'I can't swim,' I replied, waggling my toes in the water.

'No, you are in the Scotland pool,' Big Jock said. 'Tommy Doc's picked you.'

I couldn't believe it. I was only 20 and about to represent my country in a Nations Cup tie against Belgium. The Nations Cup was the forerunner of the European championship.

It was Tommy Docherty's second match in charge, after he replaced Bobby Brown. It was a major step up for me. Four Under-23 caps had come my way under Bobby. It could have been more. On one occasion Bobby took me to Pittodrie for an Under-23 game. I sat on the bench throughout and I thought my whole world had collapsed. The manager didn't explain why he hadn't used me. I know I had no divine right to play and I wasn't thinking logically. There were four other guys much more deserving of a game than I was. I sat there, bursting for a game, hoping someone would get injured, but other subs

With Marina on our wedding day, 26 November, 1974.

Early days: Celtic farmed me out to Cumbernauld United for a season (front row, far left).

My great mate, Danny McGrain, a Celtic legend.

Rangers' John Greig looks on disconsolate as I celebrate scoring for Celtic against the team I supported as a boy.

Mick Mills and Ray Clemence are floored after I had embarrassed Clem at Wembley.

Getting the better of Peter Nicholas in a 1–0 win over Wales at Hampden Park in 1982.

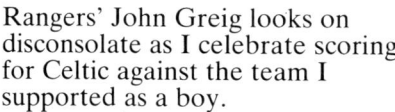

With Kelly and Kevin Keegan on his
return to Liverpool with Hamburg.

My son Paul gets an early taste of
life in football.

Sir Stanley Matthews presents me with my Footballer of the Year award in
1979.

Willie Ormond's last game, a celebration of the Queen's Silver Jubilee:
Alan Rough and Danny McGrain are next in line.

Scotland versus England was always special: here I turn Phil Thompson, my Liverpool club-mate, at Hampden Park in May 1980.

Franz Beckenbauer presents me with a solid silver cap to mark my 100th appearance for Scotland in March 1986.

I score in the 5–2 opening win over New Zealand in Malaga at the 1982 World Cup. Scotland still went out on goal difference.

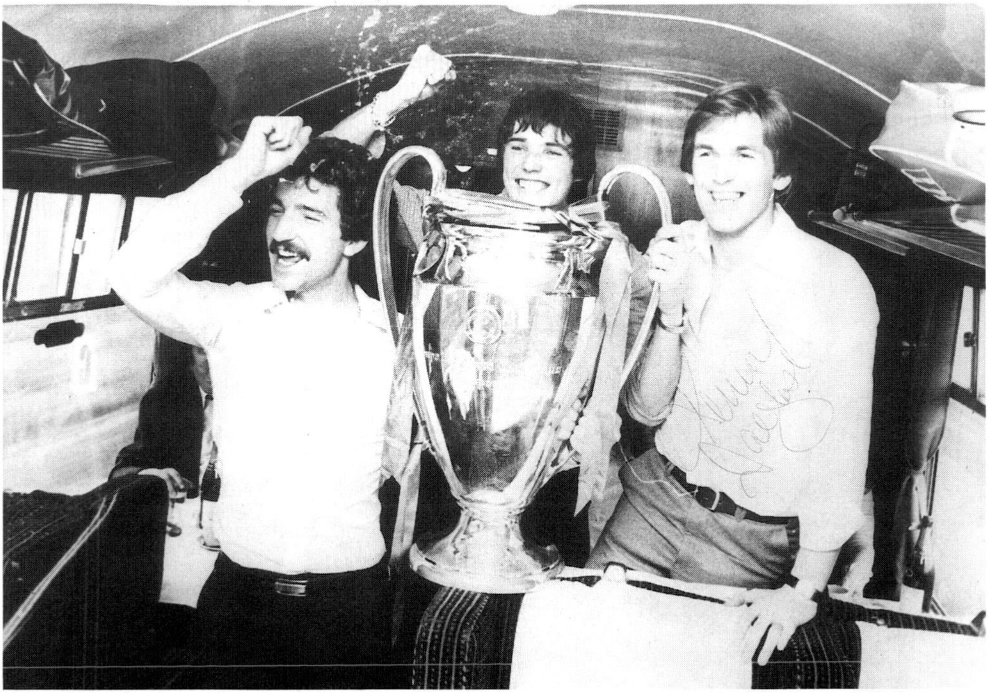

My first European Cup: celebrating with Graeme Souness and Alan Hansen on the train back from Wembley in 1978.

Two great men, Tommy Docherty and Alex Ferguson, organised teams for my Hampden testimonial in 1986.

Alan Kennedy, Graeme Souness and Ray Kennedy (right) join the celebrations as Liverpool welcome Ricky Villa (background) to England with a 7–0 defeat of Tottenham at Anfield in September 1978. I scored twice.

were sent on, not me. I was so disappointed even though I had no right to be. It was simply that I so wanted to play. Winning is vital but the enjoyment of taking part counts too. That encapsulated my career, for club and country. I just wanted to play. Let me on the park – it's where I was happiest in life.

I was lucky to be settling into Celtic's first team when Tommy Doc arrived to transform Scottish football. The Doc was great for the game in Scotland. He got everybody involved, got everybody behind the national team. He gave the whole place a lift. He gave international recognition to a lot of unexpected players. The Doc organised lots of matches, probably more for his own benefit, to keep him occupied when he started. He had Under-18s playing against League teams, League selects against other League selects. People up in Scotland, like players in the Second Division, suddenly felt more important. The Doc was full of character. His enthusiasm was infectious. When Manchester United offered him the manager's job at Old Trafford it was brilliant for him but a great pity for Scotland. He was so suited to the Scotland job. There was a great atmosphere at Scotland training. He brimmed with one-liners and jokes. It was a good time to come into the squad because there was the Doc, and a great bunch of lads, like Jimmy Johnstone, Denis Law, George Graham and Danny McGrain.

I loved the Doc; still do. Even if I had not spoken to him for ages I could phone him up tomorrow and it would be as if it was yesterday that we last spoke. Maybe we get on because we both grew up in Glasgow, maybe it was the understanding about each other's backgrounds. I respected him. We had a similar sense of humour. Some of the stories he tells about people are so funny that even the victims would laugh, but when he stands up to do an after-dinner speech, he tells an awful lot of jokes against himself. People who laugh at themselves always win laughs. The Doc will always be special to me because he gave me my first Scotland cap. He was trying out younger players in matches like these because we had no chance of qualifying for the Nations Cup finals. Belgium were a good side, buzzing with good players like Paul Van Himst. I was so keen to come on and face them. Eventually the Doc let me off the bench in the second half for Alex Cropley. We won 1–0 after Jimmy Johnstone, who was outstanding, went down the touchline and crossed for John O'Hare to score.

I must have done well enough because the Doc played me from the start in Amsterdam the following month. Holland had all their top players, including Johan Cruyff, on show. For 20 minutes, the Dutch were unbelievable. It was like the Alamo. They hit the bar, the post and finally scored. Then we began to get a few challenges in. Wee Jimmy was brilliant again that night. George Graham equalised but Holland won it in the last minute. I couldn't swap my shirt with any of the great Dutch stars because the Scottish FA only gave us one and I was determined to keep my first full Scotland shirt. Even if Cruyff himself had come up seeking a swap I would have said no. My international shirts are very precious; they bring back instant memories.

I only ever gave two away. One went to the family of Johnny Doyle, a Celtic team-mate of mine who killed himself drilling into a live cable in his loft. There was a fund-raising dinner up in Glasgow so I put a Scotland shirt up for auction. The other went to Jackie Stewart for one of his charities.

All my blue shirts retain great emotional significance. Playing for Scotland meant everything to me. International football was a real challenge. At Celtic, I played against a lot of teams who were, with respect, not very good. It was not difficult to impress in the Scottish League. Playing for Scotland against 11 really good players was more difficult. That was a great test. So I was very disappointed when, despite being included in the squad for the 1972 Home Championship, I only managed a place on the bench against England. I even went to see the Doc to express my frustration. But that was a rare disagreement. Nearly everyone loved the Doc in Scottish football. When the Doc was manager I bet there were the fewest call-offs Scotland ever had. I was delighted when the Doc called me up for Scotland's summer tour of South America. My happiness soon turned to fear. Celtic decided I was too tired to tour after an exhausting first season. I was worried the Doc would ignore me when Scotland returned but I was soon back in the team, playing in two wins over Denmark. During the second one I scored my first international goal. Sadly, the Doc then decided to take up Manchester United's offer which was such a great shame for Scottish football. At least he left an important legacy: those wins over Denmark helped us qualify for the World Cup finals for the first time since 1958.

His successor was Willie Ormond, a complete contrast to the Doc. Wee Willie was a smashing fellow, but he didn't possess the belief in himself to handle the so-called bigger names. He did a great job at St Johnstone, who were an attractive, free-scoring side, but Willie found it difficult to make the transition from club to international scene. If he had felt the confidence others had in him, he could have done the job. Even if the manager lacked it, there was strength of character in the dressing-room with Billy Bremner and George Graham, both born leaders. Bremner, the captain of Leeds, was sometimes a bit overpowering. For all the criticism aimed at Bremner's Leeds for being tough and uncompromising, they could also play, but the physical side overshadowed it. George Graham's leadership qualities became even more apparent during his very successful time managing Arsenal.

Willie Ormond's first game, in February 1973, was meant to be a night of celebration, a friendly to honour the Scottish FA's centenary. Instead, the night unfolded into one of the worst humiliations ever suffered by Scotland. We lost 5–0 to England. They destroyed us. They had such good players – Bobby Moore, Alan Ball and Martin Peters. What a nightmare! Scotland experienced a dreadful time against England that year. In the Home Championship, we lost 1–0, and a guy ran on the pitch towards Alan Ball.

'It's all right, Bally,' I shouted. 'It's my old man!'

Matches against the Auld Enemy were always exhausting, mentally and physically. England were physically stronger than us. I couldn't understand anyone saying these matches meant less to the English than to the Scots. The English players enjoyed winning every bit as much as the Jocks. That was confirmed when I came south. Emlyn Hughes used to love the battles with the Scots. After England had beaten us 1–0 at Hampden in 1978, I had a verbal exchange with Emlyn. We'd only managed to draw with Northern Ireland and Wales in the other Home Championship games, so Emlyn was determined to give us some stick for doing so badly. After the final whistle, Emlyn ran over and shouted: 'Hey, wee man.'

'What is it, Emlyn?' I replied.

'Only two points for the Home Championship!' he shouted.

I hit back with: 'If you'd got one more point in the qualifying matches you'd be going to the World Cup in Argentina as well as Scotland.'

We used to give the English players plenty of stick. It was just as well that the Home Championship was at the end of the season; otherwise we would have spent the whole season arguing. Phil Thompson used to give out as much stick as Emlyn. Phil Neal wasn't so bad. Terry McDermott never bothered. Our strength was that we were going to the World Cup while England stayed at home. All that talk about 1966 and England couldn't even qualify now – that was the focus of our attack.

Tommy Doc had set Scotland on the road to West Germany. We just needed victory in a vital qualifier against Czechoslovakia in September 1973. Willie Ormond pulled off a master-stroke by recalling Denis Law. For me, playing alongside one of my greatest idols was a special moment. Willie took me off because he said I was tiring and sent on Joe Jordan. Joe promptly dived in to head the winner; Scotland were off to West Germany. All those bleak times when we failed to qualify for World Cups were forgotten. It made it that bit more special that Scotland qualified while England failed.

We prepared for the Home Championships and the World Cup finals at Largs, our training centre out on the coast. One night, during the build-up to the game against England, there unfolded one of the more remarkable episodes in the life and times of Jimmy Johnstone. There was a line of moored rowing boats near the hotel. Inevitably, the boats proved too much of a temptation to some in the Scotland party. Somebody pushed a boat out, and Wee Jimmy jumped into it. That was no problem except Jimmy soon discovered that the boat had oars but no rowlocks and, far worse, the Clyde had a strong current. A couple of the lads decided they had better go and get him. So they took another boat, which turned out not to have oars. Eventually, they got two bits of wood and started to paddle after him. Although the impromptu rescue boat was moving out, it was also going down; Jinky's would-be rescuers hadn't noticed the boat had a hole in it until it started filling up with water. The rescue party managed to steer their sinking ship alongside some other small boats about 20 yards out and climb into them. Meanwhile, the wee man was drifting further and further out to sea.

Danny McGrain and I were tucked up in our beds. Danny got up for a drink of water and happened to glance out of the window, which looked right out on to the Clyde.

'Kenny,' Danny said, 'you'd better get up.'

'What?' I replied.

'You better get up,' he insisted, 'the wee man's out there in a boat.'

'Danny,' I replied, 'do us a favour, will you, what time is it? We need some sleep.'

Danny pretty much ordered me out of bed. So I looked out of the window and, sure enough, the wee man was a dot on the ocean. All we could hear was his voice floating back to us. 'You are a star, superstar,' he was singing, and 'Bonnie Scotland, Bonnie Scotland. We'll support you ever more.'

I said to Danny: 'Ooooh, I'm getting back to my bed.' We dived back under the covers and went to sleep.

The Coast Guard had already been called out to rescue Jimmy. Unfortunately, they couldn't keep the story quiet because a newspaper reporter lived in Largs. The next morning, Big Jock phoned up.

'Kenny Dalglish,' Jock stormed, 'you're an idiot.'

'What?' I replied.

'What are you getting involved with Wee Jimmy for?' Jock said. 'It says in the paper you were standing at the side of the water.'

'I was in my bed. Ask Danny.'

'Well, you want to sue them.'

'OK. What do I do?'

He said: 'Phone this lawyer.'

The lawyer sued the newspaper for me. I got a few bob, thank you very much.

The morning after Jimmy's midnight sail, Willie Ormond called a meeting. We all gathered, waiting a bit apprehensively for Willie. The door opened, Willie came in and looked at Wee Jimmy.

'You just gave me some look, sir,' Wee Jimmy said to Willie. 'What's that for?'

Willie glanced at him again and spluttered: 'What's that for?! It's for your behaviour last night in the boat. That's what it was for.' As a consequence Jimmy was more determined than ever against the English. He was magnificent; we won 2–0, destroying them. After the game, Wee Jimmy shouted abuse up at the press box for criticising him.

The Scottish FA warned Jinky over his behaviour. He was soon in trouble again during the build-up to the World Cup. After losing 2–1 in Belgium, we travelled to Norway. Unfortunately, there was an incident in the hotel bar with some of the press lads. Wee Jimmy became a bit abusive. The SFA warned him that if he misbehaved again he would be sent home. But there was never anything malicious in Jimmy's actions. Jimmy really did not have a piece of badness in him. It was just high spirits.

Jimmy was part of a very good World Cup squad, with players like Denis Law, Peter Lorimer, Danny McGrain, Billy Bremner, Tommy Hutchison, Willie Morgan and Martin Buchan. Everyone said that the first game against Zaire in Dortmund was Scotland's downfall because we only scored twice, but it was a difficult one to start with. Nobody knew anything about these Africans. We had to be a little bit cautious. Zaire were buzzing but we managed to beat them 2–0. We could have done better. Peter Lorimer set us on the way with a fantastic volley; then Joe Jordan headed in and we should have gone on to win by more. Early in the second half, the floodlights went out. We waited for five minutes before re-starting, but we never really got going again.

Zaire were coached by a Yugoslav. Their next game was against Yugoslavia, who thumped them 9–0 in Gelsenkirchen. It was this result that inflicted the real damage on Scotland's hopes. It could have been a fluke, although 9–0 in a World Cup game was always going to raise eyebrows. The finger of suspicion was pointed at Zaire's Yugoslavian coach. With Yugoslavia putting so many past Zaire, Scotland needed to win one of our next two games because we were so far behind on goal difference. Unfortunately, we drew 0–0 with Brazil in Frankfurt despite playing really well. Brazil were very physical. They only had Jairzinho, Rivelino and Piazza remaining from their 1970 World Cup-winners and seemed to rely on prevention rather than creativity. Afterwards Willie Ormond called Brazil 'a disgrace' because of the cuts and bruises we sustained. Willie was right. They were a disgrace. It was sad to see Brazil stooping so low.

A draw might still have sufficed against Yugoslavia, providing that Brazil did not win by more than two clear goals against Zaire. At half-time, we were still in the tournament as Brazil were only one up. It looked all over when Karasi scored for Yugoslavia with nine minutes left but Joe Jordan equalised and we headed off to the dressing-room for a nervous wait. After three minutes we learned that Zaire had conceded two more, one really weak one in the last minute. That third goal, which counted us out, was difficult to stomach – Zaire's keeper, Kazadi, allowed an easy shot from Valdomiro to squeeze past him. That sickened us. Our disappointment was tinged with anger about the circumstances of our exit. Scotland were the only team to go out without losing a game. I was particularly disappointed. I had played poorly. I was even substituted in two of the matches. The trip to West Germany had not done much for my reputation. All in all, I was very unimpressive. I just wished I could have contributed more to Scotland.

We flew back to an amazing reception at Glasgow airport. Thousands were there, waving flags and banners and scarves. That was one of the few happy moments of the trip, coming into contact with such fabulous supporters. We didn't see a great deal of them during the competition because the players were usually locked away, but we knew how popular Scotland's fans are overseas. The Tartan Army are very jovial, never much hassle. If someone upsets them, sure they will have a go back, but they would not instigate trouble. Scotland supporters were like boisterous ambassadors. When they were on our side, did they make a noise! They were more humorous than harmful.

Rangers once experienced trouble in Barcelona. Rangers fans were actually celebrating; the Spanish police panicked and deservedly got the blame. When you consider the number of times Scottish fans travel abroad, where they invariably have to endure footballing disappointment, it would be understandable if their frustrations spilled over into bad behaviour. It never happened. They vented their frustration on the players, and rightly so if we had let them down. I much preferred Scotland's supporters getting angry with us than with the venue.

A lot of fuss was made, and even more nonsense written, after Scotland fans dug up some Wembley turf in June 1977. The pitch was about to be ripped up anyway – the Tartan Army just began the job a few days early. It would have cost Wembley a fortune to have that turf taken away. They should be happy that all these Scots came in and took the pitch away for free! Some of the guys still say to me: 'Kenny, I've got Wembley growing in my back garden.' They were acting out of high spirits, not malice. The crossbar was not deliberately broken. It cracked simply because fans were sitting in the net. Our supporters never wrecked the stadium, as some people wrote. The reason why the media coverage focused on the fans was that it took the pressure and spotlight off England's defeat. I don't condone people coming on the pitch but no English player was threatened.

Those who followed the team around the world always made me proud: proud of Scotland, proud of them, proud of football. When we played Brazil in 1982, our supporters played their fans as well; in the street and in the car parks, Scot against Brazilian, echoing the real fixture – except that I think we won the matches off the pitch. Scots, Welsh and Irish can go away and enjoy themselves but the English fans often can't. It's nothing to do with the teams, who always conduct themselves in the proper manner, on and off the pitch. It's just the way these people are. It is obvious that England's problem lies not with the England football supporter, but with those who travel with the express aim of causing trouble. They are not football supporters. They are not interested in how England get on. They are solely interested in the story they have got to tell about their behaviour when they return. The Scots, like the Welsh and Irish both north and south, are more patriotic than the English. Maybe it's because of their countries' size that they express their nationality so fervently. In the Home Championship, it was always a great achievement for Wales, Scotland or Northern Ireland to beat England. It was also a great thrill. People talked about Scotland being desperate to beat England, but so were Northern Ireland and Wales; so were the Republic when they played England in those qualifying matches. So great are the expectations placed on the English to be successful that England have become an even greater prized scalp. I relished putting one over on the Auld Enemy.

Perhaps the greatest success came in 1976 at Hampden when Scotland defeated England to become undisputed Home Championship-winners for the first time in nine years. It was a very special moment – perfect for Scotland, perfect for me as I scored the winner. Joe Jordan went down the line and whipped a cross in. I went to hit it, Mick Mills lifted his foot, I touched the ball again and then hit it. I didn't hit it that well but still strongly enough to beat a man of Clem's calibre! It trickled through and into the back of the net; well, nearly to the back of the net. We should have had a penalty before half-time when Clem brought me down. It wasn't so much a penalty as an assault! As usual, I took the referee's decision with the dignity it deserved. At the end Danny McGrain and I were jumping up and down and somebody came up and gave us a cup. Danny said: 'What's that for?' I said: 'I don't know.' We learned later that it was the Home Championship trophy. We'd never seen it before.

During the championship I had been looking forward to the game with Wales, because I was about to break the record of 34 consecutive caps set by George Young, a great Rangers and Scotland captain. We congregated in the dressing-room, full of talk and life, but everyone fell quiet when Willie read the team out. I was sub. Of course, Willie didn't have an obligation to play me, but none of the players could understand it. I even had a good scoring record against Wales. During the match, there were a couple of injuries but Willie still didn't put me on. I couldn't believe it. What made Willie's decision seem even stranger was that I appeared in the following game. They beat the Welsh without me and then Willie changed a winning team to accommodate me. That was really suspicious. I was very disappointed, but when I eventually broke George Young's record, the circumstances of being denied the first time made it even more pleasurable.

What angered me even more than the decision is that no one had the manners or bottle to explain the situation to me. Maybe Willie dropped me for political reasons, not footballing ones. Maybe there was pressure from above. Such decisions should be made for footballing reasons alone; otherwise, the manager might as well relinquish the job. By not making the decisions, the manager's time in the job is inevitably shortening.

It was a year of upsets. After being denied George Young's record, I was denied the possibility of setting another mark. Again it involved Wales, although this time I was playing. It was a World Cup qualifier in November and we won 1–0. Danny McGrain cut the ball back and I scored with a back-heel that went in off Ian Evans, who was sliding in. For some reason, the authorities never credited me with the goal. It went down as 'Evans' own-goal'. If that goal had been credited to my tally, as it should have been, I would eventually have taken Denis Law's record of most goals for Scotland. I don't mind sharing the record with Denis. He wasn't a bad player!

The Willie Ormond era came to an end in the spring of 1977. Willie, or 'Donny' as we nicknamed him after Donny Osmond, had been a partial success. Scotland qualified for a World Cup, but, despite being unbeaten, still returned home with that now familiar feeling of 'if only'. Willie's last match in charge was the Silver Jubilee Celebration Match between a Glasgow Select and the English League at Hampden. Being captain, I decided to give Willie a bottle of his favourite liquid. 'There's a wee present, you can sit and have a quiet drink one night.' We had had our disagreements but Willie was a nice man. I wanted to show my appreciation somehow. At the final whistle, there was a trophy to collect, so I told Willie to go up and receive it.

'No, no, no,' he replied, 'you go. You're captain.'

'Willie, I remember when you started, you lost 5–0 here against England. This is your last one. You go up and get it, then you'll have a happy memory of Hampden.'

Willie's face lit up. He was really chuffed.

'Thanks,' he said. That's all he needed to say. All the boys in the Glasgow team enjoyed seeing Willie go up.

His successor could not have been more different. Ally Mac-Leod was extrovert, publicity-conscious and lasted only 18 months. He was fortunate that Scotland began well under him with that day at Wembley when we took England and their pitch. That created a really good mood. An acclimatisation trip was planned for South America. In Chile, where we weren't allowed out on the streets because of Pinochet's curfew, we won 4–2. Drawing with Argentina in Buenos Aires was a very good result, given that the same players were 12 months away from becoming world champions. I became slightly distracted because of speculation about my future with Celtic. When I rang home to discover my name being linked with Liverpool I was overjoyed, but along with everyone else, I came down to earth with a thud at Maracana. We were absolutely battered by Brazil, losing 2–0 – we were lucky to get nil.

Going on such a reconnaissance trip without the guarantee of qualifying was slightly tempting fate, but that was typical Ally. We returned to the task of actually getting there with qualifying games against Czechoslovakia and Wales, both of which Scotland needed to win. We beat Czechoslovakia so convincingly that Helmut Schoen, West Germany's manager, got a film of the game to show his players. I had a good game; Schoen was kind enough to say nice things about my performance. One reason for my improvement was that I had moved to Liverpool. I had gained confidence. I was now a senior international playing for the champions of Europe. That helped me as a footballer and as a person. I was no longer in awe of the players in the Scotland camp. The arrival of self-belief at last helped me to fulfil some of my international potential.

Then came Wales in October 1977. The Welsh FA decided to move the game. The capacities of Wrexham and Cardiff were too small, so they chose Anfield because of its proximity to North Wales. I could understand the Welsh FA's action. Of course, they would make more money by going to a bigger venue but they also had the safety aspect in mind. Their decision turned a Welsh home tie into a Scottish one. The Tartan Army bought every ticket they could and travelled south in their thousands. Having just moved to Liverpool, I was inundated with requests for tickets. I had never known such a demand. Scottish fans were even going down to Wales to buy them.

One of my new Liverpool team-mates was Joey Jones, an experienced Welsh international. In the run-up to the game, Joey kept saying: 'Wait till you see the Welsh support.' Every game at Anfield Joey would run on to the pitch, sprint over to the

Kop and clench his fist in salute. He had a tattoo on his arm which he would show to the Kop. Joey thought he could repeat his normal warm-up for the Welsh tie. He thought the Kop would be all Welsh. Joey ran out, took a couple of steps towards the Kop and stopped. It was all tartan and blue. Squeezed into one corner was a little bunch of Welsh supporters. It was the same all over Anfield; thousands of Scots and as many again in the car-park outside. It could have been Hampden.

With that sort of support, Scotland had to win. People questioned the legitimacy of our opening goal. A crowd of players went up for a high ball and someone's hand touched it. The Welsh said it was Joe Jordan's hand but, fortunately for us, the referee decided it was Dave Jones's. Don Masson scored from the penalty. The arguments became academic when I scored a second, a great way to celebrate my fiftieth cap. We were off to Argentina. But none of us forgot the contribution from our goalkeeper, Alan Rough. He made a magnificent save from John Toshack when it was 0–0 to lay the foundation for our victory.

The Scottish public gave us a tremendous send-off at Hampden Park. It was just as well we did that before we left; we would never have got it when we came back! The problem was that Ally never got the thing in perspective. He told the press that we would come home with medals dangling from our necks. It was never realistic to expect Scotland to come up to his rhetoric. Maybe Ally did believe the claims he was coming out with, but he should have been careful in saying it. I don't think the public even wanted to hear that their team were off to conquer the world. The players were certainly more realistic than Ally, who had delusions of his and Scotland's grandeur. He put us under pressure. It is bad enough going to a difficult country to play the best teams in the world, without the manager saying we're going to come back with the World Cup.

There seemed to be no end to our problems. It was disastrous in Argentina. The situation was made worse by so many untrue stories appearing in the papers back home, alleging incidents that simply never happened. The boys were forever phoning home and trying to convince their wives that the papers were printing packs of lies. I know everyone has to do their job but I can't understand why the press couldn't be more supportive of the team. The stories were crazy. When we were having our accreditation passes sorted out, two of the players were photographed quite innocently talking to the accreditation girls. The picture appeared in an Argentinian paper above a caption which stated the players were being entertained in a nightclub.

Another story particularly worried the families back home. We had just arrived in Argentina and were staying in Alta Gracia, our hotel near Cordoba, where we were due to play Peru. The hotel didn't have much but it did have a casino in the grounds. After dinner, Ally said anyone who wanted to walk over to the casino could do so, provided they were back by 10 p.m. Most of the boys decided to wander over in their tracksuits, although few gambled. I certainly don't. It was just an excuse for a walk really. So we strolled out of the front door, walked round the hotel, and back round to the casino, which was fenced off from the rest of the hotel. On the way back, some of the boys decided to take a shortcut and jumped the fence. Immediately, two security guards dived out of the bushes with guns. 'Don't shoot,' our guys shouted. It was unbelievable, like a scene from a spy film. Confusion reigned. The guards didn't speak English or recognise the players. Fortunately, it was eventually sorted out when some officials came by and everyone got back to their rooms in one piece. The story grew dramatically on its way to Britain's printing presses. We were in danger of death because the fence had become electrified and the security men were about to shoot us. The presence of guns seemed extraordinary, though. We used to sit on our balconies at night and watch the bushes move. Behind each bush was an Argentinian guard with a gun.

Alta Gracia was a crazy hotel. We should have known that things weren't going to work out there when the bus broke down *en route*. The hotel had looked good in the brochure which showed a swimming pool, tennis courts, and training facilities in the grounds. It turned out to be different. The swimming pool had no water in it for a start and was covered over. It wasn't the SFA's fault. They were promised the hotel would be ready in time, but it wasn't. Team spirit was affected by the hanging

around, the dreadful training facilities, the long-distance expla-
nations dismissing reports in the press.

We couldn't wait for our opening game but here Ally made a
bad mistake. He was so busy building us up that he ignored
assessing the opposition. Ally told us next to nothing about Peru,
although players should still be able to play without a report on
the opposition. I knew that they had one very good player in
Teofilio Cubillas. After Peru had beaten us 3–1, I swapped shirts
with Cubillas, the only time I got close to him all day. He scored
twice and Ally's predictions were already beginning to look
foolhardy. All this talk about being potential champions and
we couldn't even beat Peru.

It went from bad to worse. After the game Willie Johnston and
I were summoned from the dressing-room for routine drug tests.
They plied us with drinks to produce some urine and then we
went back to the hotel. Later on all hell broke loose because
Willie had failed. Willie had been taking some tablets called
Reactivan, which, in innocence, he failed to tell the Scottish
doctor about. That was stupid because we had been told
repeatedly to notify the doctor if we were taking anything.
Reactivan contained a banned substance so Willie was immediately sent home in disgrace. If we had beaten Peru we would
have had the points taken away. We woke up in the morning to
discover the cover on the swimming pool was deflated, a bit like
our mood.

Things didn't get any better. Ally gave us no information on
our next opponents, Iran, despite being briefed by Mike Smith,
the Welsh manager, and Andy Roxburgh, the Scotland coach.
Ally then made the further mistake of telling the press Scotland's
line-up before us, which did nothing for team morale. So
unfolded the worst result of my football career. We never even
scored against Iran despite being awarded a penalty which was
missed by Don Masson. An amazing own goal from yards out,
by Eskandarian, gave us the lead until they equalised late on
through Danaifar. At the end, we were booed off by the Tartan
Army, who had travelled thousands of miles and spent a small
fortune to witness another hopeless, gutless display by Scotland.
Sitting on the team coach, as all around they booed and jeered, I
could understand the fans' anger. We had gone down without

so much as a whimper. The papers were equally critical. That was no problem. If you can't beat Iran you deserve to be slaughtered.

At least we went out in style, beating Holland 3–2 with Archie Gemmill scoring one of the greatest goals seen in a World Cup finals. It made a difference having Graeme Souness in the team but it was Archie's goal that was truly special. He danced around three defenders before bending the ball past Jongbloed. It was not enough. We had needed to win by three clear goals. Once again Scotland bowed out on goal difference. An eventful trip still had one last episode in store for us. Before the flight home from Buenos Aires we were booked into a poor-standard hotel. We insisted on changing. It seemed to sum up a poorly planned, chaotic trip. Finally we flew home. What a mess the tournament had been. The win over Holland, who reached the final, simply showed up how badly we had played in the first two games. The players must take some of the blame but a lot of it must lie with Ally MacLeod. He was a decent fellow but he got carried away, creating exaggerated expectations that the players knew weren't realistic. I don't think Ally actually believed that we would win the World Cup. Even Brazil wouldn't say they were going to win the World Cup. It backfired on us. Scotland had needed to be better prepared, better led than Ally managed. But the players had a responsibility, too.

Scotland's squad have been accused of being full of cliques, but it was not true. There was certainly no divide, as everyone believed, between the Anglos, those who played for English clubs, and those employed by Scottish clubs. Often, when we were staying in hotels, we would all gather round for some serious banter. There would be stories and jokes bouncing between the players. We are all Scots, who take great pride in representing our country. It was only some newspapers trying to create divisions between Anglo-Scots and Scots; divisions mean stories to fill papers.

Talk of dissent in the camp was wrong. Most of the Scots who live outside Scotland are probably more patriotic than those back home. Moving away from home makes people seize any association with their homeland. The ones at home take it for granted, because they are living there. That's why it angered me when people said playing for Scotland didn't mean so much to me. I'm really proud to be Scottish and Glaswegian. I felt honoured to be given the Freedom of the City of Glasgow. This was an honour from the people I grew up amongst, and was a really emotional moment for me. I don't know whether I would go back to Scotland to live; I'm not desperate to return, I'll go wherever I think it best for my children, where they want to live their life. I don't need to be in Scotland to feel part of Scotland.

I love Scotland. It hurt deeply not playing as well for my country as I would have liked. The real reason was nothing to do with motivation. It was simply my lack of self-belief and being in awe of the people around me. Anyway, to place the issue into some much-needed perspective, although I didn't play well for Scotland in every game, I didn't play well for Celtic or Liverpool in every game either. I still can't understand the mentality of those who booed me at Hampden in June 1979 when we were turned over by Diego Maradona and Argentina. Jock Stein had made me Scotland captain soon after he replaced Ally the previous October. Yet here were Scotland supporters jeering my every move. They slaughtered me. Jock soon gave the captaincy to Archie Gemmill. For all those boos, I still helped Scotland to a third consecutive World Cup finals.

We approached Spain in confident mood. Things were much smoother off the pitch. Big Jock saw to that. Scotland had a good team, with players like Roughie, Danny McGrain, Big Al, Graeme Souness, Gordon Strachan, John Wark, Ally Brazil and John Robertson. But we realised that a group containing Brazil and the USSR would be difficult. Scotland were based in the south of Spain. Rod Stewart lived nearby, on the road from Marbella to Sotogrande where we were staying. It was easy to spot his house – there was a big Scottish flag flying outside. One day we were driving back in the bus from training and someone suggested we stop by. Rod was delighted to see all the boys. I asked him how he was doing for tickets. He replied that the Scottish FA had given him two tickets amongst the supporters, which was madness. Rod would have been mobbed. I gave him mine.

Many celebrities who go to matches aren't really supporters but Rod is. In Argentina he was nearly shot in a bar when some joker let a gun off. His passion for Scotland and football is genuine. He played in a testimonial at Aberdeen once and was gutted when he was taken off. He played wide right, and looked pretty decent as well. Rod also played in one of those Wembley curtain-raisers before a Scotland–England game. We both ran in on goal and I slipped the ball to him. In the act of scoring, Rod was caught by the goalkeeper who had slid out to block his shot. Rod went down in pain and I feared he was badly hurt, but as I approached all I could hear was Rod repeating in that famous voice: 'I've scored . . . I've scored at Wembley.' He was so delighted.

We began well in Malaga, beating New Zealand 5–2, but then came Brazil in Seville. In training a day or two before, Big Jock told us he wanted to play one up front. When Jock used Steve Archibald in training I knew I wouldn't be playing against Brazil. My team, the lads who weren't now in the first team, were ordered to play like Brazil. The 'mugs' team, as I called us, didn't have enough players, so we played Roughie up front; off we went, with me and four others in midfield, and just Roughie in attack. Embarrassingly for the first team and Big Jock, Roughie scored twice and we won 2–0. When Jock's team had the ball at the back, I shouted to Roughie: 'Just leave them and drop back.'

Big Jock stopped the game, came over, and asked me: 'Kenny, what are you doing?'

'Well,' I replied, 'you said play like Brazil. I thought that was what you wanted us to do. They always drop off.'

Big Jock said: 'You've always got to be clever, Kenny.'

But I wasn't. It was true. Brazil did use that tactic. Although I was on the bench, I had to admire the lads' spectacular start against the South Americans, but David Narey's goal was the worst thing that could have happened. It got Brazil angry. They had so much skill. Junior, Falcao, Zico and Socrates were soon strolling past blue shirts as if they weren't there. Brazil scored four goals, pinging them past Roughie from every angle. I was allowed to see the destruction at first hand, when I came on for Gordon Strachan, at 3–1 down. Brazil were magnificent. Maybe we should have played Roughie up front.

When I was left out for the next game against Russia, the papers printed the usual rubbish, this time alleging that I stormed out of the dressing-room. That was nonsense. I left Scotland's dressing-room to hand the players' tickets to their guests. I was going off on errands for the team, not in a huff. I went back to the dressing-room to help the players change their studs. There were no demonstrations of anger. I never let it show, but inwardly I was disappointed; not just because Jock had dropped me but because of the manner in which he did it. It would have been courteous for him to have explained why he was dropping me. Some people thought it was the end of my Scotland career but I never did. I was hardly in decline. The season after the Spanish World Cup I won Player of the Year and Footballer of the Year.

My main aim now was to reach 100 caps and Denis Law's goalscoring record. Whatever people might remember of my international performances, they could at least look back at the records I set or shared. Against Spain at Hampden in 1984, I equalled Law's tally of 30 goals with my final goal for Scotland. Many people say it was my best. Then came one of the saddest moments in my life, the death of Jock Stein. I wasn't playing for Scotland that night at Ninian Park, when Jock collapsed and died of a heart-attack. I was at Ipswich with Roy Evans, watching England's Under-21s, seeing what young talent there was. It was a trip which first aroused our interest in Barry Venison. Anyway, I phoned Marina from Ipswich and she told me about Jock. I couldn't believe it. I still cannot believe Jock Stein is not here. I think his stubborn nature contributed to his untimely death. Just before he died, Jock went on television talking about the Mexico World Cup. He hadn't been feeling well but he still turned up. He should have gone to see the doctor. 'I'll be all right,' he kept saying. That was typical Jock, but he should have been thinking of himself for once.

Jock had brought Alex Ferguson in to help coach. Fergie had been doing wonders at Aberdeen, playing good, successful football. What a formidable duo they presented in their brief time together. Imagine having Jock and Fergie in your corner when you went to play abroad. The opposition would look at the visitors' bench and think: 'Oh, oh, that's a great partnership.' It was a pity Jock and Fergie didn't have longer to work together. They were a great team. Fergie took up the reins that had fallen from Jock's grasp. Alex Ferguson was good to me. On the night of my 100th cap, at Hampden against Romania in March 1986, Fergie made me captain. It was a special night, made perfect before the game when Franz Beckenbauer came on the pitch to present me with a silver cap from the Scottish FA. I then missed the World Cup because of injury. I still managed two more games, against Bulgaria and Luxembourg. Then my Scotland career closed.

I am not happy with what I achieved at international level. Then again, I helped my country to four World Cup finals, one of which I missed through injury. For a nation of Scotland's small size it was an achievement for us simply to qualify. But, if my self-belief had been stronger, maybe I could have helped Scotland to achieve more. It was such a contrast to my success overseas with Liverpool.

—7—

LIVERPOOL IN EUROPE

G ROWING UP amongst the Lisbon Lions, listening to their stories of great nights in distant places, fired my desire to win in Europe. Sadly, during my time at Parkhead, Celtic were never strong enough to reach a European Cup final. The Lisbon Lions had faded although the memory of their triumph over Inter Milan still stirred me and countless others. Celtic had become good enough to dominate Scotland but had limited success in Europe. Within 10 months of joining Liverpool, already champions of Europe, my dream had been fulfilled.

My European odyssey in the red of Liverpool began on 19 October, 1977, against Dynamo Dresden. We won the home leg comfortably enough, 5–1, but the trip to their place proved to be an extraordinary night, one that is still talked about at Anfield. Dresden had a player called Dorner, an East German international, who spent the whole evening pinging passes of 30, 40, even 50 yards over our full-backs for his two wingers to chase. These were real fliers, determined to reach the byeline and cross the ball. Fortunately for us, Ray Clemence was in magnificent form and we lost only 2–1. Strangely, when Stevie Heighway scored for us they just sank without trace. There was some suggestion that the East Germans were so hyped up they were on something illegal. Maybe they were on a big bonus. When we scored, Dresden collapsed. They wouldn't have done if they had been pumped up with drugs; they would have carried on. The only stimulant in the

Dresden bodies was natural adrenalin. These Germans were just fuelled with the desire to turn a difficult tie around.

The quarter-finals brought us up against Benfica, unbeaten in 46 games. Running out into the Stadium of Light, an awesome arena, the situation looked none too promising. The weather was awful, lashing down with rain, and there were 70,000 Portuguese shouting their heads off at us. Although Nene scored for Benfica early on, we never panicked. Jimmy Case and Emlyn Hughes scored in reply. Emlyn's was ridiculous; he scored from nearly the left touchline. He tried to convince us it was intended. What happened was that Benfica's goalkeeper, Bento, who was quite small, missed Emlyn's cross. Whenever Emlyn scored he would take off on a long celebratory run. Nobody could ever catch him. It was like trying to catch a mad swallow. When we finally did catch up with him that night, he was shouting: 'What a goal. What a goal.' He swears to this day that he meant it.

The second leg was pretty much a formality, but we really turned it on, winning 4–1, one of the goals beginning my account for Liverpool in Europe. We had reached the semi-finals. My decision to head south was going well, Europe-wise. Barring the way to the final were Borussia Moenchengladbach, old foes of Liverpool. We lost the first leg in Germany 2–1, where Rainer Bonhof scored an amazing free-kick which rose like an aeroplane taking off. Ray Clemence bent his knees to catch it on his chest, but about three or four feet away from him it just climbed. If it had hit Ray on the head he would still be unconscious. The press criticised Ray, which was harsh. It was simply an exceptional goal, with the ball's movement impossible to track. Anyway, we were confident we would over-turn the deficit at home, particularly when we looked into the eyes of Borussia's players. It was obvious they didn't fancy it. They hated Anfield. My opponent that night was a lad called Hannes who shadowed me everywhere. The strange thing about him was that he had one eye. It was a magnificent achievement to play at that level with such a handicap. He also represented West Germany. I really admired him. It can't have been that offputting for me; I scored in a 3–0 win. We were through to the final.

It helped that Wembley staged the final. Those Twin Towers felt like a second home to Liverpool. We had been there twice already that season, although we'd failed to score on either occasion. So near to achieving my ambition, I became very nervous. My normal match-day afternoon routine was disrupted because I was unable to sleep. All I could do was lie on my bed at the Sopwell House Hotel, near St Albans, and think of what lay ahead – the atmosphere, the opponents, whether chances would fall my way, whether I would get to touch that famous old trophy.

Standing in the way were Bruges, who were little changed from the side Liverpool overcame in the Uefa Cup final two years before. The Belgians were very negative. It seemed their only plan was to try to block us out. Their defensive attitude was surprising. Maybe their coach, Ernst Happel, wanted to ensure that while Bruges may lose, they would not be embarrassed. Bruges were good enough to have defeated Atletico Madrid and Juventus on the way to Wembley. With internationals from Belgium, Holland, Denmark and Austria, Bruges clearly had some talent, even if two of their best players, Courant and Lambert, were missing. The word always used to describe Bruges that night was 'dour'. There is really no other adjective for them. It was all very well playing cagey football in two-legged, home-and-away ties but this was a one-off, the culmination of a long campaign. Bruges's approach was disappointing. Happel had his men play a spoiling game, re-grouping in numbers, putting up the barricades the moment we gained possession, all very negative. It was frustrating to play against. Goodness knows what it was like to watch.

Although Bruges proved difficult to break down, we managed to slip through a couple of times but had no one to turn the final ball in. It was such a tight game, one goal always looked likely to settle it. Fortunately, one chance fell to me, just as I had dreamed it would. I was determined to take it. I noticed a habit of the Bruges goalkeeper, Jensen, that proved to be his undoing. Each of the two times Terry Mac ran through and shot low, Jensen dropped down to block the ball. So when Graeme Souness played me in, Jensen came out as he had for Terry and I knew he was going to go down early. I dummied to play it, Jensen fell for it, allowing me the opening to lift the ball over the top of him. As the ball fell sweetly into the net, I continued my run, leaping the hoardings to go and salute the Liverpool supporters who seemed to have taken over Wembley. It was a wonderful moment, the feeling of pleasure doubling when Bruges showed no sign of attempting to redress the deficit, which was pretty pathetic really. Phil Thompson was forced to clear off the line, but otherwise nothing. Complete elation overwhelmed me at the end. I had taken a gamble in leaving Celtic, and within 10 months I was the owner of a European Cup winners medal. The gamble had paid off.

The Holiday Inn at Swiss Cottage staged one of the best celebrations London has ever witnessed. What a party – long and loud. It was one of those parties which started and finished in daylight. Eventually, with dawn well upon us, we made it to bed. We hadn't been in bed long when Marina slipped downstairs to get the papers. On returning to the room, Marina said: 'Graeme's up for breakfast.'

'Graeme? You must be kidding!' I replied, knowing what sort of night we had all shared.

'Honest to God,' Marina insisted, 'he's up for his breakfast. I saw him.'

The next thing we knew there was this almighty banging on the door. Charlie – one of Graeme's many nicknames – fell through the door.

'Marina,' I said, 'he's not been up for breakfast. He's just not been to his bed yet!'

Graeme was standing there, leaning against the door-frame.

'Charlie, you better have some breakfast,' I said, 'I've already ordered some for us.'

'What have you ordered?'

'Oh, just tea and toast. Do you want some?'

'Aye, all right,' he said.

I gestured to the phone so he could order some more. He picked up the phone, dialled the number.

'Room service?' Graeme enquired. 'Could you send up a bottle of champagne.'

'Charlie, steady. Don't start that. We've just finished.'

But there was no stopping him. He continued down the phone: 'Do you have any fresh orange juice?' The room-service lady replied that yes, the hotel did stock orange juice.

'Well, make it two bottles of champagne,' Graeme said, and put down the phone. I just looked at him.

'Oh, Charlie, do me a favour. Not at half-eight in the morning.'

But he was adamant. So he sat there in our room, with Marina and me, waiting for his champagne. After a bit, he stood up.

'I'll need to go to my bed.'

'But Charlie, what about the champagne?'

'For God's sake, Kenny, I cannot drink champagne at this time in the morning. What are you thinking about? I need to go to my bed.'

Graeme went out the door and, moments later, his champagne arrived. I looked at Marina. She looked at me.

'I cannot drink that,' she said.

But it wasn't wasted. We took the bottles on the bus for the tour of the city.

My dream had always been European success followed by a tour of the city. Now I could revel in both. We returned to Liverpool on the train, where we had a carriage all to ourselves. Everyone was laughing and singing. The tour was everything I'd hoped it would be. It must have been even better for the guys whose home city it was, players like Thommo and Terry Mac. Lining the streets were people I recognised, even though I had only been on Merseyside for less than a year. What was amazing, and heartwarming, was the sight of blue and white colours amid the red. Everton fans would much rather their own team had won but many were still happy to salute Liverpool. I thought this was wonderful and so different from Glasgow, where differences ruled. Many Liverpool fans feel the same way. If they can't win something, they want Everton to do it. This attitude must come from the powerful sense of community on Merseyside. I liked the way that Everton supporters came along to show their appreciation for what we had achieved, but they also made sure, by wearing blue, that we were left in no doubt where their real allegiance lay.

Joy turned to frustration the following season. Liverpool were drawn against Nottingham Forest in the first round. UEFA, the governing body of European football, should have given us a first-round bye, but probably disliked the thought of a monopoly by one nation. Forest were a club we didn't want so early. Winning the League the season after promotion was a magnificent achievement, one we all admired; they were a good side.

Before the tie, Brian Clough went through his usual routine of insisting his inexperienced side had no chance, that Liverpool were the holders, the greatest in Europe, blah, blah, blah, the normal Cloughie nonsense. We never listened to that. Liverpool were not a club where players took anything for granted, certainly not the outcome of any football match, against any level of opposition.

Cloughie is such a strange man. I respect his footballing achievements. I respect the teams he produced, especially his Forest teams, but I don't know him as a man. He talked a lot, always giving his forthright opinions in the papers. I wouldn't criticise him for that; if everyone was as quiet with the press as me there wouldn't be many newspapers. Cloughie has been critical of me in the past, but he's never intimidated me as he did other people. That style of his wasn't for me. I made sure he never kissed me. Ronnie Moran used to take it and laugh.

I was a player the first time I met Cloughie. We were both attending a toy fair in Leeds because we had endorsed balls. Cloughie started banging on about a game I'd played in against one of his sides. I'd won a fair penalty which he claimed should never have been given.

'Well,' I said to him, 'if you read the papers you will realise it was a penalty. When I went past the first one of your players and he kicked me, I stumbled but kept going past the second defender. He had a bit of a nip at my legs but as I was going into the box I tried to stay up. When I passed the third one and he had a pop as well I thought it was time I went down. Three's not bad.'

Cloughie didn't know what to say. He was silenced, which must go down as some sort of record. The thing with Cloughie is that he was not used to people standing up to him. He could be so cruel to people verbally.

For a team supposed to understand the nature of European competition, Liverpool made a very basic error in the first leg at the City Ground. Having gone behind to Garry Birtles' goal, we foolishly went chasing the game. This naive reaction probably stemmed from the fact that we were playing familiar League opponents. In the League you always go for victory because of the points. In a game settled over two legs, a 1–0 reverse in the away leg is not normally a bad result. We had recovered from a one-goal deficit the previous season, against Borussia Moenchengladbach. But we went looking for an equaliser and got punished in classic Forest fashion when Colin Barrett scored late on. All Forest had to do was to come to Anfield and put up shop which they did brilliantly, the game finishing goalless. It was their first European Cup tie and they made the holders look like the newcomers to the wiles of European football. I think beating Liverpool gave Forest the confidence to go on and win the trophy. They must have known that one of their toughest obstacles had been the first.

The game was on Granada Television with Gerald Sinstadt commentating. It was not his doing but at the end of their transmission, as they showed pictures of Liverpool's defeated players walking off the pitch, Granada played 'The Party's Over'. On the next occasion when we were winning, the Kop sang 'Gerald Sinstadt. Gerald Sinstadt. How's the party going now?'

There is no doubt that Liverpool made a mistake against Forest, one which was ruthlessly punished. A myth has arisen around Liverpool that they never changed their tactical approach, but this is simply not true. Liverpool often used different styles in Europe. Before I arrived, Ian Ross would man-mark people. He used to follow Alan Ball in derby matches. Liverpool did change if they thought it was important. Even in my time there, when we drew 1–1 at Bayern Munich, Sammy Lee man-marked Breitner. In away matches, we played one up, and I dropped off a central striker, like Rushie. The rest of the time I filled in the left-hand-side position, just in front of the midfield four.

The following year Liverpool again fell at the first. Dynamo Tbilisi came to Anfield and they were an excellent side. They ran out first and deliberately warmed up in front of the Kop to show they weren't intimidated by the place or people. Some journalists suggested the Kop were mesmerised by their show of skills during the kick-in. That would never have adversely affected the Kop. We won narrowly, 2–1, which meant an awkward trip to Georgia. The ban on massed gatherings in the Soviet Union had clearly been lifted for Liverpool's visit. We were woken by a demonstration at 4 a.m. We lay in our beds trying to get back to sleep but it was difficult with all these people outside shouting

'Dynamo, Dynamo'. I peered through the curtains to see hundreds of people marching past with torches. We just laughed at it. That was not a contributory factor in our losing 3–0. We deserved to fail. Dynamo were full of Soviet internationals, all very skilful and capable of fast, flowing football. Liverpool were simply beaten by the better side.

Nothing was left to chance on away trips, like the one to Tbilisi. All Wednesday-night matches followed the same build-up. We would train on the Tuesday morning and then head straight to the airport. A charter plane would fly us to the venue, we'd settle in, stretch the legs with a walk before dinner. Early bed and then a loosener in the morning, around 10 or 11, just to prepare the body for the night match. I would spend all afternoon in bed, have some tea and toast, and head off to the game. It was all very low-key. Some people were surprised that Liverpool did not travel until the day before the game, but European trips were not supposed to be sightseeing jaunts. We were going to do a job. By leaving on Tuesday we could get in a proper training session at Melwood, where the surface was good, the balls were the right pressure and there was none of the hassle that you often encountered at the other end. Some clubs leave a day earlier than we did, but Liverpool didn't like spending too much time away.

I was never curious about the places we went to. They were simply cities containing stadiums, another stepping-stone to a potential final. The team was of the utmost importance to everyone at the club. When I became manager I realised just how ingrained the team-first doctrine was. Liverpool's board understood that a successful team meant a successful club.

Liverpool always went well prepared. Two Irishmen came with us, Alan Glynn and Harry White. They used to bring us breakfast in our rooms. Harry and Alan were clever operators. They used to go into the kitchens of these foreign hotels with a couple of bottles of whisky, just to get the local people on their side, and make sure they kept an eye on things. In poor countries, the locals would be friends for life if you gave them whisky. In Scandinavia there was never any problem with food. On trips to Eastern bloc countries, we always took our own food. In Poznan once, Bob Paisley said: 'Don't drink that tea. You don't know what they might have put in it.'

We also had to contend with difficult playing surfaces, like that at Oulun Palloseura, an awkward name and an awkward pitch. These champions of Finland represented our first-round opposition in 1980–81, which after two disappointingly brief European Cup campaigns was to prove a glorious one. It was freezing in Finland, where we were happy to draw 1–1 against a bunch of very fit opponents on a tight pitch. It was said that 1–1 was not the greatest of results, given the Finns' standing in world football, but that ignored the nature of European football; 1–1 away from home against anyone represents a good result. The plan is to win the home ties, which we did pretty convincingly by beating the Finns 10–1. Perhaps we were stirred up by Bob, who told us that we had made a mess of the first game. 'Now is the time to show your true colours,' he said, and it was all red that night. Terry Mac and Graeme scored hat-tricks. I didn't find the net.

The second round paired Liverpool with Aberdeen. Thanks very much UEFA. That was never going to be easy. Scotland versus England would be hard-fought even if it was a friendly. In the run-up to the match, Graeme, Big Al and I were trying to stir the other Liverpool lads up, saying Aberdeen would be really up for this and desperate to beat us. We had to win. Graeme, Al and I kept telling each other that if we didn't get a result, we were going to be crucified, completely slaughtered every time we went back to Scotland. They would rub it in for ever. In fact, we three Scots got a lot of verbal abuse during that match, as expected. Alex Ferguson had prepared Aberdeen with typical thoroughness. They were a decent outfit, with good players like Miller and McLeish, Strachan and Rougvie. The fact that Aberdeen were soon to win the European Cup-Winners' Cup gives a fair indication of their quality. But we were equally fired up and won 1–0, Terry Mac scoring a wonderful goal, chipped over Jim Leighton. It could have been more but for Leighton's reflexes. Bob Paisley had said a lot of nice things about Strachan before the game; he really praised him. Bob was sincere in his compliments about Gordon, but at the same time he hoped his 'little bit of toffee' would have an adverse effect on Gordon's performance. He had a quiet game. Aberdeen came down south and really attacked us. Early on, Mark McGhee made a great run but his shot was blocked by Clem. That really seemed to stir us up and we ran all over them, winning 4–0.

The quarter-finals brought on CSKA Sofia, the Bulgarians who had conquered Nottingham Forest. Because of their winter shutdown, it was often best to play these Eastern European teams in March when they were a bit rusty. So it proved at Anfield where we destroyed them. Graeme was magnificent that night, scoring his second hat-trick of the tournament with a classic collection of shots. Arriving in Bulgaria with a 5–1 advantage, we were never going to be unduly troubled. They came at us briefly but when Davie Johnson turned in a shot from Sammy Lee that had struck the post, the fight went out of the Bulgarians.

Four clubs remained – Real Madrid, Bayern Munich, Inter Milan and Liverpool. What an illustrious line-up! These semi-finalists had won the European Cup on 13 occasions between them. Whoever we drew were going to be tough opponents. We were paired with Bayern, a team with an impressive generation of great German internationals like Karl-Heinz Rummenigge and Paul Breitner. They came to Anfield looking for a draw and got it. Breitner made a big fuss, calling us 'unimaginative' and 'unintelligent'. It might have been unintelligent football, but it was an even less intelligent statement. Breitner's arrogant attitude contributed to Bayern's downfall. Breitner's decision to shout his mouth off to the newspapers wound the lads up. We couldn't wait to get over to Munich. Just before the start, Bob told Sammy Lee to follow Breitner all over the place, make his night a misery, ensure he never played. Sammy was brilliant; wherever Breitner went, there was Sammy. When Breitner tried to run down a channel, wee Sammy turned it into a cul-de-sac. Breitner disappeared, he couldn't handle the attention, which made his earlier comments even more laughable. It serves him right for criticising us in public. Liverpool would never do that to the opposition. Why stir them up?

Yet the odds were stacked heavily against Liverpool that night. Our defence was patched up, with Richard Money and Colin Irwin covering for the injured Phil Thompson and Alan Kennedy. I only lasted five minutes, limping off after Del'Haye caught me on the ankle and nearly broke it. Howard Gayle came on and was absolutely magnificent. He gave Dressler, Bayern's full-back, a torrid time. The Germans hadn't prepared for Howard; they knew nothing about this man who was running them ragged.

The German supporters were screaming but no one had an answer to Howard until he was booked and then taken off. Seven minutes from time the game turned our way. Despite toiling with a torn muscle, David Johnson managed to sprint down the line and cross for Ray Kennedy, who controlled the ball and volleyed it in. Scoring so late on meant there was little Bayern could do. Rummenigge equalised but the away-goals rule saw us through.

Because of Del'Haye's tackle, I was doubtful for the final. It was a very frustrating six-week period. I certainly couldn't play competitively in the build-up to the showdown in Paris with Real Madrid, who had seen off Inter. All I could do was undergo treatment and join in the staff matches, where tackling was unknown. These were funny occasions. At Melwood, Liverpool had a pitch they called 'Wembley'. Injured first-teamers would have to guest at 'Wembley' for the staff side, whose core was Bob Paisley, Joe Fagan, Tom Saunders, John Benison, Ronnie Moran and Roy Evans. Now that was hard training, real work. The graft we injured first-team 'guests' had to put in was unbelievable. We had to do all the running. We used to pass the ball 30 yards to Old Tom. He used to get it, have a dance on it, and wait for us to run up. He would then lay the ball off for one of us who had sprinted up from behind to have a shot on goal. When one of us had a shot, there would be Joe at the back shouting 'get back'. Bob used to play in goal wearing sheepskin mittens. He never caught the ball, he always punched it. We used to play against the kids and that was how I got fit for Paris. I hadn't played a competitive match for six weeks before the final, but I was determined to play.

I was never going to allow lack of match practice to prevent me from playing in a European Cup final. I recovered in time, passed all the fitness tests, and set out for Paris. We went on the Tuesday, as usual, this time with the wives on the plane. They went to their hotel; we went to ours. It was strictly business until the game was played.

Our opponents were Real Madrid, who had a clever coach in Vujadin Boskov, and some special players including Camacho, the assassin, Stielike and Laurie Cunningham. They had a great attacking reputation but they must have been a bit afraid of our reputation, particularly after we had gone to Munich and got a result. It was never a classic match, although the atmosphere was amazing with the fans making a tremendous noise. It was like playing a game of chess, with both sides moving cautiously. Some tough battles went on – Sammy Lee was duelling with Stielike while Camacho was trying to get involved with Graeme. My time out injured slowly caught up with me. Cramp gripped both my calves, so Bob sent Jimmy Case on.

I was still on the pitch when Alan Kennedy set off on his run into the history books. Ray Kennedy threw the ball towards Alan and he started to run forward. I thought: 'Where's he going?' Alan got past Garcia Cortes and just kept going. What a strike he finished with! I don't know if he knew what he was doing, but the ball ended up in the back of the net. He ran behind the goal and we all just looked at each other, stunned. We were so pleased for Alan, who is a smashing fellow. It was a sign of his popularity that he had an amazing assortment of nicknames. We used to call him 'Barney' after Barney Rubble from 'The Flintstones'. Then there was 'Belly', too, because Bel Mooney wrote an article about him; and 'Billy', after Billy Bungalow, because he had nothing upstairs!

Real Madrid are one of the glamour sides of Europe. Their reputation had always been for winning with style. Yet here the club of Puskas, Gento and Di Stefano were beaten by a galloping full-back called 'Barney'. Liverpool's celebrations were long and hard. One moment of the revelry stood out. Richard Money, who had played in Munich, was with us and I kept asking him: 'Richard what have you got in your pocket?'

'A medal, Kenny.'

'No, you've not,' I replied, 'you've got a winner's medal.'

'Aye,' he smiled, 'a winner's medal.'

Then we came back for my favourite part – another tour of the city. It was great to be European champions again. After that first success in 1978, Nottingham Forest replaced us as England's best side in Europe, then Aston Villa. We had no complaints. Liverpool never begrudged anybody their success if it was done properly, and Cloughie achieved his success with Forest the right way. Forest's example had set us a challenge. It was up to Liverpool to improve and we succeeded.

The next season we went out in the quarter-final, to CSKA

Paul, Kelly and Marina share my pride and pleasure at being awarded the MBE in February 1985.

Together with son Paul and daughter Lynsey on a tour of the city after Liverpool had won the FA Cup in 1989.

Kelly, Lauren, Paul and Lynsey join Marina and I to celebrate the 1994–95 championship and my winning the Manager of the Year award.

I would have liked to have done better for my country; here I am playing against Holland.

My self-confidence amongst Scotland players started improving only when I moved to Liverpool in 1977.

I score our first goal in Scotland's 3–2 win over Holland at the 1978 World Cup.

Denis Law was my first real idol. He had so much style.

The great Jock Stein, who was such an influence on my career.

Bob Paisley in familiar pose: holding up another championship trophy.

Wembley is a special place for me, here playing against Manchester United in the 1983 Milk Cup final.

How inviting: a loose ball on the edge of the opposition's penalty area.

My desire to play for Scotland never waned. Here I am in 1985, fourteen years after my international debut.

Joe Fagan's last match in charge ends in horrific circumstances at Heysel, in 1985.

Phil Neal was a fine full-back but he moved on shortly after I became manager.

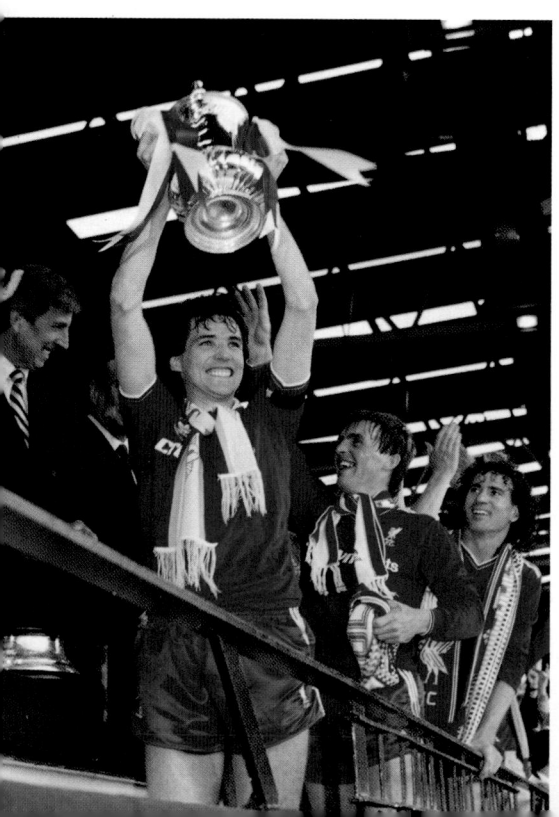

The 1986 League game at Chelsea brought the first half of the double.

Alan Hansen, my friend and former team-mate, was a magnificent captain. Here he lifts the 1986 FA Cup, followed by me and Craig Johnston.

This is Paul at Anfield, wearing his Juventus top, after Liverpool won the League championship.

Sofia. Then we had to make a trip to Tokyo, of all places, to play in the World Club Championship against Flamengo. The Brazilians battered us, 3–0. It was a mad idea to play it in Japan. The distance we had to travel was ridiculous. We woke up at 4 in the morning not knowing where we were. Because of the differing journeys across different time zones, the whole thing was much more suited to Flamengo and it showed.

The Polish champions, Widzew Lodz, proved our downfall in the European Cup quarter-finals in 1983 but the next season we were back in business. We started Joe Fagan's first campaign in charge in Odense, appropriately the birthplace of Hans Christian Andersen, which allowed everyone to make jokes about fairytales. It was chaos in Odense, because Liverpool were so big in Denmark. Odense's ground was small and they couldn't accommodate even a quarter of the people outside. Fans were climbing up on roofs, seeking any vantage point to see a match which I settled. Back at Anfield, Liverpool were far more dominant. I scored two of our five to break the record of most European goals scored by a British player. The lads were very kind to me that night; they laid the goals on for me.

We didn't make it easy for ourselves in the second round. By failing to score at home to Atletico Bilbao we knew we had our work cut out in Spain. Some people wrote us off, saying Liverpool would be turned over again, and that a third season in a row would end in European disappointment. But the important thing about a goalless draw at home is that the opposition haven't scored; many good teams have fallen out on the away-goals rule. All we had to do was nick a goal in Spain and they needed to score twice. When Rushie scored with a header, it was all over. The Bilbao supporters were brilliant to us. The Basques were noisy but sporting with it. When we came off the pitch, they gave us a standing ovation. I was playing against Goicoechea, who had gained notoriety for a dreadful tackle on Maradona. He was eventually punished with an 18-game domestic ban for that challenge, which almost ended Maradona's career. I never had any problems with the so-called 'Butcher of Bilbao', for Liverpool or when Scotland played Spain.

Liverpool must have spoiled people with their performances. After the Anfield leg of our quarter-final with Benfica, we were again criticised for winning only 1–0. Not enough, decreed the wise owls in the newspapers. They said we would struggle out in Portugal, but fear was not a word that ever featured in Liverpool's dressing-room, wherever we were playing. Every team, however illustrious, is there to be beaten. Why should Liverpool fear teams? Benfica didn't know what hit them. Craig Johnston ran amok in a 4–1 win. It ranks with Liverpool's greatest European performances. The finals were great results but not great games. Along with the 1–0 win in Bilbao and the draw at Bayern Munich, this victory at Benfica was probably the best display in my time at Liverpool.

Punters back home began getting very excited at the possibility of an Anglo-Scottish final because Dundee United were going great guns. The semi-final draw intensified the excitement. Liverpool drew Dinamo Bucharest while Dundee United got Roma. The dream final was still on. We didn't know much about Dinamo when they arrived for the first leg. We soon discovered that they were a tough, well-organised team happily prepared to resort to intimidation. Unfortunately for the Romanians, they picked on Graeme, the wrong person to get naughty with. Dinamo's players went home defeated, by Sammy Lee's goal, and muttering threats to Graeme, whom they accused of breaking the jaw of one of their players.

That sent the temperature soaring for the trip to Romania. From the moment we landed in Bucharest the atmosphere was hostile. The staff and police at the airport set the tone, brimming with antagonism towards us. Graeme had clearly been turned into a huge hate figure in Romania. Of course, it didn't bother him one bit. In fact, Graeme loved it. The stadium erupted into a deafening sound of boos when we walked out of the tunnel. They booed Graeme throughout but he relished it. Boos were better than cheers for him. Dinamo's players tried every way to get Graeme, to hurt him, to avenge the broken jaw, but they never did. After Rushie scored two great goals to give us victory, Graeme came off with his socks all ripped, which says something about their tackling. But the Romanians couldn't rip the smile from his face. In the dressing-room afterwards we could hear how angry the Romanians were. Joe stood in the middle of the room and said: 'Keep calm. Steady. Steady.' Then he let out a huge cry of delight. It was great for Joe to reach a European Cup final in his first season in charge, particularly as the semi-final circumstances had been so intimidating.

We were off to Rome. Sadly for the dream Anglo-Scottish final, the Italians beat Dundee United. Roma had a definite advantage playing the final in their own stadium. I know UEFA agreed to play the game in Rome before they knew Roma were going to the final but it was still naive planning. UEFA should never have agreed to use the ground of one of the competing teams, just in case that was a problem. The odds were stacked high against us. All the Italians told us we were going to lose, which was kind. Funnily enough, the only problem we had in the hotel was nothing to do with the Italians. I was rooming with Graeme. The night before the final we couldn't get to sleep because of a terrible racket coming from the next room. We banged on the wall, shouted 'quiet', but our noisy neighbour still wouldn't turn his radio down. So we phoned down to reception to complain. Within a minute or so, the noise stopped. Reception had obviously called up and told whoever it was to turn his radio off. When we got up in the morning, we found out that it was Joe Fagan's room.

The Olympic Stadium was as we expected – filled with tens of thousands of Roma fans convinced the good times were returning at last to their ambitious club. The Italians were all in good heart and good voice. We went out on to the pitch and there were spaces at the Liverpool end. In the other three sides you could not move. It was some scene. There were flares and fires and banners. They didn't affect me. In fact, it could have intimidated the Italian players a little bit, all that expectation on them to win at home. Their fans put them under pressure. Roma's players might have looked relaxed on the outside, but internally the butterflies would be working overtime.

Big finals were nothing new to Liverpool. As we walked along the corridor towards the entrance to the pitch we broke into a Chris Rea song, 'Don't Know What It Is – But I Love It'. I think us being so relaxed, sounding like we were just off for training, unsettled the Roma players. Their coach, Nils Liedholm, couldn't believe it, but Liverpool teams often sang. 'Don't Know What It Is – But I Love It' was just picked up by the Liverpool lads. We had other favourites, like 'Come On Eileen' by Dexy's Midnight Runners and that Phil Collins song 'Can't Hurry Love'. Alan Kennedy used to come in, singing, 'Ooh, you can't hurry up'. We tried to teach him the words but they never sunk in.

Sammy Lee would normally start the singing. He was a great one for sing-songs. There was one of Sammy's that wasn't very polite, but it was mainly songs from people like Dexy's Midnight Runners, Chris Rea or Phil Collins. It would usually end up with versions of Beatles songs. No big fuss was made in the dressing-room at the Olympic Stadium. Joe just let us get on with it. If the Italian players were worried by how relaxed we were, that was their problem. Part of being a top footballer is being able to handle big occasions.

Roma's nerves were soon clear. Their goalie, Tancredi, dropped a cross in a scramble and Phil Neal rapped it in; but the Italians came back at us. Roma's centre-forward, Pruzzo, scored with a header. I came off, Michael Robinson came on, so I wasn't eligible for the penalty shoot-out, which followed extra time. Because I had been subbed, I had to watch from the bench. Astonishingly Falcao, Roma's Brazilian, didn't take a penalty for them. It was odd. Brazilians are usually pretty dangerous with a dead ball. One of the Liverpool lads joked that penalty-taking wasn't in the Brazilian's contract!

Liverpool had been practising penalties on Monday and Tuesday although you couldn't tell from our first. Stevie Nicol decided he would take responsibility and promptly hit his penalty over. Di Bartolomei put them ahead. Phil Neal scored and then Conti missed to make it 1–1. Souness and Righetti scored to keep it all square. Then Rushie put us 3–2 ahead and up stepped Graziani. Bruce Grobbelaar gave him the old rubber-legs treatment on the goal-line. Bruce was very clever, he wobbled his body, but never moved his feet. This made Graziani nervous and he duly obliged us by blasting his penalty over. Thank you very much. We just needed Alan Kennedy to score to give Liverpool a fourth European Cup. Alan had taken a few in practice and put them in the same place every single time; and he put it in the same place this time. I bet a postage stamp would not have been the difference between that one and the ones in practice. He sidefooted it with a wee curl to the goalkeeper's right.

It was another good night out. It was unfair having to play Roma in their own backyard so victory was all the sweeter. It was great to celebrate in the opponents' city; for the punters as well. We got back to the hotel and lots of Scousers were in the reception, singing away. What a party we had! Many of the boys went off to bed. I was enjoying myself too much. At 4 in the morning I rang Graeme and began singing Liverpool songs down the phone.

'Get lost,' he said.

'That's not very nice, Graeme,' I replied. 'You should be enjoying yourself.'

Then I began singing again. He shouted down the phone, telling me to be quiet. I kept singing, and Graeme slammed down the phone. I tried again and again, but I couldn't get through. Graeme had unplugged the phone. All I wanted was a wee sing-song with a friend.

Unknown to us, as we made our merry way back for another tour of Liverpool, there had been incidents in the Italian capital which had serious repercussions a year later. My European dream was about to turn sour.

—8—

HEYSEL

W HAT BECAME known as the Horror of Heysel arose partly from events that occurred in Rome. Before and after the triumphant European Cup final, Liverpool fans suffered horrendous abuse at the hands of Italian fans. Our supporters were attacked in alleys. People I had left tickets for at Rome's Olympic Stadium said they had been hammered with stones. Coaches were ambushed by Roma fans tossing bricks at them. The police were escorting the buses but they still didn't get much protection. A year later, the seeds of chaos bore fruit. Some of those Liverpool fans in Brussels would have been in Rome the year before. When Italian fans started throwing rocks and stones again at the Heysel Stadium in Brussels, the Liverpool supporters would have remembered Rome.

We learned afterwards that some Juventus fans at the unsegregated end had been throwing stones at Liverpool supporters, which was why some of our fans ran at them on that terrace in Heysel. Liverpool fans were blamed for killing the Italians but people forget the circumstances. On previous away trips, Liverpool fans had behaved themselves as well as anyone. So why was Heysel different? The stadium, the organisation and the attacks on Liverpool fans in Rome were factors in the Heysel disaster.

When we arrived at Heysel it was all very peaceful. Our route to the 1985 final with Juventus had been easy compared to the problems of previous seasons. The toughest match was in the second round against Benfica. We were already leading 3–1, thanks to Rushie's hat-trick at Anfield, but they really went for us in Portugal, desperately striving to overturn the deficit. It didn't help Liverpool's cause when I was sent off for the first time in my career. I'd had the ball on the touchline with my back to Pietra, Benfica's full-back. I knew he was there. I'd had a look as the ball was coming. I could almost feel his breathing. So I went one way and came back the other. Pietra just chopped me down. So cynical. As I got to my feet, Pietra looked like he was going to head-butt me. So I grabbed him by the collar just to stop him. Then I let him go and walked away. The referee, Michel Vautrot, sent the two of us off and I got a three-match ban. Fortunately one was the Super Cup against Juventus. Then came Austria Vienna and Panathinaikos, who we beat 4–0 in the first leg of the semi-final. Athens was no problem; they were 4–0 down. The Greeks needed snookers and couldn't get them.

We were off to Brussels. Peter Robinson went over before the final to see the stadium. He was concerned about many things to do with the Heysel Stadium, which was clearly unsuited to holding two sets of supporters who were bound to be emotionally charged for such a big game. Peter told the Belgian authorities and UEFA that he was very apprehensive about ticket allocation. Peter was also worried that they had kept a section of the ground for the use of Belgian people. He suggested that only Liverpool and Juventus should receive tickets. Allowing a third party access to tickets would inevitably mean a dangerous mixed area, with English and Italian supporters having got tickets off any Belgian wanting to make a few bob for himself. It was a very frustrating situation. Liverpool seemed to be the only ones fearful about what could happen. Liverpool made it public that they were concerned about the condition of the stadium, but UEFA said they must continue, so the ill-fated final went ahead and unfortunately everybody knows the consequences. Liverpool were so concerned that they put up information booths outside the ground in an attempt to keep our fans out of the unsegregated area. Liverpool did that, not UEFA. It angers me that Liverpool did all the warning, Liverpool made every effort to prevent trouble and when the worst happened Liverpool received all the blame.

There was no hint of trouble when we entered Heysel. As normal, we walked out on to the pitch, still wearing our civvies, about an hour and a half before kick-off. We strolled behind one of the goals. The terrace there was split in two, but the only thing dividing the sections was a flimsy barrier of what looked like chicken wire. The half supposedly kept for Belgians keen to see a final on their doorstep was where the ticket allocation had gone terribly wrong. Most of the people in that neutral Belgian section were Juventus fans. The other section behind that goal contained our people. As we walked behind the goal, one of the Liverpool fans threw us a ball. The players just kicked it around and occasionally volleyed it back into the crowd. The Liverpool fans kicked it back and so it went on. Everything was amicable. There was no indication of any bother, but seemingly while all this was happening, Juventus fans were throwing stones at the Liverpool fans. Remembering the dreadful treatment they had encountered in Rome, our supporters inevitably reacted angrily.

I can't condone the actions of some Liverpool fans but it is difficult not to react when the opposing supporters are throwing missiles at you. The fact that fatalities might result wouldn't have occurred to the Liverpool fans when they ran across. If you have been pelted with stones the year before, and suffered badly, you are not going to accept it again. That's how the trouble started. UEFA must shoulder much of the blame. The choice of Heysel was so obviously wrong. The Belgians had no idea how to stage a match of this magnitude. There wasn't a great deal of security; thousands of people got into the ground with the stub still on their ticket. The worst mistake the Belgians and UEFA made was in allocating tickets to people not from the two clubs involved. That was a recipe for disaster. Of course, it's sad when two sets of people cannot go and enjoy a game, cannot behave themselves, but you've got to be realistic. You've got to recognise the potential for trouble and do everything in your power to prevent any problems occurring. UEFA didn't do that.

Some people said Liverpool's players were hit by stones and that our fans reacted angrily to that. I don't recall anything being thrown at us. It's the type of thing you would remember. Besides, we were inside getting changed when the real trouble started. Someone in the dressing-room hinted there had been a bit of trouble but I never listen to unsubstantiated stories. I nearly missed Heysel because I was struggling with flu. I had taken Lemsip to try to get the bug out of my system and I just lay on the massage bench, preserving my strength until the call came to go out and play. In fact, I fell asleep, so I didn't know much about what was going on. Apparently there were various stories coming in and out of the dressing-room but nothing could be confirmed. Personally, I never saw any trouble.

We were all dressed and ready to go when a UEFA representative came in.

'You can't go,' he told Joe, 'there's been a bit of trouble.'

When something like that happens, chaos takes over. No one really knew what was going on. In situations like these, the people who have least information are the players. We are cocooned from everything, just told to wait until someone decides something. Some of the lads were popping in and out, but nobody really knew what was going on. Chaos hid the truth. Even people watching did not appreciate what they were witnessing. Friends of mine who were at Heysel told me afterwards they never knew there had been fatalities. They knew there had been trouble but not to what extent. When you are in a foreign country, it's difficult to find out what's going on. I don't even know how informative the PA system was. Confusion reigned.

We didn't know anybody had died, not officially. All we heard were rumours. Football's a game of huge gossip, which I just switch off from. When Phil Neal, our captain, went out to talk to the Liverpool supporters, I don't think he was informed of the severity of the situation. He was only asked to go out to speak to them, to calm them down. I don't think he, nor Scirea, Juventus's captain, were told there were any fatalities. Phil Neal wrote in his autobiography that I knew about the deaths before we played the game. I categorically did not. I had fallen asleep and didn't know that there had been fatalities. If UEFA had told the players that people had died, I don't think that the players would have wanted to go on.

But what did we know? I was never outside so I never knew the extent of the trouble. We knew something serious had happened, because the game had been delayed by an hour and a half, but it's very difficult to decide what's true and what's false. Probably the people watching on television, in Britain and in Italy and around the world, and the media present, knew a lot more about it than we did. If the people who were running the show could not tell us what was happening, what chance had we got?

Eventually, when everything had been calmed down, UEFA decided to start the final. Amid all the confusion, the one thing that was right was the decision to play the game. If the final had not been played, there was the possibility of further trouble. Another match would not have been a very clever thought either, given the circumstances. That would have been set up for more trouble.

Walking out on to the pitch, both sets of players immediately became aware of the altered atmosphere. I honestly didn't notice the rubble piled up in one corner, where the supporters had died in that terrible crush. Most of the players surmised there was something seriously wrong because there were huge gaps at that end. It's easy to understand why so many people left. If I had been a supporter in that corner, and thought people had died, I would not have stayed on to watch a football match. Some people thought it would have been a mark of respect to those who died not to play the game. But UEFA decided it had to be played for fear of even greater trouble. The decision taken at the time was understandable.

UEFA wanted the game played, so we played it. I don't even know whether we deserved to win or whether Juventus deserved to win. I don't remember the match at all. It wasn't a football contest. The players were going through the motions. No one had the stomach for it. All I can recall is Mark Lawrenson damaging his shoulder, Paul Walsh injuring his groin and the penalty incident which settled the match in Juventus's favour. It was in no way, shape or form a penalty. The foul was committed well outside the box. I learned afterwards, from someone who worked for UEFA, that they wanted a decision on the night because of what happened. I said to the man from UEFA: 'There's no way that was a penalty.' He replied: 'We know that.'

If I had known about the fatalities, I would not have wanted to play. You go along to watch a game. You don't go along expecting that sort of ending, do you? Football's not that important. No game of football is worth that. Everything else pales into insignificance. Juventus fans should not have been throwing stones. Liverpool fans should not have reacted the way they did. Yet neither set of supporters could have anticipated the terrible outcome. If they had foreseen the dreadful consequences, or thought what terrible things might unfold, I'm sure the stones would never have been thrown by the Italians and that the English retaliation would never have occurred. Every single one of them, both Italian and English, must have regretted it. I'm sure they still do now.

When we went for dinner after the match, some of the wives said they had seen bodies piled up under the stand. It must have been pretty harrowing for them. They were sitting in the directors' box while fans were running wild across the stand. They felt very threatened. For the players, we were still trying to piece together what had happened. I only really became aware the following morning, when we watched BBC television in the hotel. Then we saw the Italian fans crying, and they were banging on the side of our bus as we left the hotel. When we left Brussels, the Italians were angry, understandably so; 39 of their friends had died. We needed a lot of police to protect the bus. I remember well one Italian man, who had his face right up against the window where I was sitting. He was crying and screaming. You feel for anybody who loses someone in those circumstances.

These Juventus fans felt that Liverpool were responsible for the deaths of their friends. How could we be? We had been the ones warning UEFA and the Belgians. It was our supporters who had been attacked the previous year by Italians and were determined not to be ambushed again. I could understand Juventus's emotions because they felt the team represented those who had been involved in the trouble, but they could have directed some of their anger towards UEFA and the Belgian authorities.

It was wrong that Liverpool took all the blame. Margaret Thatcher said Liverpool should be banned from Europe, and that our fans were hooligans. What did she know? She never knew many of the facts. Partly as a consequence of Margaret

Thatcher not understanding the situation, and condemning Liverpool so quickly, English clubs were subsequently suspended for five years.

Within football, I don't think there was any resentment towards Liverpool because English clubs were banned from Europe. I think there was resentment towards Margaret Thatcher, who mouthed off before FIFA had made their decision. When the Prime Minister of a country is critical of a club, it is easy for the governing body of football to go along with it. A little bit more thought from Margaret Thatcher, and a little bit more time to get the real information, might have been more helpful. She certainly could have waited. Someone in her position should have known how much weight her words carried.

STEPPING UP

Dᴜʀɪɴɢ ᴛʜᴇ whole Heysel period I knew I was going to replace Joe Fagan as manager. I was hardly taking over in the greatest of circumstances. At my first press conference I had to answer questions about the 39 people killed at Heysel. Liverpool were banned from Europe, vilified at home and abroad. Overnight my relationship with all the players changed, which was something I found hard to cope with. I had to keep playing and yet distance myself from the dressing-room world, the banter and wind-ups I loved so much. Outside Anfield, quite a few critics questioned my ability to do the manager's job, saying my inexperience would cost Liverpool dear. More than a few people hoped I would fall on my face. It gave me great pleasure to prove them wrong; by the end of my first season Liverpool had done the double. We even broke our FA Cup jinx.

What made me laugh at the end of such a successful season was the critics saying I had done the double with a team inherited from Joe. I have total respect for Joe but the double-winning side wasn't anybody's team but mine. I hold in equal contempt the theory that I ignored the Boot Room. I didn't go into the Boot Room after matches simply because I wasn't clever enough to cope. My critics should stop and analyse properly what happened to Liverpool during my first year as player-manager. My actions were motivated only by the best interests of Liverpool Football Club. In fact, I maintained Liverpool's tradition of evolution not revolution. I worked in tandem with people who had been running Liverpool teams for years, people like Bob Paisley, who was brought back to help me out, Ronnie Moran and Roy Evans and old Tom Saunders. At the end of my first year, I honoured that most important Liverpool tradition – winning trophies.

When the Liverpool board first asked me to be manager, my feelings centred around surprise as much as honour. Peter Robinson phoned up one day and said:

'Kenny, could the chairman and I come up to the house and speak to you?'

'Yes, no problem, Peter.'

'When can we come?'

'When do you want to come?'

'We'll come Sunday night.'

'No problem, Peter.'

'What time?' he asked.

'Whenever,' I replied. 'Half-seven, eight, Peter, whatever suits you.'

'We'll come around half-seven, then.'

'Fine.'

I thought the conversation was going to finish then but Peter added: 'Don't you want to know what we want to see you for?'

'Yes,' I replied, 'if you want to tell me.'

'Well, we'd like to offer you the manager's job.'

'That's no problem, Peter, you can still come up to the house.'

I replaced the receiver and turned to Marina.

'That was Peter. Liverpool want me to become manager.'

'Oh, yeah,' Marina said dismissively, clearly not believing me.

'Honestly, Marina, they do.'

'Why?'

'I don't know.'

So I phoned my dad and told him that the chairman and Peter were coming to ask me to be manager of Liverpool. He was overjoyed.

'Kenny, that's magnificent,' he said, 'what a compliment that is. You've got to take it, haven't you? If they've got that much faith in you, you've got to have a go.'

I called Marina's dad as well. He said much the same thing.

That Sunday night, when John Smith and Peter Robinson arrived to speak to me, I didn't know whether they came with the unanimous support of Liverpool's board, or whether it was their decision. At the time, my thoughts were focused solely on playing. I loved playing. I looked after myself and was determined to prolong my career as much as possible. My love was not management but in actually putting on boots and running down the tunnel for 90 minutes of playing. Every player would say the same. But then every player isn't offered the chance to manage Liverpool. It would have been an insult to reject Liverpool's offer, even though I understood that putting one foot in the management camp would accelerate the end of my playing career. If I hadn't taken the job, I would have played more first-team games, certainly the following year and probably the year after that. I had to make a decision knowing that I would have to sacrifice playing as often as I wanted to. This obviously entailed foregoing a lot of the pleasure I derived from football. To concentrate properly, to ensure I didn't fall between two stools, the playing side had to be curtailed. My competitive nature meant I refused to contemplate failing in my new job.

There was no real soul-searching or deep thinking involved. I had to accept Liverpool's offer. It presented another challenge, another opportunity to test my abilities at a different level. So when Peter Robinson and John Smith came up to Southport, my mind was already made up. If two people I respected so much had enough belief in my ability, then I'd give it a go. If I wasn't good enough, I'd be the first one to know. Liverpool had been so magnificent to me that I would have quit if I realised I wasn't up to it. Liverpool made every effort to prevent me failing. Peter and John explained to me that Bob Paisley would be coming in to help me. Tom Saunders, a marvellous man, so full of wisdom, was still at Anfield and Melwood. That was the support I needed. I knew that Ronnie and Roy would be at Liverpool forever. Although they didn't know anything about my appointment, I knew Ronnie and Roy would be delighted to stay with Liverpool whether it was me as manager or Joe Bloggs. Liverpool was their life.

Although my thoughts were not on coaching, I should have

guessed that the board had long-term plans for me. The year before, when I was still 33, Peter called me up to his office and said that the club would like me to sign a new contract.

'No problem,' I said.

'For four years,' Peter replied.

'Four years!' I said in disbelief. 'Are you serious?'

'Yes,' Peter said, 'we'd like to offer you a four-year contract.'

'Well, get it ready! Thanks very much.'

Peter said that I had done well for Liverpool and they wanted to reward me. I don't know what was in the back of Liverpool's mind then, a year before I became player-manager. Maybe they were planning ahead. Inviting an ageing player to sign such a long-term contract, one that would commit the club to paying me until I was 37, maybe meant they had other plans for me.

Liverpool's board might have been preparing the way for me to step up. I simply don't know whether Joe was considered a caretaker. When Bob Paisley got the job he said to the players: 'I don't want the job. They have just given it to me.' Joe was a wee bit similar. He was great in the first year but didn't really enjoy it. Management wasn't Joe's scene. Joe put Liverpool Football Club before himself – if he hadn't taken the manager's job, he could probably have worked at Liverpool for longer than he did. But he did a great job as manager, especially in the first year. Before Heysel, Joe told the board of his intention to retire. So Liverpool didn't make Joe's mind up for him. He did it himself.

It was a strange time for me, knowing I was going to replace Joe. We were training at Melwood one day and I answered back to Ronnie Moran.

'Oh shut up, Kenny,' Ronnie replied, 'you're not manager yet, are you?'

But nobody knew. It was just a throwaway line. It was funny, too. Over dinner one night with Marina, Alan Hansen and his wife Janet, I told Big Al that I was going to be Liverpool's next manager. His reaction was brilliant.

'Come on, Janet,' Al said. 'Eat up and let's be on our way. The friendship's over. We can't be talking to the boss!' But Al continued to sit and finish his meal. Probably because I was paying for it!

Rumours spread before the Heysel final. Joe even called a meeting to dampen speculation. I don't know if Joe realised I was his successor. I never had any conversations with him about what was happening. It wasn't my place. There had been constant speculation about possible replacements. My name was even mentioned which was unbelievable. How could anybody outside Anfield know? Somebody within Liverpool, who knew what was going on, must have marked the journalists' card. The press wouldn't have made me hot favourite to replace Joe without inside information. The leak might not have come from the people directly involved. It wasn't me, anyway. Maybe the person who leaked the information did it to build me up as a candidate, to make it less of a shock when Liverpool announced that I was following Joe.

Speculation intensified on the morning of the final when my name was put forward in the newspapers. Of course, all that paled into insignificance in the aftermath of what happened. The announcement was originally scheduled for Friday but it was brought forward a day. On leaving Brussels, Sir John Smith told me we should go straight to Anfield to announce my appointment. I remember sitting on the plane next to Ronnie Whelan.

'You know who is going to be manager, don't you?' Ronnie said. I replied that I did.

'Well, who is it?' he asked.

'I can't tell you.'

So he started listing names.

'Is it so-and-so?'

'Nah.'

'Is it somebody else?'

'No. No.'

'Who is it?'

'It's me.'

'Get lost.'

'Honestly. It's me.'

'Yessssss,' Ronnie went, 'can I be captain?'

Everything was happening so quickly. We gathered the players together and I told them I was their new manager. Then Sir John said to me that he wanted to make the announcement to the press.

'You can't,' I said. 'I'm not wearing a suit.' We had travelled to and from Brussels in tracksuits. 'That's all I've got. I've only got a tracksuit.'

'That'll do,' he said.

He was determined to end the speculation. So we went to Anfield, where the press conference had been organised, and Sir John told the waiting world that I was taking over as Liverpool's manager. The questions I had to field were inevitably about Heysel. I tried to speak the truth. I was most mindful of talking with respect for the Italian and Belgian people who had lost their loved ones. Really, though, there was not a lot I could say, certainly nothing I could have done.

It was an eventful few days. There was the Heysel disaster on the Wednesday. The following day I became manager. On the Saturday I had to deal with Bruce Grobbelaar threatening to quit. Then I disappeared with the family on a much-needed fortnight's holiday. Coming back was equally odd. It felt strange walking into Anfield as the boss. What made it easier was having Bob there, keeping an eye on me. That was a wise move by Liverpool's board. My first day as manager was funny. I remember sitting there, in the office with Bob.

'What am I doing sitting in here?' I asked Bob. 'There's nothing happening. The phone's not ringing. There's nobody training. All the players are still on holiday.'

Bob said: 'That's part of the job at this time of the year.'

'Oh,' I said.

It didn't sound too good to me. I just sat there and talked to Bob about football, which in itself was an experience.

I was pleased to see the players back. They were brilliant to me. They gave me the respect I probably never deserved. I knew I had their respect as a player; now I had to earn their respect all over again, as a manager. Immediately, we had to address the question of what they should call me.

'You can call me whatever you want,' I told them, 'but it doesn't mean you respect me. I've got to earn your respect.' It was agreed my title would be 'Boss'.

The only real problem I encountered amongst the players involved Phil Neal. Phil was certainly upset that it was me, not him, to whom Liverpool's board had turned as their next manager. I don't know what Phil had been promised by the club, if anything. It's none of my business. Liverpool offered me the job, end of story. Anyway, Phil was clearly angry. He made a point of calling me 'Kenny'. Sometimes in training the other players would say 'Kenny, er, I mean boss,' which is fair enough; that's a slip of the tongue. Phil was different. His reaction was obviously calculated, almost like he was not admitting that I was his new manager. I pulled him up about it. 'Don't call me Kenny,' I told him, 'call me boss.' That was that. To Phil's credit, he called me 'boss' afterwards. He didn't really have a choice. I was the boss.

It also upset Phil that I had taken the captaincy away from him and given it to Alan Hansen. One day at Melwood I simply told Phil the situation. My reasoning behind changing captains was that, first and foremost, Alan is a very lucky person as well as being a talented and respected footballer. If Al is sitting at 17 playing pontoon, he will get a four. It was the right decision. Phil, of course, continued to give of his best after the captaincy decision.

Phil had to move on. He was disappointed by the way things worked out at Liverpool and clearly had aspirations to go into management. I was not going to stand in his way if managerial opportunities arose elsewhere. Oxford United and Bolton Wanderers were both looking for player-managers. They called to enquire about Nealy's position. Because Nealy had been a good player, and a great servant to Liverpool, both Oxford and Bolton knew he might make a half-decent manager. I spoke to Nealy about it and he ended up going to Bolton with the best wishes of everyone at Anfield, myself included. It was right for him to go. Everything moves on in life. Phil's place at Liverpool was in jeopardy anyway. Steve Nicol had come in and was starting to play right-back. I doubt whether Phil would have settled for being a reserve. If he had stayed at Liverpool it would not have been a problem for me.

People thought I was flexing my muscles over Phil, who might have appeared to be a disruptive influence against a new manager. But I wasn't guided by any ulterior motive regarding Phil Neal. I acted in the best interests of the club. I wasn't stamping my authority or using Phil's situation to emphasise to the players that I was boss. I'm not egotistical like that. I would never have used anybody's career to illustrate my power. I wouldn't have done that to Phil Neal or anybody. I was employed by Liverpool to make decisions and it was the right time for Phil Neal to go to Bolton, where he had a great deal of success.

There was an inevitable change in my relationship with all the players, not just Phil. I was no longer 'Kenny', a friend and team-mate sitting next to them in the dressing-room. I was their boss. The new divide immediately showed itself at team meetings. It was hard having to stand at the other side of the table to the players. Moving from listening to talking was awkward because I knew the thoughts going through the players' minds. I knew they would be waiting for me to get tongue-tied. I knew that when they reached the training ground they would be laughing amongst themselves about any rick I had made. As a player, I used to wait for ricks by Joe or Bob, so when I went over to the other side, I thought I might as well be honest. I looked at all those familiar faces, faces of people with whom I had shared so many jokes, and said: 'I know what you are waiting for. I know you are waiting for me to make a rick.' I didn't let them down.

The change I found hardest was having to remove myself from the dressing-room carry-ons. I love the jokes, the banter, the wind-ups of other people and myself. When I became manager, the players erected an invisible barrier. I hated that. I really missed the dressing-room feeling. When I walked in, the players would fall quiet. 'Oh yeah,' I would say, 'I'm not supposed to hear this, OK, bye,' and turn around and walk out. I had been involved in all that carry-on a few months before, so I knew what was happening. Now I'd have to trot off, and let them get on with it. That was sad but inevitable.

When we gathered away from Liverpool, we could still put the ball away. If there was an invitation to go out with the players and their wives, I was there like a shot. I would go out with a crowd of them in Southport, sometimes on a Saturday. At training on Monday, the Southport crew would get fearful stick for socialising with the gaffer! I don't think the players realised how much I valued those evenings when we could sit and have a good crack. But the players would still only go so far. We were not on equal terms any more. They knew I controlled their careers. So they were always a wee bit cautious. Yet they would still joke about me being the boss. 'What about you and the team-talk,' they would say. That was good. I had all week to think about the game, to get it right. So I couldn't be too critical of them getting it wrong in a split-second on the pitch.

All I ever asked of my players was that they gave of their best. I had always tried to do that as a player. I had always worked hard preparing for games. The only disappointments as a manager were when I didn't think the preparation or the commitment were correct. This, fortunately, was rare. Sacrifices have to be made to be in the best shape for Saturday. That principle should be ingrained in every footballer's approach to his profession. I could accept mistakes, but I would get frustrated if they were repeated, particularly if the players were aware of them and we had tried to rectify them. Every player has something different to offer. Players make mistakes. I made mistakes – as a player and a manager. There are a lot of things people were asked to do which I couldn't do – like defend. In the long term if they were not good enough, that was my problem. If they couldn't improve, I'd move them out. Then I would have to bring someone better in. I would tell players when they had had poor matches. Some would argue back, which is fair because we all have opinions, but the manager's opinion is the most important one. People always have arguments, but you don't sulk or lose respect for someone because they argue back.

To produce a successful team, players must do what they are comfortable doing and are capable of doing. Over my years as manager, I tried to follow this principle. As a manager, if you come up with a formation that doesn't suit the players, you have a greater chance of being sacked. For many years, Liverpool never had a John Barnes-type player. When he arrived, he gave us a different option altogether. Barnes was not the same as Ray Kennedy. John Aldridge was more an out-and-out striker than Ian Rush. Craig Johnston was not the same as Jimmy Case. The basic principles for the team were the same, but with 11 different individuals we would get a different type of performance. You could not get anyone to replace Graeme Souness. He was a one-off. Paul Walsh came in and played in my position. Walshy did a great job but he's not the same type of player as me. I can't dribble the way Walshy can. We accommodated individuals within a passing format.

I was desperate to succeed for Liverpool's supporters. I could never stand on the Kop but I tried to please those who stood on that steepling terrace. The fans want to see all the club's assets invested in red shirts. They don't want fortunes in the bank. My transfer-market policy was simple: if we could improve on who we had and funds were available, we'd go for the player. But scouting was important, too. During my time as manager, Liverpool received countless letters suggesting we check out a certain player at another club, often non-League. I would pass the letter on to Ron Yeats and someone would go along and have a look. Sometimes videos were sent in. A video came in of Don Hutchison, while he was at Hartlepool. We looked at the video, then watched him play, and eventually signed him.

My job was to make decisions. By October, I had made five changes. New full-backs came in. Jim Beglin was starting to play left-back instead of Alan Kennedy. Steve Nicol replaced Phil. Craig Johnston and Jan Molby became regulars in midfield. In September I had signed Steve McMahon. Up front, Paul Walsh played most of the time instead of myself, scoring 19 goals before the end of January. So the line-up had changed. It's funny. I was criticised at the time for changing the team. Then the same critics said I did the double with a team I had inherited. You can't win.

I made only the odd change at Melwood. There were aspects of training which I didn't want to continue. In the past we used to come in and play mixed games on a Monday or Tuesday morning, which were a waste of time. Then the staff and injured first-teamers used to play the kids on our 'Wembley' pitch. So that stopped. The staff would still play the kids after training with the pros or if the pros were off. One popular move was bringing the lunches back for the players, which gave a social focus to the working day. Preparation for matches altered a bit as well. We started the journey to away matches earlier, instead of four or five o'clock in the afternoon. I was always worried about being held up by roadworks and bad traffic. On coach journeys, that invisible barrier between me and the players was really in force. As a player, I used to sit with the others. As manager I used to sit in the middle of the bus at a table for four – by myself! Tom Saunders would occasionally come and sit with me, and we would try to do the *Times* concise crossword. Tom had been a headmaster, so he had a chance with crosswords. He worked out the answers, I filled them in.

Like Bob, Tom Saunders was very important for me. So were all the people on the footballing staff. I kept the same people in place for my first year. Then I began to restructure the reserves. Chris Lawler went and so did Geoff Twentyman. In their places, I appointed Phil Thompson and Ron Yeats. I didn't know if Phil Thompson was going to be better than Chris Lawler. I never knew if Yeatsy would improve on Geoff Twentyman. But I knew that two ex-captains of Liverpool Football Club, who were devoted to the club and still had that fierce loyalty, would be good for us. Thommo and Yeatsy had been popular players at Anfield. From the fans' point of view, here were two ex-captains of Liverpool coming back to work for the good of the club. That had to be a positive step.

It was right for Geoff Twentyman to leave. He had arthritis in his back. My decision had nothing to do with Geoff's judgement, more to do with his medical condition. Chris Lawler also had to go. Chris was very quiet and I felt I needed someone with greater charisma to bring on the kids and the reserves. They needed to be educated either by speaking to them or showing them. Thommo was given the chance. It obviously wasn't a popular decision with Chris and Geoff. They had given Liverpool great service and indicated that they didn't deserve the decision I had taken. But that was their opinion. The only opinion that mattered was mine. It was in Liverpool's best interests. I asked Chris to stay for three months to work with Thommo. It was easier for us to help Chris if he was in employment with Liverpool Football Club than if he was on the outside. Chris did not think that he could do that. I had to respect that even if I didn't agree with him. My one regret is the way Chris found out. He was talking to Peter Robinson about his bonus and Peter said that first Chris should see the manager. Chris came into my office knowing that something was about to happen. That was wrong. I should have been the one to give him the news about him going, rather than him coming into my office already realising.

I would not have made the Chris and Geoff decisions without consultation. One of the reasons I found slipping into management easier than expected was Peter's support. I talked to him every day. Sir John Smith, the chairman, had a lot of contact with Peter, so when I spoke to Peter I believed I was also speaking to the board. PBR is the best at his profession in English football. He and Sir John Smith were brilliant to me, especially when I went for players. Peter and Sir John had their own opinions about players, but once they had appointed me, they backed me all the way. If money was available, and I identified who I'd like to buy, the board would do all they could to bring that player to Anfield. Their attitude helped keep Liverpool at the top.

Anfield was a great place to work. A few punters used to hang about the ground, guys who worshipped the club and were allowed inside. I used to love the crack with them. One of Roy's mates was a hairdresser, who used to come in and cut our hair. We would go into the trainers' room. He would sit me down, put a towel around my neck and snip away. I didn't need to go to the shops; the shops came to Anfield. A wee guy would come round with fruit, another with pies, another with suits and shirts. The man from KP gave us biscuits. They used to bring the *Liverpool Echo* into the office. A man sells it in reception after Saturday matches. I used to love all that. I still miss it.

— 10 —

THE BOOT ROOM

ONE ACCUSATION levelled at me was that I dismantled Liverpool's great Boot Room. That's utter rubbish. How could I damage something that was so fundamental to the success of Liverpool Football Club, past, present and future? It was an institution, one I would never have meddled with. The Boot Room wasn't just a chunk of air enclosed within four walls or a store for boots. It was a symbol of Liverpool's approach to the game, the thinking and planning that brought victories. Ronnie Moran and Roy Evans were the guardians of the Boot Room philosophy and tradition. They were a vast library of information used for the club's benefit. As a player, I had great respect for the Boot Room. I wasn't even allowed in, except to collect boots. Becoming manager, with authority to go anywhere at Anfield, did not reduce that respect.

My priorities were pretty clear from my first day in charge. On finishing the press conference to announce my appointment, I headed straight for the Boot Room. Inside, as ever, were Ronnie, Roy, Chris Lawler and their wives.

'I need you to stay,' I told them.

'No problem,' they replied, 'we would be delighted.'

So, contrary to the media's belief, my first act as Liverpool's manager was to keep the Boot Room intact. I had total respect for Ronnie, Roy and their Boot Room. It was important for me to have their support. A manager couldn't have asked for a better duo than Ronnie and Roy. They were Liverpool; Liverpool was them. Ronnie and Roy had been through everything. My admiration for them was immense. I wanted to get up to Ronnie and Roy's level, to be close to them, get to know them and their vast store of knowledge which gave Liverpool such strong footballing foundations. I had as much respect for Ronnie and Roy as I hoped they would have for me. I meant it when I told them I needed them. If I wanted to try a new routine at training, Ronnie and Roy would see to it. Having come straight from the pitch to behind a desk, I didn't have the experience or confidence to put on a training session. That was a significant weakness as a manager. But I was lucky; there were none better than Ronnie and Roy at organising practice sessions.

I would never, ever have done anything to compromise the Boot Room. It was special because of the people in it: Ronnie and Roy, Tom Saunders, John Benison, Chris Lawler and Phil Thompson who were there during my time. Two years after I became manager, Steve Heighway was over from America, where he had been coaching. We needed a new youth-development officer, so I asked Steve. He agreed and from the moment he started, Steve would spend many afternoons in the Boot Room, talking to Tom. It was Liverpool's heart. Like the club, there were no airs in the Boot Room. The room itself was nothing special. It was simply a room with four hampers to sit on. On the walls were rows of pegs, boots dangling from each, a bit of shelving and a double cupboard where Ronnie and Roy could keep their bottles of whisky. Eventually, they put in a fridge, their one concession to modern life. It was a brilliant place. Ronnie and Roy would be sitting on top of hampers, rabbiting away about anything. The Boot Room was a university for football. It was a bunch of intelligent guys discussing football.

People who claimed I tried to reduce the Boot Room's influence ignore the fact that I went in there every day of the week to talk to Ronnie, Roy and Tom. But I never went in after games for one very good reason – I wasn't clever enough. I knew what Ronnie and Roy did to visitors from other clubs who they invited in there. After games, Ronnie and Roy would sit in their famous hideaway, chatting away, dispensing a little bit of liquid hospitality to visiting managers and coaches, who were always delighted to be

invited into Anfield's famous Boot Room. But it was so cunning.
All the while Ronnie and Roy were picking up little bits of
information about players, perhaps even about tactics. They
didn't miss much. New ideas, how other people were working, what other people were doing, anyone floating about in the
lower leagues who was half-decent; Ronnie and Roy soaked up
everything and anything. It was gossip and more. They were
brilliant at getting information out of people. Ronnie and Roy
worked as a double act, like Morecambe and Wise, playing off
each other to outwit their visitors. They would talk to people and
glean what I would think was useless information but wasn't. It
was important. We would win 5–0 and they would say, 'Oh, we
were lucky today, we need to play better next week,' and then,
ever so carefully, begin hunting for information. It wasn't a
pooling of ideas; it was like a cabinet meeting with Ronnie
and Roy as the Prime Minister and Chancellor getting information from the rest.

Most people are willing to talk. Ronnie and Roy are held in
such high regard that people thought it was an honour for them
to be in Liverpool's Boot Room. Anfield was a very open club.
Staff from other clubs could go in the Boot Room or come down
the corridor to see me in my office. They could go wherever they
wanted. Other clubs tried to emulate the Boot Room – every club
has its own place where you have a drink afterwards – but it's the
people who count. They are more important than the place. Other
clubs could recreate the setting but you can't recreate Ronnie,
Roy, Bob and Tom. They were unique.

After quietly picking the brains of visitors, Ronnie and Roy
would pool the information they had gleaned on Monday
morning. They would say there's a player here, there's a player
there, this is happening, that's happening. The philosophy of the
Boot Room was that of Liverpool Football Club: give the opposition very little and get as much as you can out of them. Life at
Liverpool was simple. No wild predictions, no arrogance, no
petulance. After a victory, Ronnie would say, 'I've got a job for
another week.' Joining Ronnie, Roy and Tom was a real education. After my first year, when Bob began to fall ill, I started to
take the Boot Room more into my confidence in nearly every
aspect of the club. They respected that. To show how much I

prized the Boot Room, Ronnie and Roy and occasionally Tom would gather in my hotel room on away trips. The week's events would be mulled over. We would talk, reminisce, and discuss anything we thought was relevant, like the game the next day, or any particular areas of the opposition's play we should pay special attention to. Those hotel-room sessions were a bit like the Boot Room, except in more comfortable surroundings.

The Boot Room thrived under me. There was no reason to tinker with any institution that had made Liverpool so successful. Continuity was paramount. I even had a bar put into my office because I knew I wasn't going to the Boot Room after games. Just after I started as manager, Sheila, my secretary, who had the misfortune to inherit me after working for Bob and Joe, asked if I wanted a new desk.

I looked around my new office and replied: 'This was Bob's desk, this was Joe's chair. Why would I need new ones?'

'We are getting new office furniture.'

'Is it expensive?'

'Oh, yes,' Sheila replied, 'it's quite a few quid.'

I said: 'Just put a bar in, Sheila.'

So they installed a full-length bar, made of wood and formica. I knew I was going to have Marina and the kids in after games and anyone else who wanted a drink with me.

It would have been nice if the Boot Room could have lived on for ever. Because of lack of space and UEFA guidelines on the size of the press room, the old Boot Room was turned into part of the press room. So journalists who had speculated for years about what went on in there finally got into the most important room at Anfield, minus the most important ingredient – the people who made it famous.

—11—

MANAGING WELL

Hatred is the essence of most derby matches, but not on Merseyside. There is no derby in the world like Liverpool's meetings with Everton. The rivalry between the two clubs separated by Stanley Park was totally different from the emotions dominating Old Firm occasions, although it was just as competitive on the pitch. Supporters of Liverpool and Everton are every bit as determined as those in Glasgow to see their team win. It's just the feelings behind it that are different. Religion taints the Glasgow derby. In Liverpool, the rivalry is far more amicable. Both clubs had a tremendous respect for each other, from terrace to boardroom. Sure, Liverpool wanted to beat Everton every time we played them and vice versa, but we were both gracious in victory, magnanimous in defeat.

In 1985–86, my first season as Liverpool's manager, the neighbourly rivalry was keener than ever. Liverpool pipped Everton for the championship. The following week, all of Merseyside converged on London for the first all Merseyside FA Cup final. Both sets of fans were unbelievable. They did so much for Merseyside that day with their behaviour. Wembley was surrounded by amazing scenes. As we drove up in the team coach, I saw a father walking along with his two sons, one wearing red and white, the other blue. That was a lovely sight, which showed how football rivalry should be. It really heartened me. In the car-park, there was a huge game going on – Everton punters versus Liverpool ones.

The fans had jackets down as posts. I think Liverpool won that one as well but I never stopped to count the goals!

In the real game, we were poor in the first half and Everton led 1–0 through Gary Lineker. One of the most important of a manager's duties is to motivate the players at half-time. I told them: 'We've been magnificent all season, there's 45 minutes to go, let's go and give it our lot.' It was not quite Churchill but the players responded. Jan Molby took charge, and was involved in our first two goals scored by Rushie and Craig Johnston. Rushie added a third, just for good measure. Afterwards somebody gave me a picture of Rushie's second goal. It was taken on a motorised camera and I could see Rushie lining up to hit the ball and then there was the follow-through. In the background, in the crowd behind Rushie, there was my son Paul, noticeable because he had a white tracksuit on. He was sitting down, in the next frame he was getting up, then his arms were up in the air, celebrating the goal. It's a brilliant sequence.

The Evertonians at the end of the game must have been absolutely gutted. They had lost the League, were 1–0 up at half-time in the FA Cup final only to be beaten 3–1. It must have seemed like a bad dream. The Liverpool fans were chanting 'Shankly, Shankly', which was a special moment. Shanks started it for everybody at Liverpool. It was right that the punters should remember him. They could have added Paisley and Fagan to that list as well. The fans were brilliant. In our dressing-room afterwards, there was a punter in the bath, splashing around with all his clothes on. He kept saying: 'I don't give a monkey's. Come and take me away now. I can go happily.'

The only thing that didn't go smoothly all day was the lift at our hotel. I got stuck in it with Craig Johnston coming down for the after-match function. Craig wrote in his book that I said to him: 'Make the most of this day. It doesn't get any better.' But there are always other achievements to strive for. The most important feeling on winning a trophy is the desire to win it again.

Liverpool were champions at celebrating. We went back to the hotel for a little liquid refreshment and a sing-song. As ever, we were well looked after by the club. After the function, I wanted to go down to Trafalgar Square with the cup to join the punters but Marina wouldn't let me. We went to Stringfellow's with Rushie

Alan Hansen sets off on a celebration after scoring against Manchester United in the FA Cup semi-final at Maine Road. We couldn't catch him until the halfway line.

Graeme Souness was the type of player every manager wants in his side. He had everything.

'Jock picture': whenever we won a trophy, Graeme Souness, Alan Hansen and myself would always have a special photograph taken of just the three of us.

Doing the Double at Wembley in 1986. Ian Rush is in the centre of things as usual.

The Double of 1986: in my first year as player-manager, too.

I try to get the better of Celtic's Roy Aitken in the Hillsborough Memorial Match at Parkhead in 1989.

Sammy Lee and I celebrate during a momentous 3–1 victory over Tottenham Hotspur at Anfield.

The great Pele, presenting me with an award from the Football Writers' Association.

What a squad: Liverpool had such a marvellous group of players, it was no surprise the trophies kept coming.

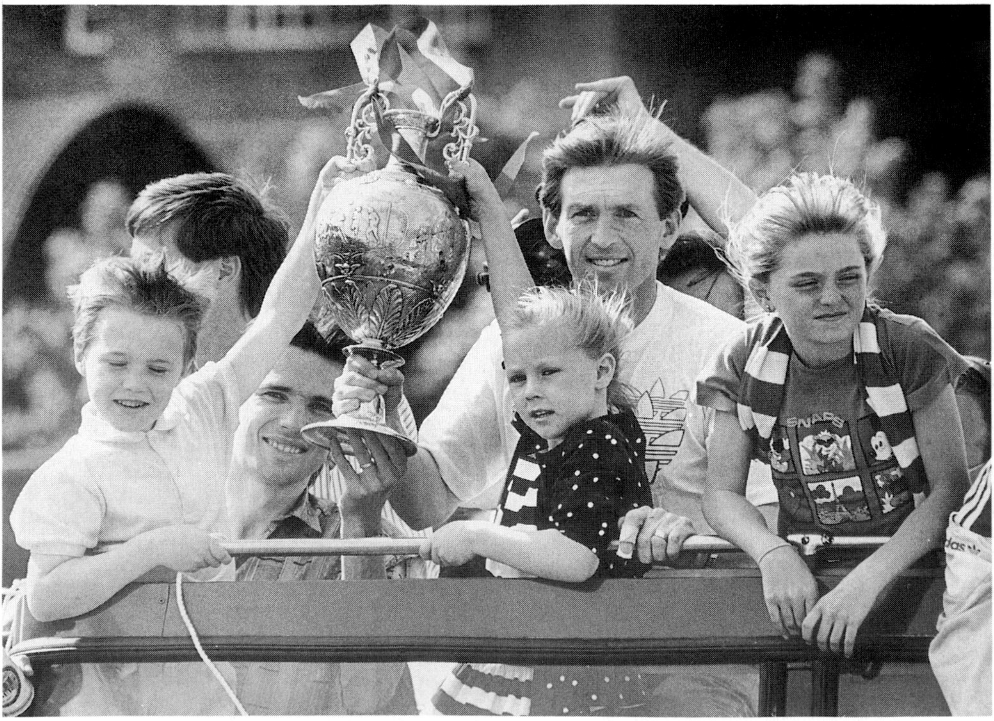

I always loved successful homecomings, marked with a tour of the city in an open-topped bus. Here I am with Adam and Alan Hansen, my daughter Lynsey, and Stacey, Roy Evans' daughter.

I learned so much from Bob Paisley, who kept an eye on me in my first year as Liverpool player-manager.

Peter Robinson (left) and John Smith (centre), made my position at Liverpool one of the best in football management.

The Anfield Rap: getting in the swing for a Liverpool FA Cup final single.

Me, Roy Evans and Ronnie Moran keep an eye on the action.

Anfield's famous Boot Room: Ronnie Moran and Roy Evans invite me into their special place.

A packed Liverpool dug-out: from the left, Steve Staunton, Barry Venison, myself, Roy Evans, Ronnie Moran, Tom Saunders (partly hidden) and John Benison.

The basis of Liverpool's success is that they employ people who are good at their jobs, like Ronnie Moran, Roy Evans and Tom Saunders.

It was great to win the Manager of the Year award and reflect on all the other Liverpool managers who had been 'cut out' to win it, like Bill Shankly, Joe Fagan and Bob Paisley!

The trauma of
Hillsborough was closely
connected with my
eventual decision to resign
from Liverpool . . .

. . . It broke my heart to
leave Liverpool.

and his wife. Amnesia begins to set in at that point, but I can just about remember walking into Stringfellow's with the cup.

We shared a plane back north with Everton. The tour of the city involved both teams this time. Everton travelled in the front bus, with nothing on it. Liverpool were behind with the two trophies. After the tour, I nipped into my local chip-shop. Everton's Paul Bracewell was in there. 'You are the last person I want to see,' he said. I diplomatically refrained from asking for double chips.

One disappointment about the whole double achievement was that Big Al never received the credit due to a double-winning captain. Because I was player-manager, the praise seemed to be focused on me. That was wrong. Big Al led by example on and off the pitch. Al earned the players' respect because, despite being good friends with me, they knew he could be trusted. The players knew that if they told Al a story, it would not get back to me. He was a great captain. All in all, it was not a bad first season – a difficult one to follow. Shortly after we had done the double, I went into a meeting with the chairman, expecting some sort of congratulations; instead I was ticked off over Bruce Grobbelaar wearing a sweatband round his neck with a sponsor's name on it. The message was clear and classic Liverpool – enjoy the moment but then get on with winning. The board's attitude was a constructive one. No one was allowed to rest on their laurels. We could have won the treble. We got beaten in the semi-finals of the League Cup, more by our own faults than by QPR. We scored two own goals at Anfield, and their keeper saved a penalty.

People wondered how we could drive ourselves on when there was no European qualification to aim for. But Liverpool did not feel much frustration about being denied Europe. We were philosophical and quite tough in our own mind. It wasn't Europe that motivated us. It was simply the desire to win whichever trophy we were competing for. If that follows on into Europe, then fine. We'd worry about that later.

In the following season, 1986–87, there was talk of crisis at Liverpool but we still finished second. After winning the double the year before, we were always going to be under pressure. Liverpool recorded a club record win in a domestic competition by beating Fulham 10–0 in the Littlewoods Cup. It was a wet night and the ball was flying; and we were going as quickly as the ball. Fulham weren't top-class opposition, but you don't see many games where one side reaches double figures. The conditions were perfect, because we liked the surface nice and fast. We got to the Littlewoods final against Arsenal where another record was broken – it was the first time in 144 games that Ian Rush finished on the losing Liverpool side after scoring. What a great goal it was as well, starting in our penalty box. But a football team needs a bit of luck to be successful.

Fortune smiled on Arsenal. Charlie Nicholas scored twice, the first one after a mad scramble; the second one went in off Ronnie Whelan's knee. It was the game Charlie Nicholas will be remembered for at Arsenal because of the goals, but he could have had so much more with us. Joe Fagan had been in for Charlie when he was at Celtic. After speaking to Big Ron Atkinson at Manchester United, Charlie decided that his choice lay between Arsenal and Liverpool, but he was frightened that he wouldn't get a game at Anfield. Graeme Souness and I both talked to him when he was trying to make up his mind, but he decided on Highbury, where he was always going to be seen as the messiah. Charlie was heralded at Arsenal as the wonder-boy who would change everything, who would be their saviour. It was unfair to put that burden on him. He was one of the best talents to come out of Scotland, but he wasn't as successful at Arsenal as they hoped he would be. If this young talent had come to Anfield, he wouldn't have needed to play well every week because there were so many people around him who could win a game. Charlie could have come to Liverpool and scored a goal every four games. Rushie would have seen us through one day, somebody else would have seen us through another. Charlie would have been great for us. Joe might have played him and Rushie up front with me just off. I would have enjoyed that.

Our defence of the FA Cup turned out to be equally frustrating but even briefer. We were drawn to play Luton Town at Kenilworth Road, where no visiting fans were permitted. Luton were trying to implement a membership-card scheme, a misguided policy beloved of Mrs Thatcher, the Prime Minister. Supporters had to fill in membership forms to get a card for entry into Kenilworth Road. But Liverpool and Manchester

United fans got hold of them too, so they could go to games at Luton. When the machines broke down, it made life difficult as 10,000 people were trying to get into the ground. It was never going to be feasible. Besides, in principle it's wrong to ban away fans. It's understandable when grounds are undergoing renovation but barring visiting fans changes the atmosphere. It makes the home crowd more hostile, more vocal. You need opposing supporters to provide a counterbalance and create a better atmosphere. It was done as a trial-and-error scheme to find out whether membership cards worked. It proved it couldn't work when visiting supporters got into Kenilworth Road anyway.

It was goalless at Luton, despite them having the advantage of their dreadful plastic pitch. We looked forward to getting them back to a real surface at Anfield, but Luton didn't make the replay. They said that they could not move because of a snowstorm. That really annoyed me. Our pitch was perfect and other people managed to travel up from London that day. Luton had booked two flights up. We had a guy at Liverpool airport who knew the times of their flights and they never got on them. The kick-off was delayed until 8 p.m. I just didn't think they made enough effort. The inconvenience caused to our club and our supporters was unbelievable.

Eventually, the delayed replay did take place. Again it was a stalemate. We wanted a neutral venue for the second replay. Typically, Luton didn't. So the clubs tossed coins and they won the right to play the game at Kenilworth Road. I thought that because of their behaviour, and the whole carry-on, we were due some luck, but it didn't turn out that way; Luton deservedly won 3–0.

I hated their pitch. Plastic pitches are very good for training, and useful for young lads to practise their technique, but there is no side in professional football who enjoys playing on them, including teams who owned them. Liverpool didn't have a bad record on plastic but the name of the pitch reveals what sort of matches they produce – artificial. The bounce was terrible. If the ball went beyond you that was it, it was out of play. I could understand it from a commercial perspective. Luton could rent it out for hockey, or have amateur teams using it, but it certainly was not a pitch that was suitable for professional football. It increased the wear and tear on player's joints, legs and backs. Even standing watching matches on it made your back stiffen up.

If Luton had got into Europe they wouldn't have been able to use that pitch, because UEFA rightly refused to allow games on anything but grass. As the FA Cup was effectively a European qualifying competition, with the winners going into the Cup-Winners' Cup, why should Luton and QPR have been allowed to use it? Everyone said I was whingeing. I wasn't. I was just stating a fact. People even came up with a joke about what was the difference between me and a Jumbo jet. 'A Jumbo stops whining over Luton.' Ha, ha. I wasn't moaning. I was just giving my opinion. The most significant indictment of Luton's pitch was that even their players hated the plastic. They used to train on grass. David Evans's experiments gave a sad, artificial air to Kenilworth Road – no grass and no away fans is getting pretty far away from what football is supposed to be about. It is significant that there are no artificial pitches or similar membership schemes in use now.

Luton was a sorry episode. Even worse followed at the end of that season. Saying farewell to Rushie, who was off to Juventus, was a very emotional moment for everyone at Liverpool. Rushie's last home game came against Watford. It was brilliant and appropriate that he scored the only goal. At the final whistle, Rushie ran over and threw his shirt into the Kop. I'm sure there were a few lumps in the throat as they sang back their appreciation of him. We all had a drink in the players' lounge and went our separate ways. Rushie had arranged to meet up with Ronnie Whelan and their wives for a quiet meal. When he walked into the restaurant, the whole team was gathered there waiting. We wanted to thank him and say good-bye properly.

Everybody wanted Rushie to stay, but nobody blamed him for wanting to go. The move would set him up for life financially. Footballers have to think of their family's security, aware that the main bread-winner's income can disappear with one bad tackle. Rushie had good reason to go. The prospect of playing in Italy, amongst the world's best, appeared an excellent step for his career, particularly with Liverpool still banned from European competitions. The players and football staff were saddened, but from a financial perspective, it was a good deal for the club. As Liverpool's manager, I knew it wasn't a good deal from a footballing perspective. Fortunately, we knew that Rushie was on his way well in advance so we had bought a replacement – John Aldridge. Liverpool had been trailing Aldo for some time, and were close to signing him, but Robert Maxwell, Oxford United's chairman, would only sell Aldo after he had played in the FA Cup. Maxwell didn't know much about football. Maurice Evans, Oxford's manager, phoned Maxwell from our hotel to tell him that the deal had been signed. Then Aldo talked to Maxwell.

'Aldridge,' Maxwell said, 'first you've got to play in the Cup against Aldershot. Then you can join Liverpool. Maybe then you will get in the England squad.'

'I'm Irish, Mr Maxwell,' Aldridge replied.

Aldo was brilliant for us the season Rushie was away. Even when Rushie returned, but was out injured, Aldo carried on scoring – 21 goals in 31 games. But that season, 1987–88, was special. Some of the football Liverpool played was out of this world. Aldo finished with 29 goals as we won the League. His anticipation and his positional sense in the 18-yard box were exceptional; still are. People compared Rushie and Aldo but all they really shared was an instinct for scoring, that awareness of where the goal is. Aldo played a lot of the time up front on his own, with Peter Beardsley dropping off. Aldo was good in the air, could link up, a perfect player to have in attack.

Aldo was one of the players I had told Liverpool I wanted in 1987. Around the time of Aldo's move, we tried to sign Ian Snodin but he chose Everton instead. I was trying to build up the team. The board had approached me at Christmas 1986 and said there was money available for players. I gave them the names of five players and I got four of them – Barnes, Beardsley, Houghton and Aldridge. It took time to buy these four. That was instrumental in 1986–87 being such a fruitless season at Anfield. It was my fault we didn't win anything. I didn't want to spend Liverpool's money rashly. Bringing in any old player for a short-term tonic seemed irresponsible. I wanted to wait until those four quality players became available. That shows how supportive Liverpool's directors were. They were also prepared to wait until the right players were ready. The board knew Liverpool might not win anything that season but that I was planning for the future. Their patience was rewarded.

We failed to bring in John Barnes before the transfer deadline in 1986–87, but when his Watford contract expired, he was entitled to talk to whoever he wanted. Some newspapers wrote that he didn't want to come north, that he was holding on for Tottenham or Arsenal or even an Italian club. When that story broke, John Barnes phoned up Peter Robinson to apologise. He hadn't said that he preferred to join Spurs or Arsenal rather than Liverpool. Peter's reaction was brilliant. He told John that if that was the way he felt 'why not come up and meet us now?' We had a later date set to finalise things but we ended up meeting sooner. John signed for Liverpool without any problem. He acted totally honourably and correctly. John would have preferred an Italian move, but that was not an issue. We had just sold Ian Rush to Italy. If it was right for Liverpool to sell a player to Italy why wasn't it right for John Barnes to seek a move there? The opportunity never arose for John, so he came to us. Liverpool fans might have been brought up to believe that players should jump at the chance to come to Anfield but football was changing. Freedom of contract was coming in. Players were getting stronger. Clubs had to become more philosophical. Liverpool had to understand the player's position. John Barnes never did anything to upset people at Anfield.

It was occasionally mentioned, or strongly hinted, that neither Merseyside club signed black players. Liverpool had only had Howard Gayle, who was a local boy. The only criterion guiding me during moves for players is, are they good enough? Colour or creed doesn't come into it. Providing the player is willing to prepare himself properly and commit himself completely to both team and club, he's in. When John Barnes arrived, racist graffiti did appear on the outside walls of Anfield, not on the inside walls as some people disgracefully suggested. We didn't know who wrote those things. It was impossible to state categorically that it was Liverpool supporters. It could have been anybody; National Front, who knows? It was rubbish to suggest, as some people alleged, that Liverpool were slow at getting rid of racist graffiti. The moment they saw it they were out there right away getting the stuff off the wall. That was hardly the first graffiti John Barnes had seen, if he did see it. Any of the sceptics would have been embarrassed when he started playing. The punters loved him. His ability was the most important thing to them.

There were bananas thrown at him by Everton fans but there was no animosity felt by Liverpool towards Everton. They can't be held responsible for their supporters in instances like that. Everton strongly criticised what had happened. John Barnes was a magnificent player who worked harder than anyone could imagine. John's class was obvious from the moment he trained at Melwood. His debut at Anfield was delayed, because of a broken sewer underneath the Kop, so we began at Arsenal with a 2–1 win. Barnes went down the line, whipped in a cross and Aldridge scored with a header. Nicol headed the winner. Barnes had done well. Our other new boy, Peter Beardsley, had a tough passage at Arsenal. Tony Adams gave him a rough time. Physical games like that were difficult for Peter. At the beginning, he never caught the people's imagination as much as Barnes did. He still made a contribution, but unlike John and Aldo, Peter took a bit of time to settle. That was no problem. While Peter was settling in, there were so many other people Liverpool could turn to for something special – Barnes, Aldridge, Whelan, Steve McMahon. Those players had a special gift of being able to change a game with one touch. Even if they were playing badly, they could still manage something decisive.

Some of the football Liverpool played that season was fantastic. In October we destroyed QPR 4–0. Barnes was magnificent. His second goal was something else. He intercepted the ball from Kevin Brock on the halfway line, took it up, shuffled his feet and then side-footed it past David Seaman. I described it as the best goal I had ever seen at Anfield. Well, the emotions were flying. Like Barnsey. Liverpool did not lose until 20 March – at Everton of all places. That was really disappointing because if we had avoided defeat in our thirtieth game we would have broken Leeds's record unbeaten start to a season. As the final whistle signalled a 1–0 defeat, I felt so frustrated I kicked a bucket placed outside the dugouts at Goodison. It was plastic, so the side buckled and the water shot up all over me. I was soaked, standing there dripping as I congratulated the other bench: 'Well done, Howard, well done, Colin.' Drip, drip. I met Howard Kendall and Colin Harvey afterwards for a drink and they gave me some stick about the bucket. There was always great respect between the two benches of Liverpool and Everton. I remember Terry Darracott joking with us after one victory over Everton at Goodison. 'Thanks very much, lads,' Terry said. 'If I want a pint tonight I'll need to go to Inverness!'

In April we beat Nottingham Forest 5–0. Tom Finney was present. 'The greatest performance I have ever seen,' he said, which was praise indeed coming from such a legend as Finney. I have a video of the match, and still get excited simply getting the tape out of the box. Houghton scored the first. Then Beardsley played in Aldridge with an unbelievable ball, sent through between the left centre-back and the left-back. Aldridge just ran on to score. What a match!

Although it was a different Liverpool side from previous years, they were guided by the same principles. The graft was as strong as ever. There was just more flair than before, with Barnes on the left. Barnsey had more style and skill than Ronnie Whelan, who moved inside. Ray Houghton was a bit more attack-minded than Sammy Lee or Jimmy Case. Some of the football was magnificent. Even I didn't know what they were going to do and I was the man who prepared them, picked them and sent them out on to the pitch. It was a very exciting team. The goals were special, like one of Peter's against Coventry, when he took on Steve Ogrizovic, sold him a dummy and ran the ball into the net. Liverpool won the League with four games remaining. We were that good.

Frustratingly we blew the double. We had reached the FA Cup final after beating Nottingham Forest 2–1. On the morning of the semi-final Steve Chettle, Forest's centre-half, had done a story headlined 'Barnes on toast', saying that Barnes would not get a kick. That was a wee bit of a mistake. Barnes destroyed him. He got a penalty off him early on, which Aldo knocked in. Then Peter knocked the ball in behind for Barnes to run Chettle. He crossed and Aldridge volleyed it in what proved to be the BBC's Goal of the Season. Wembley and Wimbledon beckoned, with us one of the hottest favourites since the War.

A lot has been written and said about the supposed verbal abuse we received from Wimbledon while waiting in the tunnel before the final. Wimbledon had never been to Wembley in the top flight before. They were so nervous that shouting was the only way for them to get rid of their nerves. We knew it was going to happen. The intimidation in the tunnel was nothing. All Wimbledon did was shout. They did it in the tunnel before the Charity Shield the next season and we beat them then. It maybe helped them but it certainly never intimidated any team I was involved with. We lost because of what happened on the pitch. They never beat Liverpool with anything they said or did before the game.

People tried to say it was a tactical victory with Don Howe putting Dennis Wise back to pick up John Barnes, but Barnsey had been confronted by players coming back to shadow him all season. The simple reason why Wimbledon won the game was because they took their chance and Liverpool didn't. I know I have a reputation for complaining about referees but there were some strange decisions that afternoon. Peter had a good goal chalked off by Brian Hill. He had blown beforehand for a foul on Peter, so we had to come back for it. That's just our luck. That year there were two referees running the line rather than linesmen, who tend not to get so involved, except for throw-ins, corners and offsides. One of them signalled for the free-kick that resulted in Lawrie Sanchez's goal. This was dangerous as Wimbledon were good at free-kicks. We had worked hard to ensure we didn't concede any. Our ability to defend against set-pieces had been harmed in midweek when Gary Gillespie and Nigel Spackman split their heads open in a collision in a game against Luton at Anfield. The wounds were stitched up and they were fit enough to play. We were taking a gamble, playing people with head injuries against Wimbledon, but we needed six-footers to compete in the air. Our marking wasn't as tight as it should have been and Sanchez scored. Then Dave Beasant made a great save from Aldridge's penalty. I thought it was a soft award anyway.

Wimbledon attracted endless criticism for being physical. They are not so physical now. They are not allowed to be. But as long as they play within the rules, they hold Liverpool's respect. Wimbledon deserve credit for what they have achieved. That must have been the best day in their history. You couldn't imagine two more contrasting clubs than Wimbledon and Liverpool but we got on well with them. The next season we went there and beat them. It was the season of Hillsborough and John Fashanu and Vinnie Jones came in and said: 'Well done, lads. We hope you go on and win the League.' They were genuine people. They respected us because we never bad-mouthed them for the way they played or their brash nature. Our approach was, 'if that's the way Wimbledon want to play, as long as they play within the rules, let the referee look after any problems, and we'll try to get our game going'. Wimbledon played within the rules most of the time, like Liverpool.

Wimbledon used to do all sorts of things to distract us. Bobby Gould, their manager, read somewhere that one of Bruce Grobbelaar's pre-match rituals was to kick the ball against the dressing-room wall to knock off the light switch. When we went to play at Plough Lane, Gould put a cover on the light-switch in our dressing-room, so Bruce couldn't knock the light off. When we came in after the game, which we'd won, Bobby said: 'I thought I had beaten you there.'

'What do you mean?' I asked.

'I put a cover on the light-switch to prevent Bruce going through his pre-match routine.'

'Bobby,' I said, 'you shouldn't have bothered. Bruce only does it at Anfield!'

At the start of the 1988–89 season we welcomed Rushie back from Turin. The Rushie deal hadn't been a bridge-builder after Heysel. He was the best goalscorer about at that time and Juventus needed him. Unfortunately, the way Juventus played was not suited to Ian Rush. I used to watch his games on satellite and he was very isolated in attack. At Liverpool, players would support Rushie; that was not the case in Italy. He would go to close defenders down, as he always did at Liverpool. The defender would knock the ball past him, which was fine, but Juventus never had anyone else coming in to win the second challenge. I could understand Juventus's way of thinking. Liverpool didn't change their style of play to suit a new player. They had a tried and trusted formula. The same with Juventus. Maybe another manager might have changed the style to suit Ian Rush more. It was the Italian style to defend deeper than Liverpool, who defend further up the pitch. If a foreigner doesn't get off to a good start in Italy, it's going to be a problem for them. Rushie struggled. He went, had a look and came back a year later. At least he satisfied himself in his own mind that he'd had a go.

I was in regular contact with Rushie, just seeing how he was doing, but I never thought he would return that quickly. Liverpool had first option but that doesn't mean anything. It just means the selling club can say no to you first. But the Italians wanted to do business with us. We always had a good relationship with Juventus. Peter Robinson was very friendly with the people in Turin and had stayed in regular touch after Heysel. Peter asked me whether I wanted Rushie back if Liverpool could get him. Considering I didn't want him to go in the first place, I said that yes, we would be delighted to have him back. We were off on a pre-season tournament in La Coruna, Spain, when the call came through from the Italians. We were actually at lunch with the press lads when the phone rang for Peter. After the lunch, Peter told me that we could have Rushie back. The journalists never knew what was going on; the phone was always ringing for Peter wherever he went. The deal was done very quietly. I picked Rushie up at Manchester airport, drove him to Anfield and he signed. He was delighted to be back. So was his wife, Tracey – and thousands of Liverpudlians were delighted to have him back.

I don't agree with those critics who argue that Rushie was unsuited to the Italian way of life. Italy was a great experience for him. I don't think he was unhappy there. Life off the pitch wasn't a problem. Although he couldn't speak Italian well, he could understand a lot of what was said. Unfortunately, the first impression he made was not a particularly good one. When he walked off the plane, there were thousands there to greet him. Rushie was asked to say something. He lifted his hands up, waved and said: 'Welcome.' They were supposed to say that! He received a real welcome off us when he returned.

That season, the season of Hillsborough, Rushie was in and out of the team. Aldo was playing well and Rushie had problems with injury. We also lost Jan Molby for a while. He went to prison for a driving offence. There were those within Anfield who thought the club should get rid of Jan, an argument I was strongly against. Kicking Jan out would not have helped him. I wanted him to stay. The club supported my opinion but at the same time they punished him severely for what he had done. A well-known employee receiving a custodial sentence inevitably tarnished Liverpool's reputation. But a club can't be held responsible for an adult's behaviour. We can't baby-sit players. It was a much bigger embarrassment for Jan and his family than for Liverpool Football Club. We just hoped that while Jan was in jail, he would have a long, hard look at himself and his unprofessional lifestyle. Jan was certainly in magnificent shape when he was released. He had really slimmed down. Sadly, Jan began having problems with injuries and his weight started fluctuating again. He deprived an awful lot of people of an awful lot of enjoyment by not being able to stay in shape. Jan could have been one of the very best because his ability was unquestioned.

Liverpool missed him in the League, which intensified into an extraordinary race. After losing at Manchester United on New Year's Day we went on an unbeaten League run until the last day of the season. Liverpool's final game was against Arsenal, our only rivals for the championship. We had had some amazing games with Arsenal. After our League Cup replay at Villa Park, Alan Ball said that the only way to beat us would be to let the ball down. We would still have scored. An Arsenal fan threw a sandwich at me. I chucked it back – it wasn't fresh. The guy it hit said he hadn't thrown it. So I said: 'I shouldn't have thrown it back anyway so I'm sorry. Drop me a line and I will get you a couple of tickets when we come to Highbury.' He was happy with that.

That punter could have been at Anfield for the last day of the season. Arsenal needed to win 2–0 to beat us to the title on goal difference. We weren't particularly defensive that day, as some people claimed. The onus was on Arsenal to come forward and attack us. They had a right good go. Alan Smith got a touch on Nigel Winterburn's indirect free-kick and it was 1–0 to them. People complained that Winterburn's free-kick had gone straight in, so it should have been disallowed. That's not true. Smith definitely got a touch. Then fate really took a hand. Kevin Richardson was injured, and hobbling around, but he still managed to nick the ball off Barnes. He gave the ball back to Arsenal's goalie, John Lukic, who threw it to Lee Dixon. Smith got involved and, as our pulses raced liked demons, Michael Thomas came through, getting a couple of lucky breaks, before taking his decisive goal well. There was no time to come back. Arsenal had beaten us to the title on goal difference. It was an unbelievable finish. The Kop applauded the Arsenal players, which was only right. Our dressing-room was pretty quiet. In the other dressing-room, Arsenal celebrated but never gloated. What a sporting night it was.

When the margin is so slender between success and failure, you inevitably look back over the season to moments when you could have got another goal or another point. But it's a two-way thing; the other team could be saying if they hadn't scored a goal earlier in the season they would not have won it. It was a magnificent effort for Liverpool to get that close. We had been asked to play too many matches at the end. It was our third game in six days, and one of them had been an emotional two-hour final against Everton. That was a really draining occasion, not just physically but mentally and emotionally because of the Hillsborough disaster. I cannot understand why we had to play Arsenal on the Friday night. When television realised in advance that the race was between Arsenal and Liverpool, they moved our fixture to the end of the season. It was a bad decision and one that probably cost us the title. Three big, tense games in six days takes a lot out of players. We were very disappointed not to win the League but Arsenal deserved to. They had one more goal than us. But if I was going to pick between the League or the FA Cup that week I would have picked the Cup because of Hillsborough. It meant a lot more to the people at that particular time that we won the Cup.

—12—

HILLSBOROUGH

I WILL NEVER, NEVER forget 15 April, 1989. I cannot even think of the name Hillsborough, cannot even say the word, without so many distressing memories flooding back. I find it very difficult to write about Hillsborough, where terrible mistakes by the authorities, both police and football, ended with 96 of our supporters dead. The memory will remain with me for the rest of my life. I was offered the manager's job at Sheffield Wednesday after I left Liverpool but I couldn't take it because of what had happened at Hillsborough. The person who offered me the job said: 'I never thought of that.' But I can never be in the stadium without thinking of all those people who died on the Leppings Lane terraces.

In mourning the victims during the heartbreaking, endless succession of funerals and ever since, my emotions have been coloured by a feeling of complete frustration. Liverpool had played in an FA Cup semi-final against Nottingham Forest at Hillsborough the year before and there had been no reported problems. The organisation was superb. The fans had to come through a barrier 500 yards away from the ground where they had to show their tickets. That wasn't the case on 15 April, 1989. A different team was in charge and the stewarding had changed. Why wasn't the procedure repeated from the previous year? If it was repeated, why did it fail? If it had been run exactly the same as the year before, those 96 people might have been alive today and there wouldn't be family after family across Merseyside struggling to live with the memory of a lost loved one.

It was obvious that Liverpool supporters should have been given Hillsborough's Kop. The smaller Leppings Lane end was clearly unsuitable. Apparently the police said it was better for the Nottingham Forest fans to come in at the Kop end of Hillsborough. To be fair to the police, our fans had stood at the Leppings Lane end the year before, without any problem. There was enough room in the ground for our fans. Liverpool had the whole stand next to the Leppings Lane end but this added to the problem. Liverpool fans with tickets to that area had to enter through the Leppings Lane turnstiles.

The previous year there had been no motorway roadworks. The police knew how many supporters were expected. With so many not inside, they must have realised many of them had been delayed on the journey to Sheffield. The police must have known about the hold-ups on the motorway. When I took the players back to Sheffield to the hospitals on the Monday we were ferried through by Liverpool police, then handed over to the Manchester police, passed on to the North Yorkshire constabulary and finally South Yorkshire police. All the police forces collaborated. Surely one force could have told another that there were problems on the motorway and that they should put the kick-off time back? It wouldn't have been the first semi-final to be delayed in football history. It will always anger me that they didn't wait for the fans. There were all these people arriving late, desperate to get inside Hillsborough so as not to miss any of the game. Having so many hundreds of people rushing into the ground caused the terrifying crush which squeezed the life out of 96 poor Liverpool supporters.

Because of the traffic, the team had set out a bit earlier than usual. Our pre-match period was routine. There were a couple of injury doubts over Al and Rushie. Alan hadn't played since August. I told him: 'You are playing.'

He said: 'What?!'

'I'll take responsibility. You are playing.'

Al wasn't too convinced, but it's a manager's job to make decisions. We went out on to the pitch, the players warmed up, and I settled back to watch the game. I never noticed any problems. Suddenly a policeman ran on to the pitch and talked to the referee, Ray Lewis, who stopped the game. Lewis sent the teams back into the dressing-rooms and told us to wait for news. Nobody knew the scale of the disaster. I ordered the players to stay inside and went out into the corridor. A few fans had gathered there. They called out to me: 'Kenny, Kenny, there are people dying out there.'

News of the horror filtered through. People who had been outside began to give a hint of the unfolding disaster. Like any man, my first reaction was to check my family was all right. I went up to see Marina and Kelly, who had been in the directors' box. My son Paul wasn't with them because he always went to cup games with Roy Evans's son, Stephen, and another friend, Alan Brown. It was a happy ritual for them, having lunch together and then going off to the match, like hundreds of thousands of young lads every weekend. I went out to see if I could find them. Imagine my relief to see Paul walking across the pitch. He could easily have been in the Leppings Lane end because, although his ticket was in the other stand, he had to go through the Leppings Lane turnstiles to get there. If Paul hadn't arrived at Hillsborough early he could just as easily have been in that area where all the fatalities occurred. I was overjoyed to see him. I took him immediately to Marina, who was so relieved.

The police asked Brian Clough and me to make an announce-ment. We walked through Hillsborough's kitchens where a radio was giving out some football scores. It was weird. They just didn't matter. We went up to the police box at the corner of the Leppings Lane end and tried to broadcast a message but the microphone wasn't working. There were two guys on the Leppings Lane end waving to us, indicating that they could not hear. So the police suggested we continue up to the DJ's booth and use his announcing equipment. I went upstairs but Cloughie didn't. Cloughie just turned and went back. He never made any announcement to the fans. Only me. Why he didn't come up to address the fans, I don't know. That was his decision. I don't think I saw Cloughie again that day. Forest left quite quickly.

I continued up to the DJ's box to make the announcement as the police requested. I told the supporters to remain calm, that there had been an accident. I told them that the way they were conducting themselves was magnificent, the help they had been giving the emergency services was equally fantastic. 'Please remain calm,' I kept saying. And they were. The punters were brilliant.

Cloughie had a moan about me in his book. After we had beaten Forest when the semi-final was eventually played at Old Trafford, I commented that there was one team who wanted to win more than the other. For our fans' sake, Liverpool desired victory more than Forest. That was to be expected. Cloughie admitted that was true but that I didn't need to say it. There was no logic in Cloughie's comments. I wasn't being derogatory to his Forest players. Because of Hillsborough, it meant a lot more to us to win it than it did to Forest. Then Forest came to Anfield to play us in the League on 10 May. Cloughie was unbelievably negative, playing with 10 men behind the ball who never moved, a wee bit pathetic really. We still won 1–0.

When they realised that people were dying at the Leppings Lane end, the Forest fans behaved superbly. They were a real credit to their club. A few Liverpool guys ran towards the Forest end, some aggressively, some simply to get away from the carnage at the front of the Leppings Lane. My immediate reaction had been that there was crowd trouble in the Leppings Lane, that Forest fans had got in there to cause hassle. Many people thought that. Once people realised that the problem was congestion, the attitude of those running at the Forest fans changed. There could have been a full-scale riot if the Forest supporters on the Kop had reacted to the angry Liverpool supporters charging at them. The disaster was bad enough but it could have been even worse if the Forest fans had thought the Liverpool fans were trying to get to them. To their eternal credit, the Forest fans showed restraint. For their conduct at Hillsborough, Forest's supporters will always have a special place in my affections.

It soon became apparent that what was going on at the Leppings Lane end wasn't crowd trouble but a major disaster. Liverpool fans were ripping down advertising boards to use as stretchers, trying to help people on the pitch, trying to lift people out from that terrifying crush. There was very little the stewards and police could do because they were on the wrong side of the fence.

It's terrible to think how long the crushing had been going on. It is unbelievably depressing to realise that as the players kicked off and throughout those six minutes while a football match took place, Liverpool supporters were already dying. The problem must have started earlier than people imagined. When we went to the hospital on the Monday, a supporter said to Big Al, 'When are you making your comeback?' Big Al started the game. So either this guy was in late or he was under pressure by that time. If he had come in late he wouldn't have been at the front, so we assumed he must have come in early. We came out at 2.55 and the game stopped at 3.06 and he didn't know Big Al was playing. The crush must have started before 2.55.

The game was eventually called off at 3.30. The one guy who was centrally involved, but who people forget about, was the referee, Ray Lewis. It was traumatic for him as well. I got his number and phoned him during the week just to make sure he was all right, to offer him a bit of encouragement or consolation, whatever he wanted. Ray was all right but I think he appreciated the call.

Ray came into the dressing-rooms and told everyone that the game could not continue. We changed and went upstairs to see the wives. It was sombre in the players' lounge. Word kept arriving of the growing number of people who had lost their lives. It was very quiet. Even on the bus back up to Merseyside. No one could speak. I never felt any anger, just a deep sense of loss, of compassion for those who had died and their families. I still find it hard to believe that there were people who had come to support us who would never be seen again by their mothers and fathers, brothers and sisters, husbands and wives. Our concern, as individuals and as a club, was for the memory of those who had died. All we did in the days after Hillsborough came straight from the heart. We just wanted to go out and help the people the way they would have helped us. They had supported Liverpool. Now it was the turn of Liverpool FC to support them.

The next day people began coming up to Anfield. They just

wanted to leave tributes and flowers at the Shankly Gates. Peter Robinson got in touch with the groundsman and told him to open the ground. Liverpool Football Club didn't want supporters standing around on the street. That was a magnificent thing to do. At 6 p.m. we all went to St Andrew's cathedral. Bruce Grobbelaar read from the scriptures. There was an awful sense of loss, confusion, frustration. So many emotions were felt. The players and their wives were determined to do something. We all went into Anfield the next day. The wives were brilliant. The same with the players; most of them were brilliant. Everything just stopped and rightly so. It comforted people coming into Anfield, talking to the players, the wives, and having a cup of tea. Liverpool Football Club was the focus of so many people's lives that it was natural they should head for Anfield. It gave them somewhere to go, something to talk about. Most of the relatives of those who had died just wanted to talk about football. They kept telling the players: 'You were his idol.'

We were talking to a family and the widow said: 'My husband's favourite was Steve Heighway.' 'Hold on,' I replied, and went off to get Steve out of his office. That was helpful to them. One of the relatives joked: 'My husband was a miserable old sod. He will be quite happy sitting up there in heaven watching all the games for nothing.' Little bits of humour from the relatives really helped them and us as well. Talking to them about football was very therapeutic. We comforted each other.

Liverpool tried to do everything it could. We gave away shirts, pictures, any memento, anything to show our support. It was the act of giving, more than what we gave, that was important. When we finally returned to playing football, we didn't even have a strip. We had to order another one because we had given all our kits away. But that was not a problem. Liverpool was a community club, where everyone was welcome. That family feel helped the city recover from Hillsborough. Because Liverpool was a club that kept very close contacts with the man on the street, we knew how to react. Peter Robinson was brilliant with how he organised things. Noel White took charge of all the funerals, which player went to which, and where to send the floral tributes. Everybody chipped in. Some of the players were magnificent, reading from the scriptures at funerals.

One morning before everyone was in, I went out on to the pitch and tied my children's teddy bears around a goalpost at the Kop end. The goals, the pitch and the whole Kop were covered in flowers, scarves and tributes. I remember describing it as the 'saddest and most beautiful sight' I had ever seen. It really was like that. It was sad because of the reason why the tributes were there, but it was magnificent to see them. On the Friday night, after everybody had gone, I walked through the Kop with Kelly, Paul and Marina's dad, Pat. Paul looked at all the tributes, the flowers, the scarves and said: 'Why did it have to happen to us?' Kelly, Paul and I stood at the back of the Kop with tears falling down our faces. Walking through the Kop was so emotional. A lot of tributes had been left by people in the place where their loved one had stood. People who had lost the person they stood next to to watch games would leave something special in remembrance. Seeing two oranges left beside one of the barriers really moved me. It was difficult not to weep on coming across little tributes like that. They were so insignificant and yet so full of meaning. Perhaps the two people took it in turn to bring oranges to matches, something to share at half-time. That really got to me. I wondered whether the person who laid the oranges ever returned to the Kop. I came across somebody's boots, left there by his mourning family. Everywhere I walked there were endless messages, each of which embodied someone else's grief. It was so difficult to pass through.

So many people left little trinkets as a memorial to somebody else, I realised that they stood in the same place week in, week out. The variety of ages and backgrounds was amazing. There was a married couple, each around 60 years of age.

'You don't stand on the Kop,' I said to her.

'Every week,' she replied, part indignant, part proud. 'Just on the right-hand side, up behind the steps, behind the barrier, that's our spot every week.' They used to go to the same place every week to meet their mates. They left their tributes in the places where their friends had stood. I should have known that about the Kop before Hillsborough. When I went to matches with my dad at Ibrox, we always went to the same passageway, more or less the same crush barrier, to meet his work-mates. It must have been heartbreaking going back to the Kop and noticing little groups standing in their familiar places, but with familiar faces missing.

Every day, throughout that week, there was a long line of shocked people paying their respects. Thank goodness for the Salvation Army, who were brilliant. They helped people, showed them the way, supported them physically if the grief became too much. I cannot thank the Salvation Army enough. Marina got really friendly with them.

So many people visited this shrine. John Toshack returned from Spain, Craig Johnston from Australia. Prince Charles came after everything had finished; got his picture taken on the Kop. Some politicians just wanted to jump on the bandwagon, wanting to be seen as concerned people. That sickened me. One politician who impressed me was Neil Kinnock. He was very unobtrusive. Arrived, paid his respects, and left. No fuss. No pictures. He really gained my respect for that.

On the Monday, we went to Sheffield to visit the hospitals. Every single one of the players went; every single one of them was emotional. It was such a harrowing trip. We went into a room with four or five kids lying there in comas. The doctors and nurses had been playing tapes of Liverpool matches to them, anything to trigger some response. We spoke to one of them. We had moved on a couple of beds when that wee boy woke up. People said it was my presence that stirred him, but it was nothing to do with me. It was the doctors who were treating him, not me. The doctors have the medication and the expertise. The boy would have woken up anyway. His mother was in tears. 'We'll just leave you,' I told her. Obviously everybody was ecstatic that her son was waking up but we left them because it was a private moment. It was difficult to walk through the hospital wards past all those beautiful faces just lying there. There was one wee boy lying in a coma without a mark on him, looking so peaceful. His name was Lee Nicol. He died that night.

I still become emotional just talking or thinking about it. Most of the players were magnificent – John Barnes, Bruce, Aldo, Steve McMahon. Some of them couldn't handle it. They had to stay away. It didn't mean they felt any less for the people who had suffered. Everybody did as much as they could. It hit Aldo really hard. Coming from Liverpool, Aldo was a lot closer to it. Steve

McMahon and Ronnie Whelan are still friendly with families they got to know after Hillsborough. All the players were affected by Hillsborough. Some of the players grew up faster than they would otherwise have done. Hillsborough accelerated the maturing process. I didn't find anything new out about my players. Their true character comes out on the pitch, whether in adversity or triumph. People saw the private side of my character, a more caring one, rather than the professional one.

The country's view of me might have changed during Hillsborough, but most journalists couldn't see what was happening. Unless people had witnessed the aftermath, the mourning, the funerals, the grief, they couldn't form an accurate opinion of the situation. Those people who sat in London, writing about how Liverpool dealt with Hillsborough, could not possibly appreciate what was going on. They weren't writing with any knowledge of the situation because they hadn't come up to witness it all in person.

I don't know how many funerals I went to. Marina and I went to four in one day. We got a police escort between them. All the funerals were harrowing. All those families mourning the loss of their loved ones. Most of the church services finished with 'You'll Never Walk Alone'. I couldn't sing through any of the songs or hymns. I was too choked up. The words would never come out. I just stood there in a daze, still trying to come to terms with what had befallen the club and the people I so admired. The families were really appreciative that the players came along. If they had a favourite player, Noel White would try to make sure that particular player was there. The last funeral I went to was as harrowing as the first. I didn't get used to the grieving. Every funeral devastated me, as another family bade farewell to somebody they loved and shared life with. As I sat at each one, all I could think of was how I would feel if it was my family. It was a feeling of 'there, but for the grace of God, go I'. I find it very difficult to talk about death. If the conversation turns that way, I immediately leave or try to change the subject.

I did what I had to do after Hillsborough, certainly not through any delusions of grandeur. I could handle the demands placed on me by Hillsborough because Marina's mum and dad were down looking after the kids. They said to me: 'You've got to do this for a fortnight, go to funerals, be there to help and support.' We knew the kids were all right. I just had to go out and help people. If I had to face consequences of stress at a later date then so be it. All that mattered was to support the people of Liverpool because they had always supported me.

Someone even sent a stress counsellor in to talk to me in my Anfield office.

'Do you think you are all right?' this woman counsellor asked.

'Aye,' I replied.

'Well,' she continued, 'you may think you are all right.'

'What are you talking about?' I said.

'I think maybe you should sit down and talk about it.'

'Listen,' I said, 'go upstairs and see Peter Robinson, will you? I am all right. Go and see if Peter's all right.'

So she went up to see Peter. A few minutes later Peter phoned down and said: 'Thanks very much, Kenny. I don't need a stress counsellor.'

After seeing so many parents bury their children, my family took on even greater importance to me. Shanks used to say that football was not a matter of life and death, that it was more important than that, but it wasn't to me. I never felt that way, even before Hillsborough. Shanks genuinely meant it. That was the way he felt. That was the way he was. A lot of Liverpool supporters also believed that. I don't know if Hillsborough changed that viewpoint for them. Some of the things people were saying when we talked were unbelievable. Some of the things they were asking me to do, like 'Go on and win the Cup for us.' The overwhelming majority of the families were saying, 'You have to stay in the Cup.' I couldn't even think of our next match, whenever it would be.

To me, football wasn't important. But it was important to the Football Association, who were talking about the Cup on the television before 4 p.m. while the bodies were still being taken out from behind the fence. That was despicable. All the FA's talk about deadlines was stupid; there was only one side who was going to win, and it was going to be Liverpool. There is no way in the world that the FA could have done anything other than listen to Liverpool Football Club. Liverpool were the only ones who could gauge the mood after Hillsborough. The FA would never,

ever have had a shred of credibility again if they had gone against what Liverpool wanted. Liverpool were going to set the deadline. Not when the players were ready, because they might not have been ready, but when the people of Merseyside were ready, when there had been a reasonable length of time for mourning.

People outside Merseyside wanted to help, too, but didn't know how. So they gave money because that was the most obvious way. People had barrows out collecting money. Ian Woosnam shot for birdies at Hillside Golf Club, my golf club in Southport. People did anything to raise money. Alex Ferguson was one of the first on the phone. Fergie sent a group of Manchester United supporters over to pay their respects. That was a wonderful gesture. Any help we needed was forthcoming because every other club knew they could have been in exactly the same position. They could relate to it. There were dyed-in-the-wool Evertonians who had never set foot inside Anfield coming to pay their respects. Sadly, I knew it was only a matter of time before the game's togetherness dissolved, before age-old differences reappeared. At the time it was very encouraging, especially the gesture by the Manchester United fans; there had been tension and trouble with them in the past. I thought this might help to re-establish bonds between two sets of supporters who normally loathed each other. But people have short memories. They soon went back to their self-same ways. The hating continued.

No club put us under pressure to play. Nottingham Forest were under greater pressure to stand aside when Everton won their semi-final, so the final could be an all-Merseyside affair, but that would have been wrong. It wasn't Forest's fault. Their players might never get to another semi-final. I could understand the point of view but Forest had to run their lives as well. They were helpful over the re-arrangement of the game; they weren't pushing too hard. People tend to forget that Forest had been affected. They had witnessed the deaths. The Forest directors were upset and compassionate. They are still friendly when we see them.

The press coverage was difficult to comprehend, particularly the publication of pictures which added to people's distress. There was one photograph of two girls right up against the Leppings Lane fence, their faces pressed into the wire. Nobody knows how they escaped. They used to come to Melwood every day, looking for autographs, and that photograph upset everyone there because we knew them. After seeing that I couldn't look at the papers again.

When the *Sun* came out with the story about Liverpool fans being drunk and unruly, underneath a headline 'The Truth', the reaction on Merseyside was one of complete outrage. Newsagents stopped stocking the *Sun*. People wouldn't mention its name. They were burning copies of it. Anyone representing the *Sun* was abused. *Sun* reporters and photographers would lie, telling people they worked for the *Liverpool Post* and *Echo*. There was a lot of harassment of them because of what had been written. The *Star* had gone a bit strong as well but they apologised the next day. They knew the story had no foundation. Kelvin MacKenzie, the *Sun*'s editor, even called me up.

'How can we correct the situation?' he said.

'You know that big headline – "The Truth",' I replied. 'All you have to do is put "We Lied" in the same size. Then you might be all right.'

MacKenzie said: 'I cannot do that.'

'Well,' I replied, 'I cannot help you then.'

That was it. I put the phone down. Merseysiders were outraged by the *Sun*. A great many still are.

I was invited to Walton jail where the prisoners were having a service for Hillsborough. Before I went in, the governor asked me to give them words of reassurance. The inmates were very upset by what they had read. It was a creepy experience. There was silence apart from the clinking of keys, the rattle of doors sliding back. I went into the chapel and the inmates were sitting there, with hardly a murmur from anybody. Then they clapped me in. It was really appreciative applause but unnerving as well. I remembered the governor's words and told them not to be upset by what they had read in the papers, because it wasn't true.

The *Sun*'s allegations were disgraceful and completely groundless. Ticketless fans try to get into every game. Any well-supported club playing in a semi-final is going to attract ticketless fans. If handled properly, as they had been at Hillsborough a year earlier, ticketless supporters do not present a problem.

The shameful allegations intensified the anger amidst the

trauma. We spent that week consoling the bereaved and attending funerals. On the Saturday we held a service at Anfield. At six minutes past three there was a minute's silence across the country. Then everyone at Anfield sang 'You'll Never Walk Alone'. We tied scarves between Anfield and Goodison. We just wanted to show the unity existing on Merseyside. The following day, there was a final service on the pitch. It was really quiet, just the wind rustling the scarves tied to the crossbar. When somebody shouted out 'We all loved you', we all broke down.

The length of grieving was about right. The following week was international week which took away some players. Peter Beardsley went off to join England but John Barnes withdrew. He was too distraught. Ray Houghton teamed up with the Republic. Aldo stayed behind. He couldn't go anywhere, he was so traumatised. Aldo took longer than any of the players to recapture the desire to play again. People cope with traumas at different speeds. Eventually Aldo's appetite returned. Liverpool would never have hurried him, or any of the players, but on Friday 28 April, 13 days after Hillsborough, we resumed training. I have never seen tackling like it in my life, certainly not on a training ground. The players really got stuck into each other. Maybe it was a physical way of releasing the pent-up emotion. On Saturday the team travelled up to Glasgow, where we were going to play a fundraiser and remembrance game against Celtic on Sunday. We took all the wives up as well. It was such a relief to get away. By then, it was also important to get a game, to find some semblance of reality. It was fantastic that it was at Celtic. The way the day went, the magnificent manner in which people conducted themselves, was a tremendous credit to both clubs but more importantly to football itself. During the minute's silence, you could have heard a tear drop. When all the supporters sang 'You'll Never Walk Alone' I nearly broke down again, it was so emotional.

It was a good trip to Parkhead, made even better because Celtic had played the day before and were exhausted, so we beat them by four goals. The score wasn't important. The band Wet Wet Wet, who are friends of mine, had sponsored us for every goal we scored plus extra if I scored. Which was why I had pushed Steve McMahon out of the way from five yards; plus I didn't fancy him from that range – he would have missed.

Afterwards Liverpool took all the players and wives out to an Italian restaurant to thank them for their efforts after Hillsborough. Everyone let rip that night.

It was an extraordinary evening. A Welsh choir were in the hotel bar. We were all trying to sing and they said: 'We'll do it for you.' When they sang 'You'll Never Walk Alone' and 'Abide With Me', everyone burst into tears again. Someone set the fire alarm off – not one of the players – and a fire engine drove up. After that, I can't remember a thing. But I woke up with a fireman's hat by my bed. Apparently I had told everyone that I always wanted to be a fireman. The players seriously wound me up the next day, making fireman jokes.

Outside the hotel, Aldo had had a couple of words with his wife, Joan. He was really depressed; Joan was in tears. So Marina said: 'John, we've all been through a lot, try and be nice to her.' He said to Marina, 'You can push off,' or words to that effect. When Marina and I came down in the morning for brunch, there was Aldo sitting with Joan. He looked up, looked embarrassed and then said: 'I'm sorry.' I just burst out laughing. Everyone needed to release the tension that had built up after Hillsborough.

The wives went home and we went to Blackpool for a couple of days to prepare for football again. It was fitting that our first competitive game back should be Everton, who had been so supportive to us. It was a 0–0 draw.

The Merseyside Cup final was played in beautiful weather with the two sets of supporters united. There was a slightly strange atmosphere. Because of what had happened at Hillsborough, the fans did not know whether it would be disrespectful to shout. Aldo scored our first. We would have been delighted if anyone had scored but we knew how much it meant to Aldo. Everton came back to force extra time. By that time there were punters sitting on the dog track, watching the game. I was on the bench with all these supporters sitting beside me. There was no problem whatsoever. We went ahead, Everton equalised again. A Scottish policeman was standing next to me and said: 'Don't worry, wee man.' Then Rushie scored to make it 3–2. 'You're all right now, wee man,' the Scottish policeman said. Amazing.

At the final whistle, fans came flooding on the pitch. That unfortunately deprived the players of a lap of honour but I could understand the fans coming on. It was as much an emotional day for them as it was for the players. I tried to run for the tunnel while the lads went up for the cup. One of the fans grabbed me, lifting me up, but I didn't want it. They had done the same thing at Old Trafford, lifted me up on to their shoulders when we won the semi. They tried to do the same thing at Wembley. One guy lifted me up and we banged heads. I eventually got halfway down the tunnel and met our security man, Tony Chinn, a real character who used to look after the players when we went away. He was at the dressing-room door, tears flowing down his face.

'I can't be hard all the time,' he said. Tony was so moved. He hugged me, stood back, looked at my face and said: 'What happened to your eye?'

'What do you mean?' I asked.

'Your eye's cut.'

The blood was running down my face. It did not matter. It was an unbelievable occasion. Everton must have been so disappointed but they would have understood. It had to be Liverpool's day.

They took the fences down for the Wembley final. I don't think there was a better time to do it. There had to be some security for the players, but the fans had to be safe as well. They had to be able to get out in case something went wrong. Taking fences down didn't create security problems. Nobody came on to the pitch during the game, although they did at the final whistle for understandable reasons. Fans knew that a pitch invasion would have been an affront to the 96 fellow football supporters who died at Hillsborough. The tragedy forced the end of standing. The Taylor Report made stadiums all-seater. Often punters don't sit anyway. If there is an incident down the other end, the guy at the front stands up, then the one behind him and so it ripples back. The Taylor Report caused a lot of people a lot of problems when it came out. It placed a financial burden on all clubs, but it was essentially right.

I remember discussing the subject with Trevor Hicks, who lost two daughters at Hillsborough. Some people want to stand at matches – they still do at a lot of smaller grounds – but when you think of somebody like Trevor and his wife who lost their beautiful children, no one could argue with the Taylor Report. It would be great if there was some way that fans could stand and watch the game in safety. Safety is of paramount importance. If going all-seater was what it took to guarantee safety, fine. It's been magnificent for the grounds.

My one real fear about all-seater stadiums is that the game might be being taken away from the man in the street. One legacy of Hillsborough is that the game has become less accessible to the working classes. The prices are too heavy, particularly for a family wanting to go. All clubs must have their commercial side, their hospitality suites and big sponsorships, but there has to be a place for ordinary supporters. They should never be forgotten. Hillsborough, and the ensuing Taylor Report, definitely changed the atmosphere of grounds. With smaller capacities, no one standing and a wealthier audience, grounds have become quieter. It is difficult to tell at Ewood Park because Blackburn never had large crowds before; we have gone from 8,000 to 28,000. But at Liverpool, the Kop has definitely changed, atmospherically. Each ground changes, when they re-build a stand. Clubs should set aside an area for those who cannot afford season-tickets but want to go whenever they have enough cash. Poorer fans should not be discouraged. Blackburn Rovers have got it right but then we've got the space. We can let kids in for a pound. We should never forget the wee boy in the street whose father cannot afford to take him. One has to be mindful of the fans of the future.

I have been at three matches, as a spectator, player and manager, where there have been disasters – at Ibrox, Heysel and Hillsborough. Although not directly involved, with the number of matches I have been at, the chances of it happening to me or somebody in my own family are probably well above average. I feel fortunate that it wasn't me or one of my kids. Parents will always be protective even when their children become adults. That's human nature.

In the aftermath of Hillsborough, I appreciated my family even more. Marina says that at times I was difficult to live with, that I was clearly under strain. I didn't realise at the time. Tom

Saunders told Marina that he was going to keep an eye on me, but he always did anyway. I did not know how tense I was being at home. Without my being aware of it, the strain of Hillsborough was beginning to catch up with me.

— 13 —

LEAVING LIVERPOOL

Although i didn't realise it at the time, Hillsborough was a most important factor in my decision to leave Liverpool in 1991. During that period, I didn't appreciate the scale of the pressure. I would admit to the deep emotion that I felt because of Hillsborough, but I would not admit to any pressure. I thought to myself, 'Why should I feel pressure?' The people under pressure were those who had lost loved ones. All I had lost were tears. But I was under pressure; I realised how much just before I left Liverpool. I had become unpleasant company at home. I was shouting at the kids. I didn't want to be this tetchy father who kept bawling his children out. I would have a drink to relax me, maybe even make me mellow with the kids. It became pretty obvious that I had to get out. In truth, I had wanted to leave Anfield in 1990, a year before I eventually resigned.

In the 22 months between Hillsborough and my resignation, the strain kept growing until I finally snapped. It was a very difficult period. Returning to Hillsborough in November 1989 was creepy. Nobody enjoyed it. The Leppings Lane end was empty. Big Al and Chris Turner, the Wednesday keeper, laid wreaths there. I could excuse my players the ensuing defeat; I couldn't focus either. We tried to concentrate on the game, tried to get our minds off the disaster that had unfolded behind one goal; but we couldn't. I said publicly that all the Liverpool boys were professionals, that they would go out and do their best to put the horror of what had happened to the back of their minds. They did try their best but it was impossible. My attention kept turning to one end being empty. My mind just wandered, recalling funerals, people, those harrowing visits to hospitals and conversations with bereaved families. Then I would look at the Leppings Lane end and think that's where they all lost their lives. It was impossible to concentrate on the game. We got away from Hillsborough as quickly as we could. I drove back with Steve Nicol, his wife Eleanor and Alan Hansen. Nicol kept asking: 'Gaffer, can we get some chips?'

'No,' I kept saying. I just wanted to get home. I didn't have an appetite for anything. I stopped eventually, but only at the motorway services where Nicol was picking up his car.

It was impossible for me to notice whether there was any pressure building up inside me. I was too busy being manager of Liverpool Football Club. The position I held was called 'the unmanageable job', but being manager of Liverpool was never complicated. I wasn't running the commercial or administrative side. It was one of the most straightforward jobs in English football because of the quality of the administration around me. People like Peter Robinson were so good at their jobs. I just concentrated on the football side. Of course, there were great expectations placed on me, but I shared those expectations. I wanted to meet them. As a player I had helped create them.

I was too focused on reaping more success to realise the stress I was under. We won the League that season, Aldo's last. He was off to Real Sociedad. For his last game Aldo was on the bench next to me during the 9–0 defeat of Crystal Palace. When we were awarded a penalty, I turned to Aldo. 'Do you want to take it?' I asked him. 'It's at the Kop.' I have never seen him move so fast.

'Yeah, yeah,' he said, peeling off his top.

I jumped out of the dugout, got Aldo on, he placed the ball on the spot and scored. It was a brilliant moment. I knew how much it meant to him to score in front of the Kop on his last appearance in a Liverpool shirt. Aldo didn't thank me for selling him but I'm sure he appreciated that gesture. After the game he threw his shirt into the Kop. They threw it back! No, they didn't. Aldo was truly loved at Anfield. In the players' lounge afterwards, Marina, remembering what Aldo had said to her in Glasgow, went up to him.

'Aldo,' she said, 'why don't you push off!'

He just burst out laughing. It was sad but Aldo went on a fitting note, one that characterised his time at Liverpool – with a ball in the back of the net.

Palace took a right hammering that day. A couple of days later, I phoned Steve Coppell, their manager, because Palace had only just come up.

'If there's anything I can help with, just say,' I told Steve. 'If you want me to send a letter saying that the scoreline didn't reflect the performance of your lads, I'll gladly put pen to paper.'

Steve said that would be great. So I scribbled something, sent it to them. I should have kept my mouth shut. Palace knocked us out of the FA Cup.

We still had the championship in our sights. When we began slowing up a bit, with injuries, I brought in Ronny Rosenthal. Ronny gave us momentum. He had five starts, three appearances as sub and seven goals. That was a very good return which helped to win us the championship. Having secured the title, I even allowed myself a trip off the bench, on 1 May against Derby County, who were so negative and played 10 defenders. It was the end of my playing career and I just wanted to show my appreciation to the supporters at Anfield. So I went sub. The staff said the fans would love that. I don't know about the players! I came on at 0–0 with 20 minutes left and swung the game! We won 1–0. On the last day of the season, we travelled to Coventry City. In the dressing-room beforehand I told the players: 'Look, you've won the title, don't embarrass us by finishing with a defeat. Go out and relax, but compete.' They relaxed a bit too much. Coventry scored in the first minute through Kevin Gallacher. 'Oh, no,' I thought. But after that the lads were magnificent. We won 6–1.

Such success simply hid the strain. I wanted a break there and then in that summer of 1990. Days after winning the title, I was thinking hard about leaving. During the season Sir John Smith had offered me a new contract which I wouldn't sign. It was no reflection on Sir John for whom I had great respect. I kept delaying because what I really wanted was a break. I was also conscious of a statement I had made to Marina when I took the job that, because of the enormity of the job, it would probably be for only five years. That period had taken in the aftermath of Heysel and Hillsborough. I was ready for a rest but because Liverpool had been so good to me and my family, I felt obliged to carry on.

During discussions relating to my contract, I requested shares in the club which would give me some sort of continued attachment to Liverpool if I felt forced to leave. I really wanted some shares in Liverpool. I felt that if I couldn't sustain the job and had to resign, at least I would have some shares in the club I love, some permanent connection. I told Liverpool's board: 'It's great what you've offered me in this new deal, I've no problem with that. But give me shares instead of money and I'll take it. I want to give something back.' There was nothing untoward or underhand about my request for shares. It would all have been totally above board. Sadly, the Liverpool directors said it couldn't be arranged. They said the shares weren't there. I was disappointed. I know that shares in a football club were not a good investment financially at that time, but that wasn't why I wanted them. I wasn't worried about that. I wanted to feel part of Liverpool, an investor in its future. Maybe the board thought I was trying to get more power, but that was never my intention. I don't have a great ego that needs constant feeding. I never had any ambition to run Liverpool Football Club. It did superbly without me being there. Why would I want to butt in?

I had enough on my plate looking after the football side. It would have been insulting to Peter Robinson, John Smith and the board of directors if I wanted to change how they ran a very successful club. I don't think I would have been respected if I had tried to muscle in on their action because they never intruded on mine. My responsibility was for the football. Maybe they had the same opinion as myself, that it was best if I concentrated on the football, that I wasn't equipped to be involved in other parts of the club. Some managers want to have many roles in their club; and some clubs want managers to be involved in everything, like negotiating transfer fees, players' wages, and financial details. In John Smith and Peter Robinson, I had two of the best negotiators around. There was no need or desire for me to concentrate on anything but football. Anyway, the board said that it wasn't possible for me to have shares in the club, which saddened me. So they paid me in cash and I carried on working.

I nearly died, that June of 1990. Marina bought a strimmer,

which wasn't wired up. She said to the guy in the shop: 'Kenny's hopeless at DIY, can you wire it up?' So the guy attached all the bits together. I decided to do a bit of edging. When I plugged it in, the strimmer wouldn't start, so I switched it off and disconnected it. I had a look at it, re-assembled it, switched the power back on and pressed the button on the strimmer. It still wasn't working. So I pulled the cable apart, forgetting it was still switched on at the mains. That should still have been OK except that the guy in the shop had wired it up incorrectly. Fortunately, Marina heard me screaming. She ran down, switched the plug off and then touched me. That broke the circuit. An ambulance took me to hospital, where they patched up my thumb which had taken the initial shock. There was a hole where one of the pins had poured electricity into me. In the end, I needed a skin graft to cover the hole in my thumb.

I don't know whether that shock added to the stress I was under. By Christmas my body was covered in big blotches. A few even appeared on my face. I saw a doctor nearly every day for injections. He used to come to the ground, bend me over, give me an injection in one cheek, and send me home feeling like a pincushion. Tom Saunders had to drive me home. I would go to bed, wake up the next morning, go back to the ground and try to start again. I was sent for allergy tests but I knew I wasn't allergic to anything. I don't know whether the rash resulted from the general strain. My lack of tolerance towards the children probably upset me even more than it did them. I hated to see the looks of surprise and hurt on the faces of my children when I bawled at them. I hated myself for shouting at them. I love Paul, Kelly, Lynsey and Lauren so much that I wanted to do something to make me less edgy when we were together. As a player, I was pretty much teetotal because I was dedicated to my profession, but in the period before I resigned I used to drink wine so I could be more sociable with the family. After Hillsborough, Marina began learning about counselling and tried to counsel me. If I didn't give the right answer to one of her questions on dealing with stress she would crack up laughing, saying I was definitely mad.

But my family could see how desperately I needed a break. I was unwell and under strain. I started having doubts about myself and my ability to make decisions. I would wonder why I made a particular decision. Was it the right one? In the past I would just make the decision, usually more right than wrong, and move on without thinking. Now I agonised over everything. I didn't like myself for that. I didn't think I was being fair to the club because if I couldn't make decisions, who was going to make them for the team?

I made good buys in Jamie Redknapp, Don Hutchison and Steve Harkness, which people tend to forget. About the same time, people questioned what turned out to be my last two purchases as Liverpool manager: Jimmy Carter and David Speedie. Jimmy Carter had a good start, won man of the match in his second game. Jimmy Carter had everything: good technique, he could dribble, get past people, whip in crosses. Jimmy could have been a tremendous asset. The mental side was his problem. Maybe Liverpool was too big for him. The critics might have had a point about Jimmy Carter being a bad buy, but I thought it was a bit harsh when the players joked that it was Jimmy Carter who pushed me over the edge. At this time, Peter Beardsley was not 100 per cent fit, so I bought David Speedie. We needed someone with a proven track record for goals. In his first three games, Speedie scored three goals – one in the draw at Old Trafford and two in the League victory over Everton. Then we drew 0–0 with Everton in the Cup, I left Speedo out for the replay and Peter scored twice in the 4–4 draw.

There was a lot of nonsense talked and written about why Peter had been left out, that there must have been a falling-out between us. The conspiracy theorists were wrong again. Peter had been injured with a stress fracture for the previous games. His shin was sore and he was reluctant to play. He had been sub a few times, which he wasn't too happy about, in case we needed him to come to our rescue. According to some people, the 0–0 with Everton was bad management by me because I didn't pick Peter. That's rubbish. Speedie was in better form, so I picked him. It didn't work out so I recalled Peter for the replay. He scored twice. Is that bad management? I thought it was quite good judgement. Peter Beardsley wanted to play, so I let him play. Bang. He scores. There's my answer. Thanks very much, Peter. Speedo was a threat to Peter's position, so it gave him an extra edge.

In Peter's autobiography, he says that he wishes he was more ruthless. He could understand why I left him out for certain matches. When we went to Wimbledon or Millwall in the Cup, where Ray Houghton was also left out, sometimes even Arsenal, Peter could understand not being used for tactical reasons. They had big players. We needed strong players to play against them. I didn't always leave Peter out against physically strong teams. I can recall him playing against Wimbledon and Arsenal a few times. He scored a wonderful goal against Arsenal at Anfield one night – nutmegged the defender, drew the keeper, gave him one of those famous shimmies and lifted the ball over the top. Other than when he was injured, the main reason I left Peter out was tactical.

Against Everton in that famous 4–4 fifth-round replay, I was the only person at Goodison that night who knew it was my last match. Before the game, I lay on my hotel bed and decided that I had to get out. The alternative was going mad. I promised myself that I would inform Noel White and Peter Robinson of my decision at our usual meeting the following morning. Irrespective of the outcome against Liverpool's oldest rivals, I was going to tell them that I was resigning. If we had won 4–0 I would still have resigned the next day. I could either keep my job or my sanity. I had to go.

We should have beaten Everton. It wasn't that Tony Cottee kept scoring against us. It was us who kept giving them the opportunities. All credit to Everton who kept coming back, playing with the sort of commitment we expected, but drawing was our own fault. At 4–3 I was going to make a positional change. Because Everton, and particularly Cottee, were causing us problems, I wanted to push somebody back into defence. Turning to Ronnie Moran, I said: 'We'll move Jan back to sweeper.' Ronnie replied: 'Hold on.' So I left it. I still blame myself now for not doing it, for being weak-willed when normally I was so decisive. It was my fault that Liverpool did not win that game. If I had been 100 per cent right in my own mind, I would have made the decision. We needed to get a hold of Cottee. But I failed to take command. All my old decisiveness drained from me. I don't blame Ronnie. I blame myself. I should just have done it and faced the consequences. In my own mind, that hesitation confirmed I was right to quit. Liverpool needed somebody who was going to be authoritative, somebody who could make a decision. I couldn't do that anymore.

So, the following morning, I went in for our usual meeting. Noel was already there. Peter was still in his office. I just chatted to Noel for a bit. Peter came in, and they started talking about the business side. I couldn't hold back any longer.

'Hold it a minute,' I said. 'I cannot go on. I am telling you now that I want to give up.'

Obviously, they were a wee bit surprised, but there wasn't a lot Noel and Peter could do. They just had to accept it. They did suggest I 'take a couple of weeks off'. That wouldn't have solved anything. The break had to be clean. I wouldn't have rested if I'd known I was coming back. If I'd been off on holiday, the games would have still been going on, the results still happening, I would still have been thinking of them. A clean break was my only way of reclaiming my equilibrium and recharging my batteries.

Resigning was a decision made primarily in my best interests, but I was also thinking of Liverpool. A manager who cannot make decisions has to go. Some people could hide or con people or get others to make decisions but I couldn't do that. Not to Liverpool. I would have been glad if it had never happened, but it was inevitable, given the strains and stresses of the previous few years. I left the club I loved out of necessity, not choice. Events and emotions had overtaken me. I was no longer in control. I said I felt my head was going to explode. That's what it really felt like. There was a feeling of intense relief throughout the afternoon before the Everton game, because I knew respite was hours away. It was like emerging from a darkened room.

That Thursday was hectic. I spoke to Tom. Then Tony Ensor, Liverpool's legal man, came in and said: 'Kenny, can I speak to you as a friend?' I told Tony I was determined to leave.

'Well, Kenny, I've got to put my official hat on now and tell you what the repercussions are for you.'

'I don't care what they are, Tony. I've just got to go. Just let me go. I'm not going to cause any problems. I've got to go.'

Tony realised just by looking in my face that I had reached the end of my tether.

Finally I went home. Marina already knew that I was going to resign, but nothing could prepare me for the reaction of my kids. I thought I had done the best thing for everybody until I came home and saw Kelly and Paul in tears. Then I thought: 'Oh God, what have I done?' But it had to be done. I could not have gone on. Coming back after matches, I had been snapping at the kids for no reason. No one deserved my behaviour. When I saw them so upset it got to me, but there was no going back. It was strange. I felt both relief and disappointment. Relief that I was nearly free. Disappointment that I had let down both Liverpool and my family, the two most important groups of people in my life. I felt sad at leaving Anfield, a place which had been so very, very good to me, Marina and the kids. Liverpool had been part of our lives for such a long time. But it would have been a bigger disappointment if I hadn't made the decision.

On Friday, I returned to Anfield. First stop was the dressing-room, where the lads were changing before taking the bus to training.

'I'm off,' I said. 'That's me finished with the club.'

I walked out, leaving them in stunned silence. I went into Steve Heighway's room to say goodbye to him and Big Yeatsy. I went to the press conference, did my bit and then retreated to Southport.

It was the fairest way to leave Liverpool. I just hoped people would accept that my stated reasons were true. What was hurtful afterwards was that newspapers concocted all sorts of reasons. They hinted that I might not have been telling the truth. That was hard to deal with. People called the press conference 'brief'. It certainly wasn't brief to me. It was agonising. I felt I was squirming with humiliation in front of the eyes of the world. It angered me that people didn't believe me. I really did feel that my head was about to explode. I told the press that; still they searched for other reasons. Everybody threw in their twopenny worth. All the journalists became amateur psychologists. Amid all the fuss and pontificating, a consolation was that I knew the reasons why I left and so did Liverpool and they accepted them. That was the most important thing.

The Gulf War was raging and people were devoting pages to unbelievably inaccurate analyses of my decision. Michael Parkinson had a pop at me. He wrote that pressure was having no home or hope, working at a coalface or on an emergency ward. He said that what pressure is not is being paid a good wage to manage one of the most famous football clubs in the world. How does Michael Parkinson know? How does he know what I'm like, what sort of strain I was under? Of course there is pressure if people have no money, no job, no house, no food for the kids, but that's not the only pressure. It doesn't matter what a person's financial position is; if they are exhausted, they need a rest. Getting £10 a week or £100 doesn't make it any easier. I'm not disputing that I made a good living from being manager of Liverpool. Everyone said I gave value for money, but I had reached a stage in my life when I couldn't do it anymore. I was being honourable in telling my employers so. I don't have to justify myself to Michael Parkinson. I listen to criticism from people I respect, but if it comes from people I don't respect or who don't know what they're talking about, the best thing is to ignore it.

At least there had been no speculation beforehand. All the reporters got the story at the same time. That was the way I liked to work. A lot of people wrote afterwards that they could tell the stress I was under because I looked ill during the Everton match, but they only said that with the benefit of hindsight. Sometimes if I train too hard, or work out too much, my face becomes thin like that. A surgeon friend came over to our house on the Saturday. He told Marina that I had made the right decision.

The implications of what I had done sank in firstly when I returned home to see the tears on my children's faces. Then it hit me again when we were coming back from Orlando, and it was announced that Graeme Souness was going to take the Liverpool manager's job. Of course, I had no right to hope Liverpool would come back to me. Besides, at that time I thought Graeme was the best man for the job. But if Liverpool had waited until the summer, and then asked me, I would have gone back. Like a shot. Liverpool will always be in my family's heart.

— 14 —

RE-BUILDING
BLACKBURN

P ART OF THE BEAUTY of Blackburn Rovers was the naivety of the place, almost innocence. A really down-to-earth atmosphere pervaded Ewood Park. The first time I signed a player – Alan Wright on my first Thursday to catch that week's registration deadline – the then secretary of Rovers, John Howarth, got a bit of a sweat on. Soon it was: 'Come on, lads, it's Thursday. Who are we signing?' They started to get into it, but the people at Blackburn were never ostentatious, even when the success started. They are good, honourable people, respected throughout football. If Blackburn's board told me something, I wouldn't need it in writing. Their word is as good as their bond; just what I was used to at Liverpool.

Ewood Park was the perfect place for me to return to football. After a few months I was ready to get involved again. Filling the time hadn't been a problem. Immediately after leaving Liverpool, I took the family off skiing. Marina was always on to me about skiing; it was a banned activity as a player, too much potential for a season in plaster. Now was the time to go. On the first day I was halfway down the slope and shouted to the instructor: 'How do I stop?'

'I haven't taught you how to stop yet,' he replied.

I was the class idiot. I went from bad to worse; it really was all downhill! We took the kids to Disney after that. It was the perfect break, one that recharged my batteries. Soon, I wanted to return to football.

Before the Blackburn enquiry, there was only one possibility that I was seriously interested in. A middle man approached me, saying: 'Do you fancy a job at a big club?'

'Aye, I'd be interested if it was Marseille or Milan!' I replied jokingly.

He went off and a few days later contacted me again.

'Are you serious about Marseille?' he said.

'Aye.'

So I went to Switzerland to speak to Bernard Tapie, Marseille's owner. It was all very serious. Tapie said: 'Well, let's go and watch the French Cup final next week and then I'll announce you are getting the job.' Very nice, I thought. This was before the match-fixing scandal; Marseille sounded a good place for the football and the lifestyle. We would have lived in Provence, found a lovely place, somewhere near the beach, and there are some golf clubs near there. I'd already looked into that. So when I bade farewell to Tapie in Switzerland, I thought it was only a matter of days before I became his manager at Marseille. But just after I arrived home, the agent rang me to talk about his commission. We had an argument over the size of his cut. The next thing I heard, the whole Marseille deal was off.

Funnily enough, it was in France that I discovered who my next employers would be. Gerard Houillier, then coaching the French team, invited me to play in a Variety Club of France charity match.

'No problem,' I told Gerard. 'I'll tie it in with a few days in Monaco with the kids.'

On returning to the hotel after watching Monaco play, I received a call from Bill Fox, Blackburn's chairman. Bill wanted to know whether I would be interested in the Blackburn job. The papers had already been speculating about it but I hadn't heard anything. I never took any notice of such talk until it became official. Now it was. Bill's call to Monaco began my return to football. We agreed that he could come over to Southport when I got back. Bill duly arrived at the house and presented Blackburn's case.

'All right,' I told him, before requesting a series of guarantees. 'You'll need to confirm that all the money for players is going to be available and won't be affected by the development of the stadium, and that the ambitions of the club match my own.' Basically I wanted proof that Jack Walker was genuine. I had no reason to doubt Jack; I was just concerned with protecting myself.

When I had the confirmation that there was the necessary finance for both team and stadium, I was ready to meet Jack. He came over to the house and we discussed how we could transform Blackburn Rovers. The deal was coming together. I insisted that Tony Parkes stayed on at the club and he said that he would be delighted to do so. Tony had got some great results as caretaker after Don Mackay's departure. I had one final request. Get Ray Harford, I told them, and I'd give it a go. I wouldn't have gone to Blackburn without Ray. We were a joint package. I wanted Ray on board for his coaching and organisational abilities and for his deep knowledge of football. I had been impressed with Ray every time Liverpool played one of his teams. People said Ray's teams and mine were very different but that was not so. Luton Town and Fulham were footballing sides. They might not have been as good as my Liverpool sides, but they could play. Plus Ray had the experience of working at Wimbledon. He had knowledge of a variety of styles. We seemed to get on quite well at a couple of functions when we'd met. We enjoyed talking on the phone. That was all I needed to convince myself that Ray could come in and help us.

Blackburn had to speak to Liverpool. When I left Anfield I'd signed an agreement that they would get compensation if I went back to work within a certain time. Blackburn were prepared to pay the compensation. It was time to go to work again. Blackburn suited me. The attraction was simple. There was money to support a real change in their fortunes so I thought I would give it a go. I knew I would be under scrutiny. I'm not naive. I know Kenny Dalglish can never find a quiet job in football. My previous success with Liverpool ensured that. The spotlight would always be on me.

The situation at Blackburn differed from the one I inherited at Anfield. With Liverpool, I had just carried on everything that had been started by Shanks, Bob and Joe. When Ray and I arrived in October 1991, Blackburn were brand new. Rovers' great days were long gone, memories for only a few. It was important that the correct foundations were laid, so we set about building up the first team and the youth set-up. That had long been in place at Liverpool. One difference between Blackburn and the cities I worked in before was that there was only one club in this town. Liverpool and Glasgow were football capitals where everyone knew your team's result. In Blackburn they wouldn't know. That inspired me because I realised people hadn't looked upon Blackburn as serious. My determination to succeed never faltered but I remained relaxed. That was vitally important to me after what had gone before. There wasn't the intensity, the demand for success, that there had been at Liverpool. I felt detached from Rovers because I was not living in the town, but at the same time I felt driven to do my best for town and club. Blackburn were worth making an effort for. Lancastrians are good people and Blackburn were famous for being a very hospitable club. The boardroom, with that old table creaking under the weight of a hundred plates of cakes, was second to none. When the laundry lady couldn't get to Brockhall Village, the new training centre, Blackburn gave her a job up at Ewood. Blackburn cared.

There's no them and us at Ewood Park between the players brought in and the old staff. It was a club where mutual respect reigned between all parties. Jack, a man of unimaginable wealth, walks about without an ounce of arrogance. That sets the tone. None of Blackburn's success would have been possible without Jack. He put his financial resources behind me and the stadium. With that sort of total support, the least I could contribute was my very best. I had the utmost respect for what Jack Walker was trying to do with Blackburn Rovers. I could see his genuine love for the club and the people of Blackburn.

Not even someone as powerful as Jack could wave a magic wand and change everything overnight. It was not perfect to begin with. We made the best of the facilities, or the lack of them. Players and staff laughed about them. Everyone was in the same position. Everyone held the same aim of lifting Blackburn up again. Everybody pulled together. At lunch time we used to sit upstairs in the John Lewis restaurant in the old stand, which some of the punters also used for lunches. They would pass by and say, 'Keep it going.' When we noticed more and more of them passing by, we knew Blackburn were on the up.

The facilities were poor but no one complained. The old training ground was dreadful, covered in dog mess. It was next to a crematorium and we had to move the goals because the balls kept going into cortèges. At our first week of training with Blackburn's players, Ray Harford scored a hat-trick in the practice match. In the second one, the two of us limped off. The players took it a bit too seriously. On Friday mornings, a few hundred people would come and watch us train, even though the conditions could be really icy. One morning, Ray Harford slid in to hook the ball back and knocked an old man up in the air. The crowds thinned a bit after that incident.

Press conferences took place in an old terraced house over the road. There were snide comments in the press about the facilities, which really irritated me. That's why Jack was spending millions to develop Ewood. The press facilities there now are second to none.

Blackburn's upward movement made it inevitable that Rovers would attract a lot of speculation. The important thing was that the players knew we would tell them what was happening but not the press. When I arrived at Ewood, I warned the staff about potential pitfalls.

'Let the team do the club's talking with their football,' I told them. 'We don't need to go high-profile, just stay the way you are. Don't ever forget your roots and don't ever change. Be the same people you have always been.'

That's what had attracted me to the people at Blackburn, their integrity.

I met the players before the Plymouth game, the day I was introduced to the press. They beat Plymouth and afterwards we sat down to identify the players we needed. With Stuart Munro injured, there was an obvious problem at left-back so we im-mediately signed Alan Wright from Blackpool. Blackburn's reputation quickly changed. They had tried to get Gary Lineker before I was associated with the club, but didn't even get a look-in. People thought they were kidding but Blackburn were serious. When I took the job people began to think: 'Hold on, Blackburn are genuine about this. If they weren't serious, Kenny Dalglish wouldn't have gone there.' So that helped attract good players.

We got some players in, got ourselves organised and off we

trotted. Then it started to snowball. Soon Blackburn sat on top of the Football League, heading for the Premier League. I don't know what goals Jack had set. I just told him I would try my best. In the back of my mind, I was thinking: 'Well, it would be fair enough if we went up next year. We might have a better chance with a full season.' But nevertheless, while there was a chance that season, we thought we might as well have a real go. We went top, then hit a brick wall and started losing games. Funnily enough, we were playing better when we weren't winning. The delight that it brought some journalists to see a team of mine struggle made me even more determined. It was some problem they had with me. I explained this to the players, so they understood that it was me the journalists were wanting to crucify, not them. We got back on the winning path, and beat Plymouth 3–1 to reach the play-offs.

The players had done magnificently in recovering the way they did. David Speedie was vital to our cause. Everyone made massive contributions but his was easily seen by looking at the scoring charts. Colin Hendry was vital too. It was easy for him to come back to Blackburn, because that was where he was before an unhappy spell at Manchester City. We knew Colin's heart was in the right place. He wanted to play for Blackburn. What a magnificent servant Colin Hendry has proved to be for Blackburn. Gordan Cowans was good as gold, too. These were good, experienced players, the backbone of the team. The captain was Kevin Moran, who was very helpful to Ray and me. Anything we tried to do, he helped put it over to the players. Bobby Mimms played really well in goal but unfortunately got injured. Mike Newell and Tim Sherwood came in and some of the local lads got a bit of a run, players like Jason Wilcox, David May, Lee Richardson, Nicky Reed and Scott Sellars.

In the play-offs, we started appallingly against Derby. We went 2–0 down before running out 4–2 winners. The second leg was really nerve-racking. I thought I was OK, until just before kick-off, in the dugout. There was something on my shirt and as I went to rub it off, I felt my heart pounding away. Kevin Moran headed one in to get us out of trouble, which was a relief. I had only been in the job from October to May and I was determined not to get myself into the state that had forced me out of Liverpool. Sadly

Bill Fox, the chairman, never saw us reach Wembley. He had been ill but had tried to keep going. I can remember him in his office, hardly able to breathe. I would tell him to go home and get well. The only regret of the whole season was that Bill Fox was not alive to witness Blackburn's promotion. It was ironic that he hated the concept of the Premier League. I don't think Bill would have hated it after Blackburn had won it. Bill disliked the élitism but he was resigned to its inevitability.

Going to Wembley in May was a familiar trip, although this had a different feeling. It was my first and last play-off. Before we left the hotel for Wembley, I told our new chairman, Robert Coar, who had followed Bill, that I was going to let Tony Parkes lead Blackburn out against Leicester City. Tony had been at Rovers for 25 years. Instead of giving him a gold watch, it would be better to let him take the team out. Tony never knew. We were all in the dressing-room. I let Tony put his training gear on and then said: 'Come on, Tony, get a suit on.'

'What?' he said.

'You take them out.'

'Thanks,' Tony replied.

He didn't need to say any more. I knew how much it meant to him. It was a small gesture of thanks for everything he had done for Blackburn during my brief time and for years before that. To take a team out at Wembley was nothing new to me; Ray had done it before as well. I appreciated what an honour it was and there was none more deserving of it than Tony Parkes.

Throughout the day, I had a feeling in my stomach that we were going to get through. Mike Newell got a penalty, put it away. Leicester bombarded us in the second half. Colin knocked a few off the line. Mike had a second penalty saved. We enjoyed a bit of good fortune and were at last up in the Premier League. Afterwards we went back to a pub in Blackburn. I think everyone in Blackburn was there – directors, players, staff, punters, Kelly and Paul. You couldn't move. Once you got a spot that was it. The only way you could get in and out was through a window. It was a brilliant night.

It was time to think ahead. One group of players had got us promotion but not all of them were equipped to take us a stage further. Buying players who were better than the ones we had was not just a philosophy I had learned at Liverpool. It was common sense. We were trading up. So that summer we made a key move by bringing in Alan Shearer, who was clearly better than the strikers we had at that time. Ray worked with him at the Toulon Under-21 tournament and had first-hand knowledge of Alan's talent. We had gone for Alan the season before our promotion, but Southampton said he wasn't available. When we went up I tried again and was successful. When we met Alan, the most important thing was that he really wanted to come and play for Blackburn Rovers. He asked us to take him up to Ewood. He wanted to get a feel for the place. Of course Alan got well paid but it wasn't finance that motivated him to come to Blackburn.

The interest in money varies between players. Money was not important to me as a footballer. It was more important for me to be happy. If you are happy and well paid, you have the best of both worlds. We tried to give that to Alan. He's got the ability, he's had the plaudits, he's endured a bad injury and yet remained a really nice fellow. Alan's kept his credibility and his hunger to be successful. He seemed to embody Blackburn Rovers – genuine, down-to-earth but ambitious. Alan came from a tight-knit family home in Newcastle. He was brought up the family way at Southampton. I think he was attracted to Blackburn's family feel.

There was competition for Alan's signature; if there hadn't been competition, there must have been a few people wandering around with blindfolds on. Manchester United may have wanted Shearer but they never put a bid in for him. Anyway, part of the agreement was that Southampton wanted David Speedie, and we were the ones with Speedie. It was sad to lose him; he was brilliant for Blackburn. I told Speedo how much we appreciated his contributions, his 23 goals in 36 games. The perfect scenario would have been to give Southampton the cash and keep Speedo, but we had to sacrifice him. The game before Alan's debut was a pre-season friendly at Darlington. Blackburn's fans were chanting 'Speedie, Speedie'. Two days later, Alan joined us for our friendly at Hibs. Rovers' supporters were soon chanting 'Shearer, Shearer'. I have lost count of the times I have heard them walking in a 'Shearer-wonderland'.

Spending so much money on a player of Alan's stature made people think Blackburn were now a force to be reckoned with. We got some stick for the record money paid, £3.3 million. That didn't bother me. I didn't feel I was inflating transfer fees. Fergie paid £2.3 million for a centre-back four or five years before that. Gary Pallister hadn't even been capped but Fergie knew that was who he wanted. Everyone would have paid what we did for Alan. Blackburn were slaughtered for buying so many players. There was so much speculation over who I was supposed to be chasing that I lost track myself of who I was really interested in. I would love to count up the number of players we were associated with, compare it to the number we bought, and see what percentage was correct. I didn't even buy as many players as I could have done. I could always find a player a wee bit better than the one I already had.

It was a misconception about the wages Blackburn were supposed to be paying players. Many of the figures bandied about were miles off the mark. These writers never even thought about figures; they just put x thousand a week. Both the journalists and the figures they invented were way over the top. When other clubs competed with us for a player, they were terrified because they believed what they read in the papers about how much Blackburn were supposed to be offering. When we got back to talk to players, we discovered they were being offered fortunes by other clubs. Much, much more than Blackburn were paying. We were pretty responsible. I said to the board: 'Look, you pay the wages you think you can pay. The last thing I want is for you to give me money to buy players and then you can't afford their wages. Never mind the money you have for the transfer market, it's what money you have to pay the wages.' I didn't want Blackburn to have a financial noose around their neck. If they did their sums right, it was not going to be a problem. It was the board's responsibility not mine.

Because of Jack Walker's well-known wealth, some players we talked to made financial demands that were ridiculous. They just wanted a slice of Jack's fortune. We could say to them, in all honesty, that it wasn't true, there weren't vast funds for wages, and we could substantiate it. We would tell these players: 'You ask for what you want, but we'll tell you what we can give you – take it or leave it.' Some of them went elsewhere. The way Blackburn conducted themselves was totally above board and honest. If someone turned us down, fair enough. They are professionals and, as in any other profession, they can work where they wish.

When considering whether to buy a player, I thought of his re-sale value. We bought young players because of that, and because we were a young club. We wanted to grow up together. But Blackburn also bought experience. There was a good balance. Colin Hendry wasn't young when he returned to Ewood and he has been magnificent. His hunger is second to none. We usually looked for players on their way up, players with a future, like Blackburn. Alan Shearer had been capped once. Graeme Le Saux was in Chelsea's reserves when he came to Blackburn in March 1993. It was only a matter of time before Tim Flowers became an England goalkeeper. Colin hadn't got much recognition at inter-national level; now he has. Henning Berg was in and out of the Norwegian team. Stuart Ripley was uncapped when he arrived at the same time as Alan. He and Jason Wilcox made a great contribution to Shearer's, and Blackburn's, success. The respect that other people had for our two wingers was unbelievable. Stuart is a bright boy – he's got A-level French.

We were building a good team. Ray and I knew it would take time. Liverpool's foundations weren't laid in a day. It was an emotional moment returning to Anfield on 15 December, 1992, almost a defining moment of how far Blackburn had come and how far we had to go. Of course, I had been back to Liverpool since resigning but going there as an away manager felt really strange. Wanting Liverpool to lose for the first time was an odd sensation, too.

I got a great reception when I walked into Anfield. The staff were very welcoming. There hadn't been many changes. Fred, who used to do the tickets at the players' entrance, chatted away to me – he thought I'd never been away. Liverpool's family spirit glowed as strongly as ever. All these people I had worked with, from catering staff to coaches, players and directors, greeted me with: 'Good to see you back, Kenny. Hope you get beat.' I was touched. Then I had to make the unfamiliar journey to the away dressing-room. I had been there once before, when Scotland played Wales in that famous World Cup qualifier in 1977. I knew where it was. It still felt strange. The players got changed, I gave my talk, and suddenly it was time to go out on to the pitch. I walked down the corridor towards the 'This Is Anfield' sign. Previously, I always touched the sign for luck. I didn't touch the sign this time because Anfield wasn't my place any more.

It was a great feeling emerging from the tunnel. The reception outside was as warm as the reception inside. It felt like I had never been away – the Kop were chanting my name. That was a magnificent gesture. The Kop then did what you would expect them to; they gave Graeme Souness a great shout. As witnessed when Arsenal won the championship at Anfield, or when smaller teams got a result there, Liverpool supporters could appreciate other teams, but they never let anyone forget where their real loyalty lay. So they sang Souey's name, which was great. There was no problem between me and Graeme. I had decided to resign and Liverpool had chosen to give Graeme my old job.

As usual, the Liverpool dugout leant over to greet the visitors. Ronnie Moran shook my hand, held on to it, and tried to drag me into the Liverpool dugout. It was just a bit of fun. It was an emotional experience for me but I was more concerned with what it was going to be like for the players. With me coming back to Liverpool, there was always going to be a lot of hype. In a way, it was beneficial that the focus was on me not Blackburn's players. They could carry on with their preparations and not be distracted. It was encouraging the way the players responded to it. We lost 2–1 but my players did themselves proud. It was nice not to be embarrassed on my return to the club I still feel so strongly about.

Blackburn were always trying to improve the team. When Alan Wright got a problem with a hernia, we found ourselves short of a left-back. I always had half an inkling for Le Saux. He'd thrown his shirt at someone at Chelsea but that didn't worry me. Obviously, I want players to show respect, but I like them to have a bit of fire in their belly. Graeme's a nice lad, with a range of interests, including books and art; maybe a bit different from other players, but any walk of life has different personalities. You are not going to walk into an office and find everybody with the same interests. Graeme has come to Blackburn and done brilliantly, progressing to the England squad.

The real loss that year was Shearer, injured against Leeds in December. He didn't play again in the League but still finished our top scorer. Without Alan, Blackburn finished fourth. On the last day of our first Premier League season we beat Sheffield Wednesday at Ewood. Afterwards, we went round the pitch waving to the fans. Halfway round I said to Ray: 'This is the first time I've been on a lap of honour for finishing fourth.' The championship had been won by Manchester United and deservedly so. I was pleased for Fergie. He had also endured a lot so he deserved his success. But Blackburn's achievement in finishing fourth was still greater than United's in finishing first. We'd come up a division, they'd only come up a place. Blackburn came from nowhere. United played in a cathedral. Our ground was a building site. The only club I can remember having such a good first season is Nottingham Forest when they got up into the First Division and won it in 1978. We only just missed out on Europe.

For a newly promoted club, finishing fourth was pretty impressive. We spent the whole season looking at the fixture list to see who was coming up next – United, Liverpool, Leeds, Arsenal. Every match was tough. Blackburn's success was helped by the magical atmosphere in the dressing-room. Everybody helped each other. The new boys were helped to settle in by lads who had only just settled in themselves. It was easy for guys like Ray and me to do our jobs when there were so many good characters in the dressing-room.

Back at Anfield, the season finished on a less happy note with mounting criticism of Graeme. My name was linked with a return, which was nonsense. The press thought I went on a golfing holiday with David Moores, Liverpool's chairman. The truth is less dramatic. I had bumped into David at a game and mentioned I was off to Marbella in a couple of days.

'I'm going to Marbella then,' David replied. 'We'll have lunch.'

So we met up for lunch and a drink in Marbella. The story about us discussing Liverpool was rubbish. Why should I meet David Moores in Marbella when he lives two miles up the road? I've had drinks with David in restaurants in Southport. We talk about games but he would never discuss business matters. David Moores was 100 per cent loyal to Graeme and he's given the same complete support to Roy Evans. That whole story was a big insult to David Moores, Graeme and me.

It gave me no satisfaction to see Liverpool being slaughtered from every quarter. Graeme was harshly criticised. Graeme said he had inherited an ageing team from me, a suggestion I cannot allow to stand unanswered. Their ages were there for everyone to see, but there was still a great deal of life left in them as footballers. Apart from Glenn Hysen, who returned to Sweden to join Gais, and David Speedie, who through permanent and loan moves helped Blackburn, Leicester and West Ham into the Premiership, the others continued in the Premiership, underlining their ability in the top flight. They included Peter Beardsley, Steve Staunton, Gary Gillespie (who went to Coventry via Celtic), Barry Venison, Ray Houghton, Gary Ablett and Steve McMahon. At the same time we were obviously conscious of the fact that you need young players and I signed Don Hutchison, Jamie Redknapp and Steve Harkness. With an eye to the future, Robbie Fowler and Steve McManaman also came to Liverpool FC. As mentioned before, some people said that Jimmy Carter was a bad buy on my part, but Liverpool sold him to Arsenal for £500,000. A team considered old were top of the League when I left. Graeme Souness won the FA Cup within a year. He should take the credit for that; so I should not take any criticism for an ageing team.

Back at Blackburn, we had Shearer on the road to recovery. The most difficult part was restraining Alan at the start of the 1993–94 season. He had done so well in pre-season training that we took him on tour to Ireland. In training at Drogheda one day, Alan tore into a real bone-cruncher of a tackle. Normally there was never much tackling in training. I thought: 'Al's trying to tell us he's all right.' I asked him if he fancied being on the bench for our next friendly. He was naturally very keen.

'Well, just go on the bench,' I told Al, 'but don't be bending my ear with "When am I getting on, boss?" Just sit and enjoy the game.'

Al promised he would. Anyway, I had it in my mind that I was going to put him on. With 15 minutes to go I turned to Ray and said: 'Let's throw Alan on.'

'I don't know,' Ray said, being cautious.

'What's the difference?' I said. 'Let's see how ready he is.'

So I said to Alan: 'Do you want to get on?' He was up like a shot. Went on and scored twice. Typical Alan.

We still had to protect him and also be fair to the rest of the lads, who started the season quite well. So Alan was eased back in, playing games as sub. Al was dying to be more involved, particularly after coming on and scoring against Newcastle, who were his team as a kid. I would rather he was champing at the bit than saying 'oh no, I'm not ready'. Psychologically, it was useful having Alan as a sub. Opposing players would think: 'Jesus, even if I'm doing well against these, they've still got Shearer to come on.'

Ray and I knew we still needed new players. Paul Warhurst came in September; Ian Pearce and David Batty in October. I knew all about Batts, having played in the same team as him when he was 18. Rushie and I turned out for Leeds against Everton in a testimonial for John Charles and Bobby Collins. Batty is a really good player, a good passer. Howard Wilkinson curbed his style at Leeds, made Batts more disciplined than expansive. He was a good complement to Gary McAllister. Someone told me he might be available so I phoned Howard up. Howard was in a bad position. Leeds had a problem with finance, needed the money quick, so the deal was done in 24 hours. Batty is a real Leeds lad and probably didn't want to leave Elland Road.

'That's football,' I said to Batts. 'Howard doesn't want you to go from a footballing point of view, but there's a problem with finance.'

The timing of the deal was right for Leeds and us, even if it all came about for Leeds for the wrong reason.

Blackburn were also in the market for a good goalkeeper. That meant Tim Flowers, one of the best around. Liverpool were also in for him. Tim is very friendly with Alan so when Ian Branfoot, Southampton's manager, asked him where he wanted to go, he said Blackburn. 'OK,' said Branfoot, who then went and phoned Liverpool, trying to sell Tim to them. Graeme was interested and even offered David James in part-exchange, but Tim wanted to come to Blackburn and he has proved to be an important signing for us. He spent much of his early career working with Peter Shilton at Southampton and works very hard. Tim's on a par with David Seaman and Peter Schmeichel. He hasn't conceded many daft goals since signing for Blackburn. The first bad goal Tim let in was the one against Sweden at Elland Road – and that was for England, some time after signing for us.

Just after we bought Tim, Marina was complaining I hadn't bought her any flowers.

'What are you talking about?' I replied. 'I've just spent two million quid on Flowers. I can't do much better than that for you.'

A few nights later, Marina and I were on the Orient Express which was running an excursion around Derbyshire. David Moores was on it too. He sent an orchid over for Marina. Marina sent a wee note back saying: 'Is that all you can send me? When Kenny goes out for Flowers he spends two million quid.' David took it in the spirit it was meant.

We finished second to United that season, two places higher than the previous year. The one really disappointing result came in the FA Cup, when we lost at home to Charlton in the fourth round. You would expect to beat a team from the First Division. People said that Charlton played as if they had nothing to lose. That's a fallacy. Smaller teams always have something to lose, even if it's only money. The rewards of a cup run are even more important for a smaller club. Blackburn should have been a good cup team because we always tried to be difficult to beat. But you need a bit of luck. Maybe the luck we missed in the Cup, we got in the League. Liverpool weren't lucky in the FA Cup for 20-odd years but the championships kept coming in. It was about to come to Blackburn.

=15=

BLACKBURN'S CHAMPIONSHIP

For the championship to come to Ewood, for us to outlast Manchester United, Blackburn required players of quality. Chris Sutton, playing marvellously for Norwich, was exactly who we needed. He was so adaptable. The previous season, Rovers drew 2–2 with Norwich when Chris had done very well. He impressed me in his role up front, a change from his old position of centre-half. Sometimes when footballers acquire the taste for goals it's difficult to get them back in defence. The one time Chris went back to defending, when we had a defender dismissed, he was brilliant. But the glory is up front, scoring goals and making headlines.

The options Chris offered looked even more attractive when David May, one of our centre-halves, left. David May's contract had expired and we couldn't agree terms. Fergie stepped in and signed May, although United weren't exactly short of good centre-halves. They had Steve Bruce, Gary Pallister, Paul Parker and Gary Neville. Fergie probably thought he needed cover but I'm sure, in the back of his mind, there must have been the thought that 'us buying David May weakens Blackburn a wee bit'; which didn't prove to be true. Anyway, we got Ian Pearce in, who was brilliant.

Fergie beat us in the Charity Shield at the start of the season, but we had so many players out injured that the game didn't provide a realistic taste of how the season would pan out.

The only lesson to be learned was that the referees were cracking down after the American World Cup. I had been to see Philip Don before the kick-off, with Brian Kidd, Fergie's No 2. It was just the normal pre-match chat. I had missed an earlier meeting to discuss with all the referees the implications of the World Cup. Philip Don had also just returned from holidays.

'What's the change in the interpretation of rules?' I asked Don.

'None,' he said.

'So there's no change?'

'No,' Don said.

'Very good,' I said and went off.

There were about seven booked in the first half. It was ridiculous. It set the tone for a season of red and yellow.

Blackburn did not enjoy much luck with referees against United that season. The important refereeing decisions could have helped our cause if they had been favourable. We were hard done by on two occasions against our closest rivals, costing us at Ewood Park and Old Trafford. Henning Berg was sent off at home, for colliding with Lee Sharpe, a bad decision by Gerald Ashby. We had been leading 1–0 and eventually lost. At their place, Tim Sherwood's legitimate goal which would have given us a point was chalked off. The cause? Alan Shearer fouling Roy Keane. That was a ridiculous decision. Their players' lack of reaction told it was a good challenge. There was another bad decision at Elland Road, which denied us points. Alan was brought down in Leeds's box but the referee never gave the penalty. Shearer was never going to dive – he was six yards out with only the goalie to beat and somebody square of him. Why should he go down? That could have been a vital decision against us. We would have gone 2–0 up. But I suppose it makes Blackburn's eventual success all the more honourable.

It was just as well the League worked out for us because we had no joy in the cups. The hysteria that followed our UEFA Cup defeat to Trelleborgs was a bit over the top. We had enough chances to win the Trelleborgs game. Without trying to justify the manner of our dismissal, Trelleborgs were a half-decent team. In the next round they had what looked like a legitimate goal cancelled at home to Lazio. When they went to Rome, they lost to a goal in the fifth minute of injury time. I know we didn't cover ourselves in glory but Trelleborgs were a well-organised side to run Lazio that close. Our critics even wondered whether Blackburn's approach was suited to Europe. In fact, at home against Trelleborgs, we had more than 20 shots at goal. Not to score from one of those was a wee bit unusual. The Trelleborgs players even had a pop at us. On the night we were poor, but the pundits were ridiculous. After that result, they said: 'Money can't buy success.' At the end of the season, the same guys said: 'Money won the title.' That's crazily inconsistent. I had a discussion with BBC Radio Five's Alan Green over Trelleborgs. I thought that his radio comments were disgraceful. He decried the players; and Blackburn and me for spending the money on those players. It wasn't constructive criticism. When I bumped into him at Ewood, we both had our say. If I saw Alan Green now I would still talk to him, but I didn't appreciate Alan Green's judgement.

We went out to Liverpool in the Coca-Cola Cup and to Newcastle in the FA Cup. Predictably, we received more criticism but they were hardly two bad teams to go out to. We gave a good account of ourselves against Liverpool, but Rushie was on fire, scoring a hat-trick, one of them a great volley. After the game Roy Evans, who had succeeded Graeme, said that Alan kept backing into Neil Ruddock. Shearer has never hurt anybody, certainly not big Razor, who is one of his best friends. Maybe Roy was simply playing a psychological game, trying to plant a seed in referees' minds to help Liverpool's cause because they would play Blackburn again soon. It was funny hearing Roy say what he did. Nobody used their backside more than I did while I was in Liverpool's employ as a player. Roy never complained then. Before Roy, Bob Paisley used to use psychology. He used to throw comments out to the press, to get reported. Bob did it for our benefit, maybe to give us a kick up the backside or a bit of encouragement. Bob loved to say, 'I'll give the other team a bit of toffee', which meant a compliment. That praise might lull them into a false sense of security, which he thought might be beneficial to us. If you say harsh things about another team, they will be doubly determined to beat you. Roy was a lieutenant of Bob's; he knew this psychological game. Maybe Roy was trying to emulate Bob. Psychology is a very important part of football management.

Fergie tried to use psychology during the championship run-in. People would ask me what I thought about Fergie's comments.

'I've been there,' I said, 'I've seen it, I've done it. What Fergie is doing has no effect on me.'

I occasionally turned it back on him. When he said Blackburn needed to 'do a Devon Loch', I replied: 'Is that an expanse of water in Scotland?' Devon Loch was the horse who inexplicably fell while leading the Grand National, which I knew perfectly well, but I wasn't going to let Fergie know. So it just fell flat for Fergie, as flat as Devon Loch in fact! The moment you have to explain a clever comment like that, it's lost, backfired completely. It was a compliment to us that Fergie was trying those sort of tactics. United couldn't do anything against us on the pitch so he was trying to intimidate us. They needed us to slip up, so they tried anything to sow seeds of doubt. In our dressing-room, the players had a laugh about United's mind games. At the end of the season, Fergie wrote me a nice letter congratulating me and Blackburn on our success. At the end was a PS – 'Devon Loch is a horse! I'm sure your Dad must have backed it . . . mine did!'

Blackburn's players definitely did have a touch of the jitters. The championship was somewhere only David Batty had been before. It was so close that they wanted to reach out and grab it. When you can't quite grab it there is bound to be frustration. That's when doubt creeps in.

It was unbelievably tense. The worst game Blackburn played that season came in April at Goodison. We led 2–0 very early on. Everton pulled one back, then battered us. In the last minute, with the score at 2–1, Alan Shearer booted the ball almost out of Goodison. It was ugly but it showed that the players didn't want to lose. Everton fans booed us off. That was a fair reaction from a purist perspective. It's cynical to say 'never mind the quality, feel the three points' but at that stage it's true. It would have been lovely to have played more of a passing game but it was a fierce struggle out there. Everton were also fighting for

The Manchester United Football Club plc

AF/LL

22 May 1995

Mr K Dalglish
BLACKBURN ROVERS FOOTBALL CLUB
Ewood Park
Blackburn

Dear Kenny

Now that the season is finally over I just wanted to drop you a wee line to congratulate you and your team on winning the Premier League Championship, and I'm sure that the last few games got your pulse racing........I know it did mine.

To win the Premier League is certainly an achievement, and I know that you will all still be on cloud nine, along with the whole of Blackburn, who have waited such a long time for the glory days to return to the town. I know that when we won the Championship after 26 years it seemed that the city of Manchester just partied for days, a truly wonderful feeling and I could go to bed at night and sleep!

Please pass on my good wishes to all your lads, it was a thrilling season right up to the final whistle!

Yours sincerely

Alex Ferguson

Alex Ferguson C.B.E.
Manager

PS: Devon Loch is a horse! I'm sure your Dad must have backed it...... mine did!

Manager - Alex Ferguson CBE, Secretary - Kenneth R. Merrett
Telephone 0161 872 1661   Ticket & Match Enquiries 0161 872 0199   Facsimile 0161 876 5502
The Manchester United Football Club plc, Sir Matt Busby Way, Old Trafford, Manchester, M16 0RA
Chairman & Chief Executive: C.M. Edwards, Directors: J.M. Edelson, Sir Bobby. Charlton CBE, E.M. Watkins, R.L. Olive, R.P. Launders.
Registered No. 95489 England VAT No. 561 0952 51

their lives. No one could criticise Blackburn's determination and desire not to lose. Everyone would love to play the way Liverpool or Manchester United play. During the season we did play like them; but certainly not against Everton. Our aim was to win the championship.

The run-in was very tense and not helped by former players of mine scoring against us, even before we reached Liverpool on that climactic last day. There were three games in succession in which former players of mine scored. For Manchester City it was Paul Walsh; Ray Houghton did it for Crystal Palace and Don Hutchison for West Ham. Then came Newcastle, the penultimate game of the season. Peter Beardsley stopped the rot that night! When he hit an amazing shot, first time and rising viciously, I thought: 'There's another ex-player scoring against me.' Fortunately for the hopes and nerves of everyone at Blackburn, Tim Flowers was in unbelievable form, making a magnificent save and keeping us in it. After the match, Tim was interviewed on television. The guy from Sky asked him a simple question about something else and Tim just came out with: 'Don't talk to me about bottle.' The psychology had reached the stage where people had questioned our bottle. Tim almost shouted that the performance showed Blackburn had bottle. It was like he wanted to answer Manchester United's continual questioning. Tim had played so well against Newcastle and his adrenalin was pumping. He couldn't get his words out quick enough. He was really away. Tim must have sat down afterwards and thought, 'What have I done?' He certainly got a bit of stick from the other players. Because Tim kept going on about bottle, they called him 'Ernie, the fastest milkman in the West'. The humour was a good way to release the tension.

The mind games intensified as the last day of the season approached. Manchester United had to win at West Ham, and hoped we couldn't at Liverpool, so they put every ounce of pressure on us. Suddenly there was all this paranoia about Liverpool wanting to do us a turn, to help me and spite United. You can imagine what the people on Merseyside thought on hearing Fergie saying complimentary things about Liverpool, saying how he was sure everything would be above

I may have left Liverpool but the city and club will always be part of me.

Ronnie Moran (left) and Roy Evans, both vital to Liverpool's success.

The goalmouth in front of the Kop became a shrine of tributes after Hillsborough.

So many people brought flowers to Anfield.

The aftermath of Hillsborough: people immediately began gathering at the Shankly Gates.

Here I am taking the mike and thanking all the Liverpool people who turned up for my testimonial against Real Sociedad in 1990.

A rare smile for the press.

Different characters but two great players: Bruce Grobbelaar of Liverpool and Alan Shearer, here playing for Blackburn.

I loved being amongst the people, like here in October 1991 during Blackburn's game with Swindon.

I have so much respect for Ray Harford. I told Blackburn to get Ray and then I would join them.

Returning to Anfield is always an emotional experience; here I greet Graeme Souness, my successor.

Pre-season training in 1994, where the seeds of Blackburn's championship were sown.

I present Alan Shearer with the 1995 Player of the Year award at the PFA dinner.

More from behind the scenes at Ewood Park: Jack Walker, Ray Harford and I.

Alex Ferguson: who I admire as both a man and a manager.

Relaxation takes me to the golf course, here celebrating my only hole in one.

It was a great feeling to grip the championship trophy again in 1995. Doing it at Liverpool made it even more special.

board. It was all psychological. The Liverpool punters saw right through it. I don't have any animosity towards Fergie for using those tactics. I knew it was going to happen. It wasn't personal. The season before, when we finished second to United, Fergie told his players in October that Rovers were going to be the danger. He had respect for what we were doing at Blackburn. We were just competing against each other, doing the best for our clubs. We might not have been saying anything about Manchester United in the run-in, but we wanted them to lose every game. That's only natural.

On the Friday before the final Sunday trip to Anfield, the journalists who came up during the week, the national and local guys, challenged the staff to a game. It's always good to go through the season undefeated, so we arranged to play. Umbro supplied the reporters with kits, which was very nice of them, but the press lads didn't know whose kit it was until they opened up the box in the dressing-room. Their faces were a real picture. Umbro had sent them the Manchester United strip. We had drafted in a ringer: Asa Hartford, the reserve team coach who went to Stoke. We were more than a match for the press lads. Steve Millar, of the *Daily Mirror*, played in goal for them. His fingers were bent back towards his wrist from trying to stop shots. Steve had to type upside down afterwards. They really enjoyed it. We put a couple of beers on for them afterwards and I made a speech.

'Fergie will be proud of you,' I told them. 'You've worn those red shirts with pride.'

They had lost 16–0.

The big game was getting closer. The demand for tickets was hotting up. Stephen Hendry rang me up asking for some. He's a good friend but we began to have doubts about whether we were good for each other's careers. I had been to see him play in the UK Snooker Championships when Ronnie O'Sullivan beat him. I said to Stephen: 'I'm never coming to watch you play again because I'm real bad luck for you.' Stephen came to watch some Blackburn matches and we always lost. He said he was a Jonah for me.

'Can I come to the Newcastle game?' he said. 'Because I've never seen you win.'

'Dearie me,' I thought, 'that's a game we desperately need to win and we have a Jonah coming.'

Fortunately, Stephen phoned back and said: 'I can't come to the Newcastle game, but can I come to the Liverpool one?'

'Aye, no problem.'

So when we won against Newcastle, I was thinking: 'Oh, what's happening? Stephen didn't turn up and we won. Now he's coming to the Liverpool match which has the championship riding on it.'

Sunday dawned, and what a day it turned out to be. When I first went to Blackburn, I asked my son Paul: 'What would happen if the last game of the season is Liverpool–Blackburn; and Liverpool need to win to take the championship but Blackburn have to get a result to stay up. Which would you choose?'

Paul shrugged and said: 'I'd need to go for Liverpool to win.'

'But Paul,' I said, slightly shocked, 'we'd be relegated.'

'Well, you cannot blame me, can you?'

'What do you mean?' I said.

'Well, you brought me up to be a Liverpool fan. I've been going since I was six months old. I can't just turn because of that.'

'But, Paul, we'd be going down.'

'Well, maybe I would just want a draw, then.'

'Thanks,' I said to him, 'we'd still be relegated.'

That Sunday, 14 May, 1995, was the perfect day for Paul in the end – Liverpool won the game, we won the title and Manchester United won nothing. From the moment I woke up, I knew Blackburn were going to win the championship. It was such a strong feeling. It had to be us. If we couldn't win it before our fans at Ewood, the next best place was Anfield. It was a tremendous occasion; strange with it. During the first half, the guy just behind the dugout was wearing a Liverpool strip. When we came out for the second half he had a Blackburn kit on, shouting for us. That was the mood of Liverpool's supporters; they wanted us to lose the game but win the championship.

It was a tense match. Alan scored for us but then Barnsey equalised. Three Sky TV people were sitting in the tunnel with a television monitor, so I knew the score was one each at West Ham. Then Jamie Redknapp scored with that great free-kick, which never got the praise it deserved. What a free-kick it was. I looked at Jamie, who was shrugging his shoulders. There was no celebration from him. He must have been thinking: 'What have I done?' After all, it was me who had brought Jamie to Anfield. In the heat of the moment, some people thought that because we'd lost the game, we'd lost the League. I've seen the video many times with that poor guy behind the goal racked with misery and disbelief. They had forgotten that Manchester United needed to win. Suddenly, the guy who had changed strips shouted: 'It's over, it's over. Man U have drawn. You've won it. You've won it.' I shouted to the Sky guys: 'Is it finished at Upton Park?' They wouldn't answer me. I don't know why. Then there was a huge roar. It was true. United had failed to win. Bedlam broke out.

It was the perfect scenario. Everyone at Anfield could celebrate. Those who suggested or thought that Liverpool would lay down, either for my sake or to frustrate United, should feel embarrassed. Liverpool had never laid down before. They weren't going to start now. Everyone enjoyed how that day worked out – unless they were Man U supporters. It was unusual Manchester United asking Liverpool to do them a favour – and even more unusual Liverpool doing them a favour. It made the Scousers happier still that Manchester United couldn't even do themselves a favour. Ronnie, Roy and Sammy were really made up for us. Everyone was jumping into the dugout, hugging Ray and Tony. I ran down the tunnel to find Marina. I wanted to share the moment with her. On my way through Anfield, I bumped into Peter Robinson.

'Congratulations, Kenny,' he said, 'that's marvellous.'

Peter had this great big smile covering his face. I told him I was off to find Marina.

'I'll go and get Marina for you,' said Peter, his smile growing wider, 'and I'll get a kiss first.'

I ran back downstairs where I met Stephen Hendry.

'Told you I was a Jonah,' he said. 'You always lose when I see you!'

Anfield was a brilliant place to celebrate. Liverpool's players were overjoyed for us. Neil Ruddock piled in with the champagne. I missed the party in the dressing-room because I was away talking to the press, taking champagne up for the women, being as helpful as ever! Somebody had a phone so we called a restaurant in Preston where we'd provisionally booked, to tell them the celebration party was on. We needn't have rung. The guy who owns the restaurant is a Blackburn fan; Manchester City, too, so he particularly enjoyed our success. He knew we were coming. He was already celebrating. He saved some drink for us. It was a brilliant night. The Drifters were on in the cabaret, and we had a right good time. We all piled into this big, long room with a bar in one corner. People were dancing on the tables. Players, wives, dads, mums, brothers, sisters, families, punters who'd booked tables. Everybody. Blackburn had waited so long to celebrate the championship that there was almost a look of disbelief on people's faces. I was so happy for Jack, who was sitting there crying. Emotion overcame so many people. I thought of Peter White, the Rovers correspondent for the *Lancashire Evening Telegraph*. How long had he lived in the shadow of Burnley? Imagine the stick Peter must have taken working for the *Lancashire Evening Telegraph* with Burnley flying and Blackburn grounded. Then Jack comes in and it's lift-off.

It was a wild, emotional night. I don't think the conversations were too deep. It was not a night for analysis. I certainly didn't repeat what Bob Paisley did in Rome. Bob stayed sober because he wanted to get drunk on the atmosphere after Liverpool won the European Cup.

People wondered why Blackburn played a different way from my Liverpool teams. But that had to be the case; there were different players involved. We couldn't play Liverpool's style of football. That took years to achieve. Liverpool had been playing that way since Bill Shankly. We built teams to win games. The more games you win the more successful you are going to be. I can't understand people querying what Blackburn have achieved and the way we achieved it. When I went to Blackburn, we bought some players who got us up into the Premiership. Then we bought some other players who got us into a very respectable fourth position. The following season we bought in some more new players and ended up second. If it hadn't been for Blackburn that year, Manchester United would have won the thing out of sight. We were everyone's friend because we were the only ones who came out of the pack to challenge United. During my time as manager, we've added to our achievements every year. That should be acclaimed not abused. Blackburn have only been at it for four years. You cannot expect Rovers' playing style to be as developed as Liverpool's.

Blackburn achieved success through organisation, through having Shearer up front, through everyone giving everything to the cause. I thought we played sensible soccer as opposed to copying anyone else. Some of our goals and performances were magnificent. If you have to clear your lines, clear them, don't bring the ball down and play. When you can play, play. Blackburn had two wingers going down and getting crosses in. I would call that exciting. Stuart and Jason were real wingers, not wide midfielders. There was so much more to Blackburn than simply being hard to beat. No one gave us credit for our creativity. In our first season, we had one of the best passers in midfield in the country – Gordon Cowans. He went because of his age. Tim Sherwood came in; he was a good footballer. You couldn't say that a combination of Paul Warhurst and Sherwood was not a footballing central midfield. When Warhurst went off injured, Batty came in.

Blackburn's critics accused us of being a one-player team and very predictable. Alan's been a brilliant player for Blackburn but there have been other people who have made great contributions as well. When Alan wasn't playing, Mike Newell was prolific. Alan was the focus but only in the top third of the pitch. If you were able to stop Alan, you still had to deal with Chris Sutton. We were only predictable in that we were hard to beat. You could look at every team and say they are predictable. Liverpool are predictable because they will pass it. Steve McManaman is predictable because he will run with it. Manchester United are predictable because Eric Cantona is going to drop off into the hole, get the ball and give it to Ryan Giggs going down the left. That's really predictable, exciting and very dangerous. Trying to stop it is an even harder task. People said that other teams had different options from us but that's irrelevant. It's the quality of options that counts. We had great options. If you play to your strengths it doesn't matter how predictable you are, other sides have got to be good to beat you.

Some people said that Blackburn's success was artificial, that it was cash-based. What success isn't? The success of any club is cash-based, it just comes from a different source from Jack Walker. People say Crewe Alexandra are not cash-based. And they get a few hundred grand for a player to support the rest of the kids. Everything's cash-based. What's the problem with having cash? Jack Walker should be getting a town clock in his honour for putting that money into football. There isn't a team which hasn't bought the championship. It's irrelevant whether the purchases have come over a long or short period of time. Arsenal's championship-winning side was based around their youth team but they had bought Alan Smith, their top goalscorer, David Seaman and Steve Bould. That's the way forward. Blackburn didn't start the upward spiral of fees but we understand the damage it can do. If transfer fees were more realistic, you wouldn't see such an influx of foreigner players.

Even our increased support was accused of being artificial. We didn't know where the new supporters were coming from; we were just happy to see them. There is nothing wrong in going to watch success on your doorstep. If Blackburn people were criticised for going to watch other teams in the past, they can't be criticised for coming to watch their own team. What happened with Newcastle United when Kevin Keegan arrived to set the bandwagon rolling? Their attendances improved. Their people might have been going to other clubs before Kevin came back to St James's. So what, if some Blackburn people stopped going to Old Trafford, Bolton, Manchester City, Liverpool and Everton, to come and watch the club on their doorstep. We welcomed them. The important thing is to look at how the attendances went up; look at what Jack Walker has done for these people; look at the facilities he's built for them; look at the pride he's given them in the town.

There is no other ground which has improved its attendance by 300 per cent in four years like Ewood has. We get great crowds for European ties, given the catchment area – 20,000 is magnificent for a town the size of Blackburn. Rovers let kids in cheaply, under the supervision of adults. Those seats would be empty otherwise. Manchester United can't do that because they haven't got any empty seats. Liverpool might not be able to do that. But there should be a section at all the big clubs for the guy who can't afford a season-ticket but wants to support his team when he has a few quid to spare. Rovers do that. Blackburn are one of the success stories of modern times.

—16—

STEPPING DOWN

I WAS CLOSE TO leaving Blackburn Rovers before we won the championship. At the start of that 1994–95 season, when my three-year agreement still had a few months to run, Blackburn's board offered me a new deal. I refused. Blackburn had reservations about me working on a week-to-week basis, which I wanted. I understood the board's concern, but being without a contract gave me greater control of my situation. I did not want a week-to-week arrangement so I could slip off if another job was offered to me. I would never have left Blackburn in the lurch. I wasn't thinking of leaving. I just preferred the freedom so if I wanted to go, I could.

A two-year contract is a major commitment. Leaving suddenly would have been less irresponsible if I was on a week-to-week contract; and it works both ways. If things had gone badly, and Blackburn had decided to sack me, it would have been easier and cheaper for them. But Blackburn didn't think it was a good idea, and eventually, I agreed to stay until the end of the season. If it hadn't been resolved, I would have left Blackburn three months into the season which turned out to be their championship one. If I had left, just look at what I would have missed!

Blackburn and I could trust each other. But even before the end of the season, while the championship was still in the balance, I had decided to stand down. Five days after we won the League, I met the chairman, Robert Coar, at Brockhall.

'There's no point in being anything other than open with you,' I told the chairman. 'I don't want to continue as manager. I don't want the team responsibility or heavy day-to-day involvement.'

There was not a lot Robert could do or say. My contract had expired. I could have climbed in my car and never seen Blackburn again. Blackburn had no option really. From the moment I arrived at Ewood Park, Jack Walker talked about having a five-year plan for the championship, but I only had a three-year contract. I couldn't work that one out. Anyway, I had brought them the championship earlier than Jack expected, and I wanted a lighter workload.

It wasn't difficult stepping down, because my mind had been made up some time before. When you have won a trophy the next step is to win it again. That was always the way at Anfield. Liverpool's players would come in for pre-season training to be greeted with the words: 'Last season means nothing. Let's go out and do it all over again.' But I had no desire to do that. I did not crave another trophy after Blackburn won the championship. I was leaving anyway, whether we attained our championship goal or not. The right time to go is always when you want to go, and I felt that time had come. I didn't tell Blackburn until after the end of the season because I didn't want to rock the boat. It wouldn't have been fair to have knowledge of my pending departure circulating inside the club in advance. I didn't want to put the board in an invidious position, where they might have had to lie. If the news had spread, it wouldn't have helped the players as they tried to win the championship.

My overwhelming aim was to keep as much pressure away from the players as possible. I tried to take as much of it as I could upon myself. People found it odd that I rejected a chance to manage a team in the European Cup, a competition I worshipped as a player. Europe wasn't an attraction for me at that time. I had had enough of the daily grind. I didn't want that anymore. I just couldn't be bothered. Blackburn had no cause to complain – during my time there we won promotion, finished fourth, second and then first, and I had extended my original contract.

The youth-development side had also taken off. At the same time as I was buying Gordon Cowans and building up the first team, we were very concerned about improving the youth scene. Alan Irvine joined the staff to work with Jim Furnell. In the second year, Jim Furnell moved up to co-ordinate the youth side while Alan Irvine worked with the boys on the pitch. When Jack invested in the training ground, he retained two houses as hostels for the kids to live in. I had reorganised the scouting side to spread the net all over Britain. With the first team doing well, good youngsters were attracted to Blackburn. I tried to meet all of those who were signing. We went about our youth work quietly. Via word of mouth, parents and young players learned that Blackburn was a good place to come. Re-building the youth system was very important. Blackburn's youth policy can now stand comparison with any other club, with the exception of Manchester United who have been at it longer. It would have been easy to ignore the kids because with Jack's finance we could buy the players we wanted, but it would have been irresponsible. The money could have dried up.

Some people believe that the reason for my standing down was that I had fallen out with Jack, but my relationship with him never changed. It was a working relationship: employer–employee. I admire him. After Blackburn won promotion, I flew across to Jersey to play in a golf tournament Jack sponsored. It came over loud and clear then how much of a Blackburn fan he was. No other club interested him. Only Blackburn. None of the club's success would have been possible without Jack. He wasn't on an ego trip. The huge amount of money he has poured into Blackburn is not an investment. It's a show of love, a gift. Jack gave the club success which gave the town success.

Jack's a fan. Every Saturday, he would come into the dressing-room. 'What's the team?' Jack would ask. He shook hands with all the lads, wished us all luck. Afterwards he would come in to say well done, or unlucky. If we were crap, he wouldn't say anything. He didn't need to. But Jack never came in and tried to take over. If we were having a meeting after the game, Jack wouldn't come in. There was no interference whatsoever. Jack never sat down and talked football with me or the players. He had his own opinions, but kept them for the privacy of some place else. They weren't heard in the dressing-room, which is a help to any manager.

A look at his reported wealth tells you that Jack's a very astute businessman. Jack and I had disagreements over transfers. That was inevitable. People's opinions differ and, after all, it was his money. It was said that Jack was only prepared to invest money in players who were young and English, because of their re-sale value. But we signed Gordon Cowans and Chris Price, who weren't young. We signed Colin Hendry who wasn't young and certainly isn't English. Henning Berg and Patrik Andersson are Scandinavian. Jack's money also bought Robbie Slater, Jeff Kenna and Kevin Gallacher: an Australian, an Irishman and a Scot. If you are a businessman, and Jack is a very good one, you have to look for a return. Being a football manager is no different. Of course we took re-sale into account, but you can't buy a 19-year-old kid with a 29-year-old's head on him, unless his name is Alan Shearer. If we needed experienced campaigners Jack would give me the finance.

Jack's straight. At our first meeting, Jack said to me: 'If you want to buy players, the money is there. As long as everything is above board and within reason, you don't have a problem with getting money to buy players.' When I had decided on a player I wanted, I would go to the chairman, who was my contact with Jack. The chairman would find out if the finance was there. If the response was positive, he would negotiate with the other club until we got permission to speak to the player. Then I would get involved. The chairman had the final word on the details of the player's contract. It was a very straightforward system.

My relationship with Jack was based on mutual respect and trust. There were temporary differences, but I still got on with my work. Jack signed the cheques so I couldn't do anything against his will, nor would I have tried. Sometimes Jack would say there was money available, sometimes there wasn't. That's the same at any club. I wanted to bring in Geoff Thomas from Crystal Palace in 1992. We played the first game of that season at Palace and obviously, Palace did not want Thomas to move until after the game. When we were down at Selhurst Park, the chairman had discussions about Thomas with Ron Noades, Palace's chairman, and as a consequence, the deal fell through. I don't know what happened. I certainly wanted Geoff Thomas, but you don't always get what you want in this world. If we couldn't buy a player for financial reasons, I would accept that. If the board said they didn't want somebody for footballing reasons, I found that hard to accept. It was my job to make the footballing decisions. I thought Geoff was a good player. He had just got into the England team, and at the time was better than who we had. I really wanted him; but that's life.

After I had stepped down, I was involved in the bid for the Bolton pair of Alan Stubbs and Jason McAteer, good players who would have made us a far stronger proposition in Europe. Bolton's chairman told Robert Coar that Stubbs and McAteer were a package; the price was for the two of them. Ray wanted them both, so I went with him to speak to them. We were a bit disappointed when Bolton sold McAteer to Liverpool. I suppose it was McAteer's right to choose where he wants to go, but it was disappointing for Blackburn Rovers. The unfortunate one in the whole saga was Stubbs.

Blackburn felt I could still play a part in the club's future, and I was delighted to stay. I would have gone like a shot if Blackburn's board thought that my presence would make life difficult for Ray. There was some confusion over what my new role entailed, which the media made a real fuss about. In the end, I invited four or five journalists over to explain the situation. I was there to be of help to anybody at Blackburn Rovers who needed me. I would speak when I was spoken to and help in whatever way they thought I could. There was no time commitment. I suppose the title, Director of Football, was a bit misleading. It's not a board directorship or being in charge of the football side. I am more a consultant, helping when called upon. I'm there to be of assistance. I might go training at Brockhall and see what transpires; my main contribution is working with the young kids and their coach Alan Irvine, training with them, or the young reserve lads, sometimes even with the first team. Whenever I can get in for a game, I'm in. I love that. Early on, it was important for me to stay in the background so the players knew Ray was in charge. That's why I kept a low profile. If Ray wanted, I would go to watch opponents, or a player, or even our own teams. Blackburn's players understood who was the boss.

Ray wanted to return to management so I stepped down at a good time for him. He had been linked to a few jobs elsewhere.

Ray is very highly regarded. During the championship season, the focus might have been on me but people in the game and at the club knew Ray's importance. It was natural for Blackburn to turn to him. He already had experience of managing Rovers. When I had my appendix removed at Christmas 1994, Ray did a marvellous job looking after the team. Maybe it gave him the incentive to get back into management. When Ray did take over, I deliberately kept well back. I didn't want my shadow troubling him. I remember stories about what had happened when Bob Paisley followed Bill Shankly. Shanks used to turn up at Melwood to watch training, which confused the players. That image stayed with me. I didn't want Blackburn's players to have a problem with knowing who was boss. I would never talk about the team, or seek to influence it, because at the end of the day there's one guy in charge and one voice. The way I was brought up was that the one voice was always the manager's, not a chairman's, a player's or anyone else's. People respected that when I was managing Blackburn, so the least I can do is give the club that respect back.

I have heard it said that I gave Blackburn credibility. But there's a lot more to Blackburn Rovers than Kenny Dalglish. Success on the pitch is brought about by a talented group of players, a good management team, a supportive board and a committed club. It is not the work of one individual. Blackburn has great credibility. If part of Blackburn's attraction for some players was Kenny Dalglish, then maybe I helped a bit in that way. The fact that Blackburn were champions would have helped Ray sign players like Matty Holmes, Graham Fenton, Lars Bohinen, Chris Coleman and Billy McKinlay.

Contrary to popular belief, my job was not to scout on our Champions' League opponents. Besides, you don't need to go and watch teams to analyse them. You can get videos from all over the world. You can work out all about their players, their styles. Some people like to see them live, rather than on video. I prefer to watch a player live, but a team on video.

Blackburn were not ill-prepared for Europe. Ray could only use the players he had at his disposal, and Blackburn did not have enough players. This obsession with Blackburn's poor preparations is misguided. When I played for Liverpool, we never knew too much about the opponents either. If you get your own game right, why worry about the team in the other dressing-room? Assessing the opposition was not always a foolproof procedure. Tom Saunders used to go scouting for Liverpool. He would tell Bob Paisley how good or bad a team were; but there were many times when Tom went to a game and thought 'this lot are hopeless'. You can't tell the players that; sometimes opponents who had played hopelessly then performed brilliantly in the big match.

Blackburn's failure in Europe was not through any shortcomings in preparation. We tried to play to our strengths in Europe and concentrate on our game being better than the opposition's. I felt that if we had changed our style it would have weakened us further. It is all very well having an idea of how you want to play in Europe, but if you don't have the players it's not going to work. You have got to go with who you've got. The players dictate your approach by their own style of play. You have to play a system they are most comfortable with.

It is fair to say that Spartak Moscow, our first Champions' League opponents, were technically individually better than Blackburn. That is not a criticism of anyone at Blackburn Rovers; Spartak were simply better. Watching the Russians gave us a target to aim at, both as a club and individually. Legia Warsaw were not technically better, just more fortunate. A lot was made of Rosenborg being part-timers but they trained four nights a week. Calling them amateurs is a misnomer. I don't think the 2–1 defeat at Rosenborg was a fair result. Alan Shearer could have put us 2–1 up at one point. Their goalkeeper made a great save. The last thing anyone wants to do is dismiss our displays or insist Blackburn could not have done better, but I don't think the performances were as bad as they are made out to be. Blackburn deserved to get more out of four of the six games. Spartak Moscow away and our defeat of Rosenborg at home were the only deserved results.

I admit Blackburn did slip back the season after winning the championship. We got nowhere in Europe, the League or the cups. But that didn't mean something was fundamentally wrong. After the euphoria of winning the championship you hope there is not going to be a reaction in the team the following season; but the reaction of opposition teams is always going to be different because you are the champions, the division's benchmark. At Blackburn, the players' hunger and approach to games was unchanged from the previous season. They are genuine lads. The players' ability was still there. Unfortunately, at the start of the season, the results weren't. Ray signed a few players which gave the dressing-room a lift. Unfortunately those new players were ineligible for the Champions' League, having been signed after the deadline. But our League form improved after a poor start and we just failed to qualify for Europe.

Having stepped down, I was less involved day to day. I travelled less. There was less responsibility. I saw a lot more of my family. I embarrassed myself twice on skiing holidays. I played more golf and generally just relaxed. I spent a bit of time smiling at all the managerial vacancies the papers linked me with. One of the job offers was for the Republic of Ireland position. The FA of Ireland approached Blackburn's chairman for permission to speak to me. Blackburn refused, which didn't cause me any worry. It was simply nice to be thought of. I certainly felt no animosity at the chairman's reaction. There was also speculation in the papers linking me with the England manager's job, but I thought the language barrier might have been a problem!

=17=

SUPPORTERS, REPORTERS AND MY PUBLIC IMAGE

O NE OF THE greatest disappointments of my life is that I never stood on the Kop. I always wished I had been able to join the people I so admired on the most famous terrace in football. As a player, I looked upon myself as a custodian of the supporters' dreams. When I ran out of the tunnel, I felt I was carrying out an ambition that the fans of Celtic and Liverpool couldn't fulfil for themselves. I was playing, and trying to win, for the good of the club they loved. As a manager, I was also a guardian. I was driven by a desire to win games so the supporters of Liverpool and Blackburn could go home happy, and be proud of the players and the club. I wanted everyone to have a weekend to remember, me included. I know I'm not too good at explaining things to the press, but I know where my heart lies. My desire is the same as those who pay money to come and watch the team. I always felt the servant of the supporters of Celtic, Liverpool and Blackburn Rovers.

Before I started playing professionally I was a fan. I watched from the terraces at Ibrox. When I stepped from the terraces on to the pitch, all my celebrations and disappointments were shared with the supporters. There was a common bond. Liverpool's fans accepted me because I tried my hardest. They never accepted a run of bad results but they appreciated the principles behind the football I was trying to play, as player and manager. The Kop trusted me. They knew I was motivated solely by Liverpool's best interests. Blackburn was no different. At Ewood, I had the same principle of being a custodian as I did at Celtic and Liverpool. I was trying to realise a dream for Jack Walker, who was a huge fan capable of showing his love and loyalty and desire in a financial way. The people who came, week in, week out, were also sacrificing a lot. It cost them a few quid to come to Ewood. In their own way, the supporters showed their hunger to be successful. My relationship with the fans at Blackburn was a bit different, understandably less intense than at Liverpool, because I hadn't played for their side. But my ambitions and principles were the same.

Liverpool supporters knew that I was one of them. Whatever the press might think, my public relations were good with these people; people like Jim Gardiner, a friend of Sammy Lee's. Big Jim came to many games with his mates. Sammy used to make sure they had tickets. When Sammy was transferred, I used to see the lads at games and ask them whether they were all right for tickets. They would travel everywhere pre-season. If they could get there, they would – trains, buses, boats, any means of transport would do. Jim and his mates were genuine supporters, so I trusted them. One day, I asked a favour of Big Jim.

'I'd love to do it myself but I can't,' I said. 'Can you take Paul in the Kop for me? He really wants to go.'

'No problem whatsoever, Kenny,' Jim replied.

'His mother's a wee bit worried,' I said. 'But I know if he's going in with you, there won't be a problem.'

So I got a steward to take Paul along the track to put him in beside Big Jim, who always stood in the same spot next to a pillar on the right-hand side of the goal.

Tam the steward led Paul on to the Kop and pointed him towards Jim.

'Keep an eye on the wee fellow with the Juventus strip on,' Tam told one of the Kop stewards as Paul headed out into that sea of red and white. 'That's Kenny's lad. If there's any hassle get him out right away.'

By pure chance, a photographer from the *Daily Mirror*, Albert Cooper, overheard this. He took two magnificent pictures of Paul which appeared in the *Mirror*. They were unbelievably natural photographs but I was really upset. I didn't want the fact that Paul had gone into the Kop to be advertised. I wasn't angry with Albert. Good luck to him; he was just doing his job. What upset me was that some people might have thought it was stage-managed. It was after Heysel and Paul was wearing a Juventus shirt. It might have looked like Liverpool wanted the pictures taken to help us build bridges with Juventus. That was not the case.

I was grateful to Jim for helping Paul to fulfil a dream. When I had my testimonial I phoned Jim up and asked if he'd like to come to the match.

'Kenny, I'll be going anyway. I wouldn't miss it,' he replied.

'Put your collar and tie on because there is a seat for you in the directors' box.'

The kick-off was 7.30 or 7.45 but Jim was there at 6 o'clock, sitting in the directors' box. He was there even before the pre-match kids' game. Paul played in that, for Liverpool against his own Formby amateur team. Big Jim sat there in the directors' box, all smartly dressed, watching Paul play. It gave me a thrill to see Jim like that, sitting there proud as Punch. It probably meant as much for him to sit in the directors' box as for Paul to stand on the Kop. I was really pleased to be able to repay his loyalty.

My rapport with Liverpool fans like Jim was my idea of public relations. I would give all sorts of boys tickets. I used to give Fred at the door a couple of tickets for old age pensioners. Quite a few of the OAPs, who couldn't afford the entrance fee, would hang around on the off-chance or simply to share the atmosphere. It was with people like Jim and those OAPs that I enjoyed good relations. I didn't need to shout about what I did for the Liverpool public. They knew.

To me, public relations involved being able to relate to fans, helping them in any way I could, whether with tickets or just spending a moment talking to them. I wanted to make them feel the club's appreciation of their support, make them feel part and parcel of Liverpool Football Club. My secretary, Sheila, would organise groups of kids to come down to the training-ground, and let them into the players' lounge so they could see the inside of the club. If a child was ill, Liverpool would do all they could to help. We never wanted any publicity. The kids, their parents and teachers used to ask: 'Can we take pictures with the players?'

'Yes,' we would reply, 'but we don't want them appearing in the papers.' We didn't want to see a little kid who wasn't well in the paper. If they wanted to put the picture in, fine. If it helped the kid, I certainly wouldn't object. But I would say to them: 'Don't think Liverpool want the publicity. We are just happy to help.' Every club helps its community, some quietly, some with a bit more song and dance.

My concept of public relations did not involve providing banner headlines. I was suspicious of the press from the moment I made Celtic's first team. We were playing at Firhill and some-body swung in a corner. I got a touch on it and it went in so I had scored three of our four. I came in in the morning and Big Jock said: 'So, you never got a hat-trick, then.'

'Yes I did,' I replied. 'I scored three.'

'Well,' said Big Jock, 'you spoke to a journalist after the game and said you never scored that one.'

'I never spoke to anyone after the game.'

'That'll do me,' Big Jock said, and was straight on to the journalist who had got me quoted in his column. That made me sceptical of the press. Journalists complain about my attitude but I have never missed a post-match press conference. There are some managers who can't boast that record. After we had lost the Littlewoods Cup final to Arsenal in 1987, there was nobody around to take me upstairs for the press conference, so I missed the official one. But I spoke to every reporter who was in the tunnel.

At Liverpool, I had a great working relationship with the locally based press lads like Matt D'Arcy of the *Daily Star*, John Keith of the *Daily Express* and Colin Wood of the *Daily Mail*. When I got the manager's job, I called them all into the office and said: 'This is how I want it to work. I won't give you any team news. I won't give you any team line-up before the players know. I won't confirm or deny speculation in the papers. I will work at all times in the best interests of the employees of Liverpool Football Club. I won't be giving anybody any exclusives. You will all get something or nothing. That is how I am going to conduct myself.' I stuck to my word. They accepted that – or grew to accept it. They were honest journalists, and I respected them as people. I enjoyed their company, even more so when they weren't working.

I do admit that my relations with the national journalists is one part of my managerial career I would have liked to have improved, especially at Liverpool. The club even organised a lunch in London before an England–Brazil game. Liverpool thought it would be beneficial for me to meet certain members of the national press, whom I saw only on a professional basis. The press said I never communicated with them. They claimed that my reluctance to communicate about team matters meant that the fans never got a full explanation of events. But the supporters knew where my heart lay.

My public image as a dour Scotsman doesn't worry me. Joe Fagan used to say he had a great relationship with me: 'I can't understand him, and he can't understand me!' There is little I can do about this image of the incomprehensible Scot. If journalists fling something at you often enough, it will stick. People I've met know what I'm like as a person. The other players who have written books say how different I am from my one-dimensional image. But the media won't accept it. It suits them to portray me as the dour Scot. Maybe they are doing it because I won't give them stories or quotes for headlines; maybe it's because they like my image to contrast with other managers.

Journalists criticise me for not talking and not informing the punters properly, but what are they doing by perpetuating this false image of me? They are misinforming their readers. The biggest frustration for journalists is not my post-match press conferences but the lack of integrity amongst some in their own profession. My post-match comments were never reported the same way in every single newspaper, so I would be very guarded in what I said. Otherwise the words and meaning would be twisted. When I tried to be constructive about an incident during a game, journalists would put a word like 'angry' in front of my name, which means people read it in a different context. So many times the word 'irate' was inserted when I was trying to be perfectly calm and normal about an event. But it is not in newspapers' interests for me to be perfectly calm and normal.

It is not simply the fault of those journalists attending post-match press conferences. They send their articles back to the newspaper offices where some sub-editor will put the damaging word in. Seeing this twisting of context happen to other managers convinced me how right I was to be guarded. I remember George Graham gave a TV interview, talking about a penalty, saying 'sometimes you get them, sometimes you don't'. He was being quite reasonable, but in the papers the following day it was made out to be 'Angry George Graham . . .'. Fergie had the same experience. There was one game at Goodison where Jesper Olsen went straight through, somebody pulled him down from behind and got a yellow card not a red. On live television, Fergie said: 'Sometimes players get sent off for that; this time he never. What can we do about it?' The next day the headlines were all: 'Angry, irate, whingeing Fergie'. He wasn't. It was ridiculous. Journalists cannot guarantee that what we say will appear in the same context as it was said. There is a lack of responsibility in the profession. Even the journalists admit it. I've seen them on Sky's 'Hold The Back Page'. People in the profession are slagging off the tabloids; even people from tabloid papers are slagging off other tabloids.

I once fell out with Matt D'Arcy. There had been rumours of Rushie going to Italy and I told the local press lads: 'It's a load of rubbish, it's not even worth a comment.' Rushie himself had just done a piece in the paper totally dismissing the story. Two or three days later there was a story 'Rushie for Milan' in the *Star*. I said to Matt: 'What's going on? I told you there was nothing in it. If there is going to be something, then every one of you will get it. But you knew there was nothing there.

'Here we are trying to go for the double and you are trying to cause disruption among the players. Don't come back. You're banned.'

Matt was obviously upset.

'Look,' I told him, 'I'm not doing you any great injustice. You will get the team news off one of the lads.'

Matt would come up to the ground but he couldn't come into the press conferences. One day, all the lads were filing into my office, and Matt popped his head out of the players' lounge and called out, 'Kenny.'

'How are you doing, Matt?' I said, looking down the corridor at him.

'Kenny, am I still banned?' Matt said.

'Yes,' I replied.

'Is it a life ban, Kenny?'

'Depends how long you live, Matt!'

But he was soon back in. When I left Liverpool, I received a letter from Matt, wishing me all the best, and saying I was one of the most honest managers he'd ever worked with. That was nice. I was never conniving. I didn't go behind some journalists' backs to tell somebody one thing, and others not. I was straight with them.

When I resigned from Liverpool, other reporters who I worked with day in, day out wrote to me like Matt did. They didn't get a quote off me every day because I didn't have something to say every day. I wouldn't lie in bed at night dreaming up quotes. I had a responsibility as manager to talk for Liverpool. But I had a much greater responsibility to the club and the fans to make sure that I wasn't covering papers in headlines detrimental to Liverpool. I have always been cooperative with the press, but I have only told them what I wanted them to know. Banning a journalist like Matt was hardly new. Shanks was one of the greatest media men of modern times and he once banned the press for six weeks. They had to phone Peter Robinson for team news and information. Bob banned them, too. Fergie bans journalists from time to time.

I mainly had a problem with some of the national correspondents based in London, the so-called No 1s. These football correspondents would often ask for interviews, and if I refused they would get upset. If I did one I would be restrained, and again they would not be happy. I understood that they had a job to do, a feature to write, but they had to respect my position. I had a job to do, too. Part of the reason why I would not be too forthcoming was that I didn't think it would be beneficial for the club. The more information a club or person gives out, the less the mystique. Whether that helped my cause or the club's, I don't know. Maybe if I had had more trust in the No 1s or was better able to present my thoughts in a way that wouldn't compromise the club, then I could have been more open. These lads do have an important role to fill in their newspapers but, for me, they weren't the important national journalists. The national journalists who I felt were important were those living on Merseyside, whom I saw three or four times a week. They may not be the No 1s but it didn't matter to me where they ranked on the league table at each paper. They were my contact with that paper. They were the No 1s to me.

During my first season at Blackburn, we went to Port Vale trying to end a bad run. There were people in the press box who weren't local journalists, they were from the national newspapers, who jumped up when we lost a goal. With all due respect to Port Vale, you don't get too many national journalists who support them. Those who jumped up got satisfaction from seeing me struggle. How could they write an accurate assessment if they had a dislike for a person? Even if I try to say something funny, it gets twisted. I would just restrict myself to fulfilling my obligation to talk after the match but not say much, only what I wanted to say, not what I was expected to say. That's why my press conferences are so stilted and usually short. Journalists feel I belittle them. In the end some wouldn't bother asking questions in my press conferences.

But a journalist's match report is very influential. Their opinions are read by millions of people on the street, most of whom weren't at the game and can be influenced. There is not much I can do about that. Football's a game about opinions. Like everyone else, journalists are entitled to theirs. But because people have played football for 20 years doesn't mean they have a knowledge of the game; because somebody has watched football for 20 years doesn't mean they have that knowledge, either. They just have experience, which doesn't necessarily give you knowledge. Just because you live by the sea doesn't mean you can swim.

I've been talking to journalists since I was 18, so I've got a wee bit bored with being asked the same questions. One of the most common during my time at Liverpool was 'What's the secret of Liverpool's success?' I would repeat, time and again, that Liverpool's success is based on the fact that everyone employed by the club is good at his job. Besides, if there was a secret, I wouldn't tell them. At Blackburn, I just carried on the same philosophy. Peter White, of the *Lancashire Evening Telegraph*, used to love the press conferences. Peter would love the whole game of cat-and-mouse.

The press lads at Blackburn must have been really apprehensive when I arrived, but I have enjoyed working with them as much as I enjoyed working with the lads at Liverpool. They accepted my philosophy and the way I worked. They wrote what they thought was right to report. There was no ban ever served on any of them. They had my respect.

Some journalists say I am being dismissive or letting the fans down because I cannot explain myself. That's rubbish. It would have been counterproductive for me if I had gone into details about why I made a decision. I'm not going to let others know, certainly not other managers, how I operate or react in certain situations. There were times when people would try to guess whether Liverpool were going to play a sweeper, such as when we were playing long-ball teams or physical sides like Arsenal and Wimbledon. But I wasn't going to give them any help in their predictions. Punters may be disappointed if they come along to watch a certain player who doesn't play because of an injury I haven't disclosed to the media; but the fans at Liverpool and Blackburn would be even more disappointed if the other team got an advantage by knowing in advance. If opponents know one of our players is out they might spend all week preparing to exploit his absence. If I thought it would be advantageous to Liverpool, I would withhold information. What the punters really want is a winning team.

The same applied to my players. I was not going to criticise them in public just to help newspapermen. I treated players the way I liked to be treated when I was a player. I helped them prepare properly for games and treated them with the utmost respect. They responded to that support and so Liverpool achieved more success. I would say my piece behind closed doors. I would much rather have a successful team, with the players on my side, than enjoy a romance with the media.

It was pointless criticising players in public, however mildly. The press would just blow it up. As long as they gave of their best, they could rest assured they would not be criticised as individuals. At times you have to admit that the team has played badly. That confidence gives players a better chance of being successful. Players have a responsibility to themselves, and their clubs, to behave in the best manner possible. If they do something wrong, they deserve to be criticised. If someone who is high-profile does something wrong, they deserve the adverse attention; but I cannot understand why the press belittle someone simply because he is talented. The personal abuse that was aimed at Graham Taylor and Bobby Robson was terrible. Some managers who might have been interested in the England job would have become very wary of it after those reports. No one wants that sort of persistent character assassination. It's not a reflection on how important the England manager's job is; it's a reflection on how important it is to sell newspapers.

The one consolation is that nowadays people don't believe what they read in the papers as much as they did in days gone by. I work in the game and read who's chasing whom, and who's signing whom. I would love those sports editors to count how many times they get it right. Not many. Joe Bloggs is not thick. Joe Bloggs supports one club and probably buys the same paper every day. Now, if three times in one week his club is being linked with a different player for the same position, he will get suspicious. At Blackburn we were linked with almost everybody. The problem lies more and more with the many football news agencies, who only get paid when their pieces appear in the papers. It helps create hysteria even though a story may not be true. I don't believe the papers are 100 per cent guilty. People within football like their clubs to be associated with buying players. The club contributing to something that is untrue, just to be seen by the fans to be doing something, is unacceptable. Both parties, clubs and papers, are guilty.

I have hardly ever had problems with television people, although producers would complain my team list was never ready in time. They would come down to the dressing-room door to ask for the line-up. They would never get it until I was ready. The press would criticise me for announcing my teams late, which they claimed was because I didn't know my line-up. I always knew my line-up by the Saturday morning. I announced my teams late purely because I didn't want the opposition to know who they were. The less the opposition knew, the greater advantage it was to Liverpool or Blackburn. There was no problem taking my time as long as it didn't confuse our dressing-room. The players got used to it. The television producers were panicking for their own reasons. I knew the rules. I had until 2.30 to hand the team-sheets in. We had to tell the players by 1.45. If I needed until 1.45 to tell the players, I'd take the time. That was my deadline. Sometimes I knew months in advance how I would play against certain teams. Just by watching them, or playing against them, I would know the players and tactics needed for when we met them next.

I used to look forward to the after-match interviews with Sky. After one match against Coventry in 1994, they came up and gave me a bottle of champagne because my interviews with Nick Collins were so entertaining. They enjoyed seeing Nick Collins trying to get something out of me. During those interviews, I was always on the verge of laughing. Nick used to start every question with 'how'. 'How important was that?' 'How good was that performance?' 'How good was that goal by Alan Shearer?' Always 'how'. One day, after a live match at Tottenham, I said to him: 'Nick, if you ask me a question that starts with "how" I'm going to repeat it back to you.' The interview began and Nick said: 'How disappointing was that result?'

'Nick, you promised you wouldn't start the question with "how". You've let me down.'

So he said: 'Were you disappointed with the result?' You can't win!

It was a bit of fun. One day I managed to upset Barry Davies. He was interviewing me in Blackburn's championship season, saying: 'Steve Sutton is doing really well.' Barry kept going on about 'Steve Sutton'. At the end, I had to say: 'By the way, Barry, Steve Sutton's at Derby. Chris Sutton's with us.'

'You never make a mistake, then?' he said.

'Not when it's my living,' I replied as I walked away laughing.

But it was a recorded interview and that bit wasn't shown. They are all different. John Motson is the man for the quiz question. Martin Tyler, on Sky, is all stats.

Anyway, whatever the media make of me, I am what I am. There is no sideshow with me, no Equity card. People can take me or leave me. All I hope is that during my spells as a custodian of both Liverpool and Blackburn Rovers, I looked after the clubs in a way of which the fans approved.

—18—

ALEX FERGUSON AND ME

DURING MY TIME at Liverpool and Blackburn, the press built up a myth that a feud exists between Alex Ferguson and me. Even now journalists refer to us as 'bitter rivals'. Because of such newspaper stories, some of the public probably believe that Fergie and I really are at war. It's not true. The idea of permanent discord between us is a figment of journalists' imaginations. It's a good script, great for selling papers, but completely untrue. Fergie and I are in direct competition but there is no hatred.

In fact, when Fergie was under pressure from the press, at a time when things weren't going too well in his early days at Manchester United, I spoke up for him at a Football Writers' Association dinner. I told the journalists, who must have chronically short memories, that they should be supporting Fergie because he was a good manager. I said to them: 'I'd just like to point out that there is no animosity between Alex Ferguson and myself, as you'd like to believe.' I told them the truth. I gave my opinion of Alex Ferguson's ability to manage. I told them I was sure he would get it right (although he didn't need to do it quite as well as he has!). Shortly afterwards, Jim McGregor, who works for Fergie, mentioned to me: 'By the way, the gaffer needed that.' There has never been any animosity between us.

Fergie and I go back nearly 30 years. I used to hang about at Ibrox with Alex Miller, who went on to manage Hibs. We'd meet up at Ibrox, near my home, and head into town. Fergie was at

Rangers then and he would often give us a lift. He never thought I would become a footballer. 'That wee fat boy won't make a player,' Fergie used to say. I had puppy fat then. I even played against him, in an Old Firm reserve game, when I was 18. I was centre-back, Fergie was up front for Rangers reserves. He said he scored but I don't remember any goal. We won anyway. All I remember are Fergie's elbows. They were a real nuisance. But that was the way Fergie ran. He was a competitive player. He carried that over into management. We are both very competitive.

People claim we fell out over the 1986 World Cup when Fergie was Scotland manager. Fergie was debating whether to take Alan Hansen, who I thought was an automatic selection for Mexico. Fergie phoned me at home to discuss the situation. After all, I was Alan's club manager.

'I think I'll need to leave big Hansen out,' Fergie said.

'Well,' I said, 'that's up to yourself.'

Fergie was keen to explain why. 'I need someone in the squad who's more adaptable, who can play two or three positions. They can help fatten up the squad a wee bit. I also need another left-footed player.'

'Alex, it's your squad,' I told him. 'But just remember one thing: it's all very well being able to play two or three positions but it is the standard of performance that is important. Big Hansen can play two or three positions but he'll not play them as well as he'll play centre-back. He's been magnificent for us at Liverpool. That's all I can tell you. He can play in front of the back-four if you want. But it's your decision.'

'Aye,' Fergie said, 'I'll need to have a think about it.'

I put down the phone. Shortly afterwards, Fergie rang back to tell me Scotland were going to Mexico without Alan. I didn't agree but it was Fergie's decision to make, not mine. Fergie phoned Alan to break the news.

I was disappointed Alan wasn't going to Mexico. I thought Fergie was making a mistake, but at least he phoned me up to talk things through. A couple of days later, I had to call Fergie to say I couldn't make Mexico because of injury. That caused a rumpus in the press. People claimed I was snubbing Fergie out of spite over Alan. That was not true. Those who said I pulled out because Alan Hansen wasn't picked were not only libelling me but impugning the integrity of the surgeon who told me not to go. I was hardly going to be able to play in a World Cup finals with the ligament detached from my knee. Since that summer of 1986, the papers have insisted that Fergie and I are at each other's throats. That is such a lie. Just to show the respect in which we hold each other, Fergie even helped organise a team for my Scottish testimonial in 1986, just before the FA Cup final. I scored for both Fergie's side and Tommy Doc's. Fergie made me captain for my one hundredth international. We got on well during our time with Scotland.

Of course, I have not always agreed with him. There was one match against Manchester United at Anfield in 1988, which we were winning 3–1. United had a man sent off but came back to draw 3–3. We weren't in the best frame of mind, not winning after being in such a good position; nor was Fergie evidently. Somebody said Fergie was coming up the tunnel, saying it 'makes you want to choke on your own vomit. You never get a decision here, blah, blah, blah.' I thought Fergie would have calmed down by the time he got to the press, but no. He was still having a go. I was walking down the corridor with Lauren in my arms as Fergie was giving a radio interview. I heard him saying the same thing about not getting decisions here, blah, blah, blah. As I passed I said to the radio man: 'You are better off talking to my baby. She's only six weeks old but you'd get more sense from her than him.' I kept going. Fergie stopped and had a rant. I said: 'Careful, Alex, the baby's a wee bit young for that.' And that was it.

Just because I don't have the same opinions as Alex, it doesn't mean a feud rages between us. Shortly after the incident in the Anfield corridor, Alan Hansen had a testimonial dinner. Fergie was there, on the top table. No problem at all. If I met Fergie at a match we'd stop and have a laugh. At Old Trafford we'd have a cup of tea. Marina and I went to the Football Writers' tribute dinner for Fergie in 1996 – and the press still believe a feud goes on. Marina and I could go out with Fergie and his wife, Cath, and enjoy ourselves. In fact, Fergie goes back a long way with Marina's family. Marina's dad taught Fergie the licensed trade in Glasgow.

I suppose a high-profile rivalry between two Scottish managers sells newspapers. Journalists made a fuss about me nipping in for

Glenn Hysen when Fergie was about to sign him. That doesn't create rancour; that's business. We are both going for the best players. Sometimes managers of PLC clubs, like Manchester United, cannot spend money quickly. They have to get permission from the PLC board. If United's wheels move slowly, that's no concern of mine. I certainly wasn't going to let slip an opportunity to acquire a player like Hysen. Fergie would have understood that.

I admire a lot of what Fergie's done. I enjoyed working with him at Scotland training; his coaching was excellent. Fergie was good as gold to me. His coaching sessions were always interesting and constructive. It must have been difficult, working part-time as Scotland manager and also keeping Aberdeen going. In club football, Fergie has a tremendous record. With Aberdeen, he won a European trophy, which was a remarkable achievement. For a Scottish club to beat Real Madrid was unbelievable. He has done his fair bit for Manchester United. The way he has restructured the youth set-up at Old Trafford is magnificent. He brought Manchester United their first title for 26 years, then followed up the next year. Fergie has kept up those high standards: two doubles in three years is a brilliant achievement.

They say teams reflect the guy in charge, but Fergie's Manchester United sides don't reflect the way he played. Fergie wasn't a silky player; he was an honest, industrious player. Yet his teams all play with grace and flair and organisation. Fergie has always put out entertaining teams. I can remember him at St Mirren, putting out an exciting team; the same at Aberdeen and Manchester United. Alex Ferguson is a great manager.

—19—

THE FINAL WORD

I T SEEMS STRANGE reflecting on my days as a manager when they might not be over. I don't enjoy management as much as playing. Playing was brilliant. Nothing beats it. Everything else is just a distant second. I always accept invitations to play in testimonials. I'm rubbish but I still go and play. I can't help it. If someone asks me to manage a testimonial team, I don't get the same enjoyment out of it, unless I pick myself. But when the playing days are over, management is the obvious next step.

When I was playing for Celtic, Jock Stein said he believed I would make a good manager one day because of the way I approached the game. He said my preparation, commitment, and thoughts on the game were good. But I have been very lucky with the people who have employed me as manager. I don't think I could have worked for two better sets of people than those at Liverpool and Blackburn Rovers. I have achieved success in environments where I feel confident. When I'm taken out of places with a friendly, family atmosphere, I start to feel uncomfortable. That is one of the reasons why I love living in Southport. People just accept me as a person. They respect my privacy which is very important to me. I feel comfortable living in Southport, just as I felt comfortable working at Liverpool and Blackburn.

I don't know whether I would have had the same amount of success if I had started at a smaller club. Some people try to belittle my achievements by saying I've only worked for big clubs with big resources. But my record of success as a manager speaks for itself. I've won more games than I've lost as a manager. All right, I enjoyed great resources at Liverpool. At Blackburn, Jack supplied the cash, I supplied the judgement and Ray supplied the help. Is it my fault that I had two good jobs? Of course not. I was asked to take over managing Liverpool and Blackburn Rovers and brought them success. Who do I need to justify myself to?

I have this miserable image because that's what television depicts when it zooms in on me standing by the dugout. It's an unfair picture. Very rarely is a manager seen smiling when he's in the dugout. I was concentrating on the game so I had a serious expression on my face.

Millions of people who don't know me probably believe I'm a dour Scot who refuses to sit down during matches. I always stood up at Liverpool because I couldn't see. The dugout was low. Then Ronnie Moran and Roy Evans couldn't see either, so they stood up. I think that's how Mexican Waves started! When the ball was down the Kop end, Roy used to run round the back of us to try to see what was happening. I would say to them: 'What happened there?' Ronnie and Roy would both chime back: 'Don't know.' I always stood. Opposition fans don't sing 'Sit down Dalglish' anymore because every manager stands. I thought the song was quite funny until referees started coming over and ordering me to sit down. After standing was allowed in the Premiership, we still had to watch out for League Cup games. Referees used to come in before ties and joke with me: 'Now, Kenny, you know you are not allowed to stand up.' It was only in the dugout you couldn't stand, so it was easy at Anfield. I just stood at the end of the tunnel.

During the re-building work at Ewood Park, we used temporary dugouts. There used to be a chair pushed a bit forward, so I would stand on that. The groundsman built a plinth for me to stand on to watch the games at away grounds. I used to get punters shouting: 'Sit down, Dalglish, I can't see the bloody game.' A few fans became abusive. It's easy to be abusive in a crowd; there's safety in numbers. I try to ignore it. The police have a responsibility to step in but they rarely do. I get into trouble if I'm mouthing off, so why shouldn't the bloke slagging me off get into trouble? The manager is an easy target.

What really bothered me was failing to win. I hate losing – at any sport. I can remember once being beaten at Norwich City with Blackburn Rovers. Afterwards Dennis Signy, of the *Sunday Express*, introduced me to Delia Smith, who is a Norwich fan and was doing one of those celebrity match reports. Dennis asked me if I needed any recipes from Delia. 'Yes,' I said. 'How to get three points from a 2–1 defeat!' You have to keep things in perspective.

I did have trouble keeping referees in perspective. I was accused of whingeing but it was a legitimate frustration. It angered me when one of my players was booked making a good tackle. I appreciate referees trying to protect skill but tackling is a skill too. The art of tackling is going out of football. I don't think referees can distinguish between a genuine attempt to win the ball and one that's got ulterior motives. There is no consistency, which makes a mockery of the whole situation. European and Endsleigh League referees interpret the rules differently from Premiership officials. The best referees are those who can have a joke with the players, not those who want to belittle them or be dogmatic or just please some FA bureaucrat sitting in Lancaster Gate. Players can relate to referees like Keith Cooper, who runs the game as he sees it, has a crack with the lads and understands what the players are trying to do. Players respond to such sympathetic handling. It's ridiculous that those referees are the ones who don't get recognised by FIFA. The ones who go forward are those who please paper-pushers at Lancaster Gate.

Players should understand what the referee is trying to achieve, and vice versa. It's crazy that a referee should have to control a match whilst worrying about which list he will be on next season, Premier League or Endsleigh. It's an indictment of the FA's system that Keith Cooper had to ask to stay on when he reached the official retirement age. The FA should be begging referees like him to continue. Football was supposed to be refereed in the spirit of the law, now it's just referees running around with whistles playing to the letter of the law. The authorities have removed common sense from refereeing. There are many referees who don't enjoy their football as much now because of the changes.

I don't understand what the authorities like the FA are up to. Their job is to look after those who play football. Referees used to check studs, but not now; not for the last two or three years. They say it's the player's responsibility. Sometimes a linesman checks studs of substitutes going on. That's daft as they never checked the boots of the 11 who started the game. It's so inconsistent.

There is another pressing issue facing the FA. Everyone says English footballers play too much football, but I don't think the number of games is a problem, just the scheduling of them. When English teams were winning European trophies in the seventies and eighties, just count up how many games we played – between 60 and 70 a season, the same as now. But these matches were less intense and the scheduling was better. It would help if Premier League teams entered the Coca-Cola Cup at a later round. Another problem nowadays is generated by international managers. They demand players for longer. England players meet up with the squad on Thursday night and train on Friday morning and afternoon and on Saturday morning. After lunch, they are allowed to go home but have to report back on Sunday night. The players don't know where to go. It's such a short period. If you are going to give them a day-and-a-half off, why not just call them up on Saturday? Let them have Thursday and Friday with their clubs. I've always said it's better to play international matches on a weekend anyway, which seems to be the way football is moving, and not before time. That way, the international coaches get players for a week and we get them back for a week. Everyone's happy.

The increase of Saturday internationals is a sensible change. In my near 30 years in football, I have witnessed many changes. The most noticeable is the commercialisation of football. Every tournament is sponsored. Every club has its sponsor's name on its shirts, apart from Barcelona. Football strips themselves now generate enormous sums of money for clubs. Commercialism is not a bad thing. Everybody has to move with the times. But football must bear in mind that people in the street have only so much money. The make-up of football crowds has definitely altered. The percentage of working people has dropped. The bigger clubs go more for hospitality and the corporate entertainment side, which is a money-spinner. The working man must find it difficult to relate to players in financial terms. The new corporate fan can more easily relate to the wealthier player.

Social changes are affecting football. Drugs are a social problem that should worry football. Football is losing potential players to drugs. Lads can go astray and miss out on a very profitable career. Even after some of them have become professionals, there can be a tendency to get involved in the wrong company which can lead to an acquaintance with drugs and the end of a career. Football has to make youngsters aware of the dangers of drugs and, if they are caught using them, make the punishment fit the crime. The PFA are trying to help in this area.

Another major problem for the future of football is the competition the sport faces from other leisure pursuits. When I grew up it was a case of 'get a ball, get a game, let's go'. Now, small kids have so many other distractions. Technology has moved on since my day. Computer games can fill hours of a child's week. A small percentage who might have gone on to play the game are being lost from football each year. The number of schoolkids playing football is decreasing. A lot of teachers now haven't the time or the inclination to take football matches, or encourage kids.

Football has moved with the times. It has become far more scientific, particularly in the preparation for matches, not just with training or getting to bed early; medical science has provided information on what footballers should eat. We have gone from steak to pasta. Science's impact is amazing. As football has become faster, so injuries have got more serious. When I played, you didn't hear of people sustaining pelvic injuries or medial-ligament damage. It is the speed of the modern game that causes injuries like that. There were only groin strains in my day. Now, surgeons can re-build knees. But the greatest healer will always be time. Nowadays, injured players are less prepared to play until they are ready. Players are very conscious that by returning early they could inflict more serious damage on themselves.

This reflects a change in power. The power has moved from clubs to players, particularly since the Bosman ruling gave players greater control of their careers. The Professional Footballers' Association has become very strong. But along with their well-deserved financial rewards, the players should realise there is added responsibility. They must do everything they can to work in the best interests of the club which pays them so handsomely. There is no point in managers using the best modern techniques to prepare players, plus the advice of many and varied experts, if the players aren't going to do their bit. Well-paid professionals have to be disciplined away from the ground. They must not do anything that undermines all the hard work put in on the training ground. They must also have a professional approach to training. Those who have been abroad come back very well educated, disciplined and responsible. Foreign players seem to take a greater pride in their profession than many British players.

The rules have changed too. The two most obvious alterations involve the pass-back and offside. It seems strange watching old matches where keepers pick up passes from defenders and then bounce the ball like a basketballer before kicking it. That's gone now. I don't know if the pass-back rule has improved football. It has certainly quickened games and made it difficult for teams to kill matches off. Giving the benefit of the doubt to attackers in offside decisions is definitely a positive move.

TV coverage has also changed. It is brilliant compared to what it was. They thought that the mass showing of live matches might mean gates would go down, but it has actually improved them. Television is vital to football. Without TV, there would be no shirt sponsorships, no perimeter advertising. A lot of people who can't go to matches, because they have moved or tickets cost too much or they can't get hold of one, watch their teams on television; or go down to the pub and watch the game with their mates. People criticise the television companies for rescheduling matches but there are three bodies which decide on that: television, the police and the FA. Probably the most influential group in changing kick-off times or dates are the police.

When it comes to representing your country, I don't think players' attitudes have changed. I like to think that the pride in playing for your country would never be diminished by financial considerations. Having said that, the respective FAs should ensure that their representatives are well paid. International players should be motivated by pride and passion. The money is a gesture but it should never be derogatory.

In conclusion, I would like to say that my best ever signing has been my wife, Marina. She has helped develop my finest youth policy and given me the four best presents of my life. They say that behind every successful man there is a woman. But, as far as I'm concerned, Marina has never been behind me. She has been beside me, always.

CAREER RECORD

The facts and figures of Kenny Dalglish's career compiled by John Keith of the Daily Express.

1968–69

After graduating from junior clubs Glasgow United, Possil Park YMCA and Cumbernauld United, Dalglish signs for Celtic as a full professional on 29 April, 1968 at the age of 17. He makes his senior debut as substitute for Charlie Gallagher in a Scottish League Cup quarter-final at Hamilton Academical on 25 September, 1968. Won 4–2.

Celtic went on to win the Scottish League Cup, defeating Hibernian in the final.

Competition	Appearances	Goals
Scottish League	0	0
Scottish Cup	0	0
Scottish League Cup	0 (1)	0
European Cup	0	0
Totals	0 (1)	0

Substitute appearances in brackets.

1969–70

Dalglish makes first League start for Celtic, wearing the No 4 jersey, in a 7–1 win over Raith Rovers, Scottish League, 4 October, 1969.

Competition	Appearances	Goals
Scottish League	2 (0)	0
Scottish Cup	0 (0)	0
Scottish League Cup	2 (0)	0
European Cup	0 (0)	0
Totals	4 (0)	0

1970–71

Dalglish makes his European debut as 55th-minute substitute for Bobby Murdoch in European Cup, first round, second leg v. KPV Kokkolan, 30 September, 1970. Celtic win 5–0 to complete a 14–0 aggregate victory. He also makes one Scottish Cup appearance and Celtic go on to win the trophy, defeating Rangers in a replayed final. They also win the championship for the sixth successive season.

Competition	Appearances	Goals
Scottish League	1 (2)	0
Scottish Cup	1 (0)	0
Scottish League Cup	0 (0)	0
European Cup	0 (1)	0
Totals	2 (3)	0

1971–72

Dalglish makes full international debut, in Scotland team managed by Tommy Docherty, as a substitute for Alex Cropley in Nations Cup game against Belgium at Aberdeen on 10 November, 1971, at age of 20. His first senior goal for Celtic comes in Scottish League Cup in a 2–0 defeat of Rangers at Ibrox, 14 August, 1971. He scores from a penalty. His first League goal is scored against Clyde in a 9–1 home win, 4 September, 1971.

He makes his first European start in the 2–1 defeat at B1903 Copenhagen, European Cup, 15 September, 1971.

He collects winners' medals in Scottish championship and Scottish Cup and a runner's-up medal in Scottish League Cup.

Competition	Appearances	Goals
Scottish League	31 (0)	17
Scottish Cup	4 (0)	1
Scottish League Cup	7 (1)	5
European Cup	7 (0)	0
Totals	49 (1)	23

1972–73

Dalglish wins another Scottish championship medal as Celtic record their eighth consecutive title triumph. He also collects runners-up medals in the Scottish Cup and Scottish League Cup.

At international level, Willie Ormond succeeds Tommy Docherty as Scotland manager in January 1973.

Competition		Appearances	Goals
Scottish League		32 (0)	23
Scottish Cup		6 (0)	5
Scottish League Cup		11 (0)	10
European Cup		4 (0)	3
	Totals	53 (0)	41

1973–74

Dalglish wins Scottish championship and Scottish Cup winners' medals and another Scottish League Cup runners-up medal.

At the end of the season he plays for Scotland in World Cup finals in West Germany, appearing in all three of his country's games: a 2–0 defeat of Zaire in Dortmund, a goalless draw with Brazil in Frankfurt and a 1–1 draw with Yugoslavia in Frankfurt.

Competition		Appearances	Goals
Scottish League		31 (2)	18
Scottish Cup		6 (0)	1
Scottish League Cup		10 (0)	3
European Cup		7 (0)	2
	Totals	54 (2)	24

1974–75

Dalglish collects Scottish Cup and Scottish League Cup winners' medals. But Celtic's remarkable run of nine successive Scottish championship triumphs is ended by Rangers. Celtic finish third, behind runners-up Hibernian.

Competition	Appearances	Goals
Scottish League	33 (0)	16
Scottish Cup	5 (0)	2
Scottish League Cup	7 (1)	3*
European Cup	2 (0)	0
Totals	47 (1)	21

* One of Celtic's goals in their 2–1 Scottish League Cup defeat of Motherwell on 10 August, 1974, is given in some record books as an own goal by R. Watson. Celtic have credited it to Dalglish and, as such, it is included in the above figures.

1975–76

Dalglish succeeds Billy McNeill as Celtic skipper and there are runners-up medals in the championship, which is retained by Rangers in the inaugural season of the Premier Division, and the Scottish League Cup.

Scotland register their first unbeaten season since 1948–49, winning six and drawing one of seven games with Dalglish prominent. He scores in a 3–1 win over Denmark at Hampden, again in a 3–0 home defeat of Northern Ireland and in a 2–1 conquest of England at Hampden as the Scots lift the home championship outright for the first time since 1967.

Competition	Appearances	Goals
Scottish League	35 (0)	24
Scottish Cup	1 (0)	1
Scottish League Cup	10 (0)	4
European Cup-winners' Cup	5 (0)	3
Totals	51 (0)	32

1976–77

Dalglish's final season with Celtic and he celebrates by helping the club win the Scottish Championship, his fourth title success, and the Scottish Cup. He also collects a Scottish League Cup runners-up medal.

Ally MacLeod succeeds Willie Ormond as Scotland manager in May 1977 and his team retain the home championship with Dalglish scoring twice in a 3–0 Hampden defeat of Northern Ireland and one of Scotland's goals in a 2–1 Wembley conquest of England.

Competition	Appearances	Goals
Scottish League	35 (0)	14
Scottish Cup	7 (0)	1
Scottish League Cup	9 (1)	10
UEFA Cup	2 (0)	1
Totals	53 (1)	26

1977-78

Dalglish signs for Liverpool in a £440,000 transfer from Celtic on 10 August, 1977. He is Anfield manager Bob Paisley's replacement for Kevin Keegan, earlier sold to Hamburg for £500,000.

Dalglish makes debut in goalless Charity Shield duel with Manchester United at Wembley three days later and scores on his first League appearance in 1–1 draw at Middlesbrough the following Saturday. He goes on to make 180 consecutive first-team appearances spanning three years.

Dalglish wins his 50th Scotland cap on the familiar territory of Anfield in October in the World Cup qualifier against Wales. His header clinches a 2–0 victory and secures Scotland a ticket to the following summer's World Cup finals in Argentina.

He crowns his first season at Liverpool by scoring their European Cup final winner against Bruges at Wembley and also collects runners-up medals in League championship and League Cup and a winners' medal in European Super Cup.

Competition	Appearances	Goals
League	42 (0)	20
FA Cup	1 (0)	1
League Cup	9 (0)	6
European Cup	7 (0)	3
European Super Cup	2 (0)	1
Charity Shield	1 (0)	0
Totals	62 (0)	31

1978–79

Dalglish plays in all three of Scotland's games in the World Cup finals: a 3–1 defeat by Peru in Cordoba, a 1–1 draw with Iran in Cordoba and a 3–2 win over eventual runners-up Holland in Mendoza in which he scored one of the goals. The tournament also takes Dalglish past Denis Law's 55-cap Scotland appearance record.

Two of the World Cup-winning Argentina team are on the receiving end of a drubbing by Dalglish and his Liverpool colleagues in September. Osvaldo Ardiles and Ricardo Villa are members of the Tottenham side toppled 7–0 at Anfield. Dalglish scores twice in what is regarded as one of Liverpool's finest-ever performances and he and the club go on to lift the championship. They do so with a total of 68 points from 42 games, a record under the two-points-for-a-win system, and concede only 16 goals, also a record. Dalglish scores 21 League goals. During the season he passes the 100th appearance milestone for Liverpool and 50 goals. He is voted Footballer of the Year by the Football Writers' Association.

During the season at international level, Dalglish is re-united with his Celtic manager Jock Stein who succeeds Ally MacLeod in October.

Competition	Appearances	Goals
League	42 (0)	21
FA Cup	7 (0)	4
League Cup	1 (0)	0
European Cup	2 (0)	0
European Super Cup	2 (0)	0
Totals	54 (0)	25

1979–80

Dalglish opens the curtain on the new season with a goal in Liverpool's 3–1 FA Charity Shield win over Arsenal at Wembley. He completes his third successive ever-present season by contributing 16 goals towards Liverpool's retention of the League championship. Dalglish scores in a four-game record FA Cup semi-final marathon against Arsenal only for Liverpool to lose in the third replay. On the very day of the club's agonising defeat, 1 May, 1980, they make a signing which proves to be of huge significance. Ian Rush, who is to form a legendary partnership with Dalglish, arrives from Chester for £300,000.

Competition		Appearances	Goals
League		42 (0)	16
FA Cup		8 (0)	2
League Cup		7 (0)	4
European Cup		2 (0)	0
Charity Shield		1 (0)	1
	Totals	60 (0)	23

1980–81

Dalglish's long sequence without missing a first-team game since joining Liverpool ends when injury rules him out of the League Cup second-round, first-leg game at Bradford City in August. It ended his 180-game ever-present run. He returns to score twice in the return and in every round to the final when he hits one of the goals in a 2–1 success against West Ham in the Villa Park replay.

In Europe, Dalglish suffers damage to his left ankle and is substituted after only nine minutes in the European Cup semi-final second leg at Bayern Munich. A 1–1 draw takes Liverpool through on the away-goal rule and he is fit for the 1–0 win over Real Madrid in Paris to give Liverpool the trophy for the third time.

Competition		Appearances	Goals
League		34 (0)	8
FA Cup		2 (0)	2
League Cup		8 (0)	7
European Cup		9 (0)	1
Charity Shield		1 (0)	0
	Totals	54 (0)	18

1981–82

Dalglish scores Liverpool's 100th European Cup goal in a 7–0 rout of Finnish club Oulun Palloseura in the first round, second leg at Anfield in September. Liverpool go on to reach the quarter-final but lose on a 2–0 aggregate to CSKA Sofia.

Dalglish helps Liverpool retain the League Cup, now called the Milk Cup, with a 3–1 conquest of Tottenham at Wembley.

He scores in the 3–1 home League win over Tottenham in May that recaptures the championship.

Dalglish helps Scotland to reach the World Cup finals in Spain in the summer of 1982 and scores in the 5–2 opening win over New Zealand in Malaga. He goes on as a substitute in the 4–1 defeat by Brazil in Seville but misses their final group match when a 2–2 draw with the USSR put out the Scots on goal difference.

Competition	Appearances	Goals
League	42 (0)	13
FA Cup	2 (0)	2
League Cup	10 (0)	5
European Cup	6 (0)	2
World Club Championship	1 (0)	0
Totals	61 (0)	22

1982–83

Another ever-present League campaign by Dalglish, his fifth in six seasons at Liverpool, helps the club retain the title. He scores 18 goals in the championship triumph.

Dalglish also collects another Milk Cup winners' medal after a 2–1 defeat of Manchester United at Wembley.

In Europe, his absence from the European Cup quarter-final second leg against Widzew Lodz through illness ends his unbroken run of 35 European games, including four Super Cup, since his arrival from Celtic. It was only his 11th absence overall from Liverpool in that time.

Dalglish is named Footballer of the Year for the second time to complete a personal double after his election earlier in the season as the PFA's Player of the Year.

Bob Paisley, the manager who signed Dalglish, retires at the end of the season after an unprecedented haul of 19 trophies in nine seasons. He is succeeded by Joe Fagan.

Competition		Appearances	Goals
League		42 (0)	18
FA Cup		3 (0)	1
Milk Cup		7 (0)	0
European Cup		5 (0)	1
Charity Shield		1 (0)	0
	Totals	58 (0)	20

1983–84

Dalglish helps Liverpool win the treble of League championship, Milk Cup and European Cup, a unique managerial feat by Fagan in his first season in charge.

Dalglish's two goals against Danish side Odense in the first round, second leg at Anfield sets a new European Cup scoring record for a British player of 15, surpassing Denis Law's previous best of 14. It was also Dalglish's 54th European Cup appearance, more than any other British player.

He scores his 100th League goal for Liverpool at Ipswich in November on his 259th appearance. He is the first player in history to complete a League century in both England and Scotland with only two clubs. Neil Martin also scored 100 each side of the border but his goals came for Alloa, Queen of the South, Hibernian, Sunderland, Coventry and Nottingham Forest.

In January, Dalglish suffers a depressed cheekbone fracture in a collision with Manchester United's Kevin Moran at Anfield and is out for two months but returns in March to help Liverpool to their triple success.

Their 15th championship win also completes the first post-war hat-trick and their European Cup triumph comes after a penalty shoot-out against Roma in the Italian club's own Olympic Stadium.

Liverpool's Milk Cup success, achieved by beating Mersey rivals Everton 1–0 in a Maine Road replay, after a goalless draw at Wembley, is the club's fourth consecutive win in the competition, an unprecedented feat in English football.

Competition	Appearances	Goals
League	33 (0)	7
FA Cup	0 (0)	0
Milk Cup	8 (0)	2
European Cup	8 (1)	3
Charity Shield	1 (0)	0
Totals	50 (1)	12

1984–85

A season that ends in tragedy with the deaths of 39 supporters, mostly Italian, at Liverpool's European Cup final against Juventus in the Heysel stadium, Brussels.

Dalglish makes his 400th senior appearance for Liverpool in a 3–1 defeat at Arsenal in September and the following month he is dropped for the first time by Liverpool when Fagan omits him from the live televised Friday night game at Tottenham, who win 1–0. It is only the 28th game he has missed for the club and he wins an immediate recall. November is a month of mixed fortune for Dalglish. He is sent off for the first time in his career after retaliating in the European Cup return with Benfica in Lisbon's Stadium of Light. He receives a three-game ban but returns in the semi-final against Panathinaikos, making his 50th European appearance for Liverpool in the second leg against the Greeks.

A week after his dismissal in Portugal, Dalglish hits a memorable goal to give Scotland a 3–1 win over Spain at Hampden Park. It was his 30th at international level, equalling Denis Law's record.

In the 1985 New Year Honours List Dalglish is awarded the MBE for services to football. He receives it at Buckingham Palace the day before his 750th club appearance for Celtic and Liverpool in the 7–0 FA Cup replay win over York City at Anfield in February. Three days later he makes his 300th League appearance for Liverpool in the 2–0 home League win over Stoke City.

The Brussels meeting with Juventus on 29 May is a sad watershed for English football and Liverpool. English clubs are banned from European competitions after the disaster. A Michel Platini penalty gave Juventus a 1–0 victory in a match rendered irrelevant by the tragedy. Less than 24 hours later Dalglish is named as Liverpool's new player-manager in succession to Joe Fagan who informed the club he would be retiring as manager before the events of Heysel.

Competition	Appearances	Goals
League	36 (0)	6
FA Cup	7 (0)	0
Milk Cup	1 (0)	0
Charity Shield	1 (0)	0
World Club Championship	1 (0)	0
European Cup	7 (0)	0
European Super Cup	0 (0)	0
Totals	53 (0)	6

1985–86

Sadness for Dalglish early in his first season as player-manager when Jock Stein, his manager at club level with Celtic and international level with Scotland, dies immediately after the World Cup qualifier against Wales at Cardiff's Ninian Park, which ends 1–1 and which Dalglish misses through injury.

Alex Ferguson takes over as Scotland manager and a goalless draw with Australia in Melbourne, a game Dalglish misses through club commitments, ensures qualification for the finals in Mexico.

At club level Dalglish responds magnificently to his new challenge in management by guiding the club to a championship and FA Cup double. He scores the goal at Chelsea in May that clinches the title, becoming the first player-manager to win the championship. A week later he plays in the FA Cup final when a 3–1 win over Everton completes the classic English double, the first player-manager to achieve the feat. He is named Manager of the Year. During the season he passes the half-century of Cup goals for Liverpool, becoming the first player to score 50 or more in knock-out competitions in England and Scotland.

At a ceremony in March in Glasgow he is made a Freeman of his native city by the Lord Provost, Robert Gray, and two days later Dalglish wins his 100th Scotland cap in the 3–0 win over Romania. Before kick-off he is presented with a solid silver cap, with nine-carat gold braiding, by Franz Beckenbauer, as a gift from the Scottish FA and Dalglish takes over as captain for the night from his former Liverpool team-mate Graeme Souness.

A Scottish testimonial match for Dalglish at Hampden Park in May between an Alex Ferguson-managed team of home-based players and an Anglo side under the guidance of Tommy Docherty draws a crowd of almost 30,000. Dalglish scores for both sides as Docherty's team run out 5–2 winners.

A knee injury forces Dalglish to withdraw from the squad for Mexico, preventing him becoming the first Briton to play in four World Cup final tournaments after his appearances in West Germany (1974), Argentina (1978) and Spain (1982).

Competition	Appearances	Goals
League	17 (4)	3
FA Cup	6 (0)	1
Milk Cup	2 (0)	1
Screen Sport Super Cup	2 (0)	2
Totals	27 (4)	7

1986–87

Dalglish's champions and FA Cup winners draw 1–1 with double runners-up Everton at Wembley in the Charity Shield. He goes on as a second-half substitute, with Ian Rush scoring a late equaliser.

Dalglish also makes a substitute appearance against his former club Celtic in the desert clash of the British champions for the Dubai Super Cup. The game finishes 1–1 and Liverpool win 4–2 on penalties.

Liverpool reach another final in the League Cup competition, newly sponsored by Littlewoods. Ian Rush puts Liverpool ahead but two Charlie Nicholas goals give Arsenal a 2–1 victory, ending Liverpool's 144-match unbeaten run in games in which Rush has scored. Dalglish's 72nd-minute introduction as substitute for Paul Walsh sets a new record of 15 Wembley appearances with one club.

Liverpool, who open up a nine-point lead over second-placed Everton on 18 March, finish championship runners-up to their arch rivals who finish with 86 points, nine more than Liverpool.

Dalglish makes his 102nd and final Scotland appearance in the 3–0 win over Luxembourg at Hampden on 12 November. A save by visiting keeper John Van Rijswijck denies him a record-breaking 31st international goal. Andy Roxburgh's succession to Alex Ferguson the previous July makes him the sixth Scotland manager of Dalglish's illustrious career following Tommy Docherty, Willie Ormond, Ally MacLeod, Jock Stein and Ferguson.

Competition	Appearances	Goals
League	12 (6)	6
FA Cup	0 (0)	0
Littlewoods Cup	4 (1)	2
Charity Shield	0 (1)	0
Screen Sport Super Cup	1 (0)	0
Dubai Super Cup	0 (1)	0
Totals	17 (9)	8

1987–88

The season when Dalglish becomes very much the manager rather than the player, making only two appearances, both as a substitute. But he has the satisfaction of seeing his team storm to Liverpool's 17th championship and their second under his command. A 1–0 home win over Tottenham clinches the title after they equal Leeds United's record of 29 First Division games unbeaten from the start of the season, the run ending at Everton in March.

Liverpool, favourites for another double, are on the receiving end of one of the all-time upsets when they lose 1–0 to Wimbledon in the FA Cup final after a John Aldridge penalty is saved by Dave Beasant, the first-ever spot-kick failure in an FA Cup final at Wembley and his first in 12 penalties for Liverpool.

Dalglish is named Manager of the Year for the second time.

Competition	Appearances	Goals
Football League	0 (2)	0
FA Cup	0 (0)	0
Littlewoods Cup	0 (0)	0
Totals	0 (2)	0

1988–89

Another season of appalling tragedy for Liverpool. Their FA Cup semi-final against Nottingham Forest at Hillsborough is abandoned after six minutes following crushing at the Leppings Lane end of the stadium in which 96 supporters die. A fortnight later Liverpool play a Disaster Appeal game at Dalglish's former club Celtic which raises more than £300,000. Dalglish plays at Parkhead on an emotional occasion, his first start for Liverpool since a pre-season friendly in Copenhagen in July 1987, and scores in a 4–0 win.

After long deliberation about their FA Cup future in the aftermath of the Hillsborough disaster, Liverpool continue in the competition and beat Forest 3–1 in the re-staged semi-final at Old Trafford to book an all-Merseyside Wembley meeting with Everton. Ian Rush steps off the substitute's bench to score twice in extra time and give Liverpool a thrilling 3–2 win and surpass Dixie Dean's 19-goal Mersey derby record.

An incredible climax to the season six days later sees Arsenal snatch the championship and deny Liverpool the double with an injury-time goal from Michael Thomas at Anfield. The London club win 2–0 to go level on points (76) with Liverpool and with an identical goal difference (37). But they are champions on superior number of goals scored (73 to 65).

Competition		Appearances	Goals
League		0 (0)	0
FA Cup		0 (0)	0
Littlewoods Cup		0 (1)	0
Mercantile Credit Trophy		0 (1)	0
	Totals	0 (2)	0

KENNY DALGLISH – PLAYING CAREER RECORD

With Celtic	Appearances	Goals
Scottish League	204	112
Scottish FA Cup	30	11
Scottish League Cup	59	35
European Cup	21	5
E. Cup-winners' Cup	5	3
UEFA Cup	2	1
Totals	**321**	**167**

With Liverpool	Appearances	Goals
League	355	118
FA Cup	36	13
League Cup (inc. Milk and Littlewoods)	59	27
European Cup	47	10
E. Cup-winners' Cup	—	—
UEFA Cup	—	—
Charity Shield	7	1
World Club Championship	2	0
European Super Cup	4	1
Mercantile Credit Trophy	1	0
Screen Sport Super Cup	3	2
Dubai Super Cup	1	0
Totals	**515**	**172**

Career totals	Appearances	Goals
League	559	230
FA Cup	66	24
League Cup	118	62
European Cup	68	15
E. Cup-winners' Cup	5	3
UEFA Cup	2	1
Charity Shield	7	1
World Club Championship	2	0
European Super Cup	4	1
Mercantile Credit Trophy	1	0
Screen Sport Super Cup	3	2
Dubai Super Cup	1	0
Totals	**836**	**339**

Scotland: Under-23

Appearances: 4   *Goals:* 3   *Youth caps:* 8

Full

Appearances: 102 (Scotland record)   *Goals:* 30 (joint Scotland record with Denis Law)
(including 8 as substitute)

1989–90

Liverpool sweep to their 18th championship, their 10th in 15 seasons and their third of Dalglish's five-season managerial reign. A 2–1 home win over QPR in April secures the title, making Liverpool the first club to be champions in four consecutive decades – 1960s, 1970s, 1980s and 1990s. The championship success sees captain Alan Hansen equal Phil Neal's all-time record of eight title medals as a player. It is also Dalglish's eighth, five as a player and three as player-manager.

The following Tuesday evening, 1 May, Dalglish makes his farewell appearance as a Liverpool player as 72nd-minute substitute for Jan Molby in the 1–0 home win over Derby County. He is involved in the move for Gary Gillespie to score the only goal. At the end, following the championship presentation, he throws his No 14 jersey into the Kop from where his 13-year-old son Paul is watching, wearing Michel Platini's Juventus shirt.

Dalglish is named Manager of the Year for the third time.

Competition	Appearances	Goals
League	0 (1)	0
FA Cup	0 (0)	0
Littlewoods Cup	0 (0)	0
Totals	0 (1)	0

1990–91

A crowd of 30,461, paying estimated receipts of £150,000, turns out at Anfield to salute Dalglish for his testimonial game between Liverpool and Spanish club Real Sociedad whose team includes former Liverpool star John Aldridge and two other English players in Kevin Richardson and Dalian Atkinson. Dalglish plays for 75 minutes, laying on the passes for Liverpool's first two goals in their 3–1 win, before being replaced by Peter Beardsley. As he walks off the pitch he gives his famous No 7 jersey to 76-year-old wheelchair-bound Eileen Leffler.

The football world is stunned on Friday, 22 February. With Liverpool top of the league and engaged in an FA Cup fifth-round marathon against Everton, Dalglish makes the shock announcement that he is resigning as manager. His last game in charge, less than 48 hours earlier, is the pulsating 4–4 draw with Everton in a Goodison Park replay. Ronnie Moran takes over as acting manager.

1991–1992

After eight months out of football Dalglish is appointed manager of Blackburn Rovers only hours before the Ewood Park club's home game against Plymouth Argyle on Saturday, 12 October. They kick off 11th in the Second Division and, with Dalglish sitting in the stand, win 5–2. The new manager appoints Ray Harford as his assistant. The famous old Lancashire club climb the table and a 1–0 Wembley win over Leicester City in the Second Division play-off final the following May takes Blackburn back into the top flight for the first time since 1966 and in time for the launch of the new Premier League.

1992–93

With Blackburn's ambitions financed by vice president and lifelong supporter Jack Walker, Dalglish signs Alan Shearer from Southampton for £3.3 million, a new British record. He is the key arrival in a flurry of new signings at Ewood and proves to be a bargain investment. Blackburn top the table in the autumn but finish a creditable fourth. Although Shearer is injured mid-season, his goal return for the campaign is a remarkable 22 in 26 appearances.

1993–94

With more new faces, including £2.75 million David Batty from Leeds United and £2 million goalkeeper Tim Flowers from Southampton, Blackburn mount a dramatic pursuit of Manchester United for the championship. At one stage they claw back a 16-point deficit on United and set a new club record of 13 consecutive home wins. But United hold on and retain the title with 92 points, Blackburn finishing runners-up on 84. Shearer scores 31 League goals in 40 appearances.

1994–95

Dalglish breaks the British transfer record again by paying Norwich £5 million for Chris Sutton in July 1994, his 27th signing since becoming manager at a cost of £27.55 million. Sutton and Shearer are dubbed the 'SAS' and they shoot Blackburn to the championship with 34 and 15 League goals respectively.

Blackburn lose their final game at Liverpool 2–1 but Manchester United's draw at West Ham the same day means that Dalglish carves yet another niche in football's roll of honour. It is his ninth championship success in England, five as a player with Liverpool, three as player-manager of Liverpool and now another as Blackburn manager, a unique record. He also becomes only the third manager in the history of English football to win the championship with different clubs following Herbert Chapman (Huddersfield 1924, 1925; Arsenal 1931, 1933) and Brian Clough (Derby County 1972 and Nottingham Forest 1978).

As the championship flag proudly flies over the impressively rebuilt Ewood Park, Dalglish relinquishes the managerial reins on 25 June, 1995, to become Blackburn's Director of Football. Ray Harford takes charge of team affairs.

The manner of my departure from Blackburn Rovers in August 1996 disappointed me. I had made a phonecall from Spain, where I was on holiday, to the chairman, Robert Coar, because I had reservations about the level of my involvement in the club as Director of Football. I wasn't asked to help often enough to satisfy me. The title of Director of Football was a role with no authority and with little guidance. During our phonecall the chairman said a letter had been sent to my home in Southport, saying our relationship had run its course. Somebody signed for that letter at the house but I had no knowledge of it at the time I called. It would have been more appreciated, and certainly more thoughtful, to have called me, telling me of the contents of the letter, rather than just sending it to my home.

But I felt the same way as the chairman. I was ready to go because I wasn't getting enough job satisfaction. If they wanted more out of me, they just had to ask. I did virtually the same mileage in my car as Director of Football as I did as manager. I watched plenty of games. I helped to recruit a lot of the young players. I wasn't in day to day but they didn't expect me to be. I wasn't absent every day either. The agreement that I would have more free time to spend as I wished was stressed to the chairman when he was given the option of letting me go after the championship success. That's why I stepped down as manager. I wanted to sit back a bit, have a holiday with the kids, play golf, or do whatever I wanted to. But at the same time I still had the responsibility of being of help to Blackburn Rovers if and when they asked me.

I hadn't spoken to Ray Harford since the end of the 1995–96 season. I wasn't informed about Alan Shearer's move by the club, although Alan called me before he went over to see Jack Walker. Alan rang me for advice. He told me of his thoughts. I advised him to take the deal Blackburn offered, but Alan had to make his own decision. The next I knew it was being announced on television that Alan was signing for Newcastle. I sat for about three or four days and couldn't believe it. Even now, it's difficult to imagine he has gone to Newcastle. It didn't surprise me that I wasn't consulted over Alan because I wasn't consulted over every transfer.

I really enjoyed watching Blackburn evolve. I remember going down to the school pitches when I first started and having to assemble the goals; I had a spanner and would screw the bolts in. That was good. It was the other side of football from what I was used to as manager of Liverpool. I remember phoning round in the mornings, finding somewhere to train – look at the magnificent training facilities at Brockhall now.

I enjoyed watching the playing squad improve. I remember the tears in the directors' eyes when we won promotion. I enjoyed seeing the pride on Tony Parkes's face as he walked out at Wembley for the play-off final. Then there was the satisfaction on the faces of everyone, and the pride, when we finished fourth and then second; looking at the fan's face behind the goal at Liverpool when he thought we had lost the championship after Jamie Redknapp scored. His face turned to a picture of joy within twenty seconds. I wish Blackburn Rovers everything they wish for themselves, unless I'm in opposition to them. To all the players, and everyone at Blackburn who contributed to the success, I greatly appreciated them and their work. I just hope it gave them as much pride and pleasure as it did me.

K.M.D. Friday 23 August 1996

S
T
O
P

P
R
E
S
S

INDEX